Discover the
WRITER'S LIFE
in New York City

Over more than six decades of steady innovation, The New School has sustained a vital center for creative writing. Study writing and literature with The New School's renowned faculty of writers, critics, editors, and publishing professionals—in the heart of Greenwich Village.

Master of Fine Arts in Creative Writing
The New School's distinguished MFA program offers concentrations in fiction, poetry, nonfiction, and writing for children. Fellowships and financial aid are available.

Bachelor's Program in the Liberal Arts
Writing students seeking a BA may apply to the **Riggio Honors Program**. Students who are accepted into the program are eligible to receive a partial scholarship.

The Riggio Writing Honors Program is offered in conjunction with the Leonard and Louise Riggio Writing & Democracy initiative at The New School.

For more about the programs, call 212.229.5630 or visit us online.

www.newschool.edu/writing64

THE NEW SCHOOL

The New School is a leading university in New York City offering some of the nation's most distinguished degree, certificate, and continuing education programs in art and design, liberal arts, management and policy, and the performing arts.

2010–2011
Director: Robert Polito
MFA FACULTY
Jeffery Renard Allen, Jonathan Ames, Robert Antoni, Catherine Barnett, Susan Bell, Mark Bibbins, Peter Cameron, Susan Cheever, Jonathan Dee, Elaine Equi, David Gates, Vivian Gornick, Jennifer Michael Hecht, Ann Hood, Shelley Jackson, Zia Jaffrey, Hettie Jones, James Lasdun, David Lehman, Suzannah Lessard, David Levithan, Phillip Lopate, Patrick McGrath, Honor Moore, Sigrid Nunez, Meghan O'Rourke, Dale Peck, Darryl Pinckney, Robert Polito, Helen Schulman, Tor Seidler, Laurie Sheck, Darcey Steinke, Benjamin Taylor, Jackson Taylor, Paul Violi, Sarah Weeks, Brenda Wineapple, Stephen Wright.

Associate Director: Jackson Taylor
MFA VISITING FACULTY
Max Blagg, Deborah Brodie, Patricia Carlin, Gary Indiana, Dave Johnson, Joyce Johnson, Greil Marcus, Sharon Mesmer, Flaminia Ocampo, Marie Ponsot, David Prete, John Reed, Lloyd Schwartz, Susan Shapiro, Justin Taylor, Craig Teicher, Frederic Tuten, Susan Van Metre, Victoria Wilson.

Associate Chair: Luis Jaramillo
Associate Director: Laura Cronk
RIGGIO HONORS
PROGRAM FACULTY
Jeffery Renard Allen, Catherine Barnett, Mark Bibbins, Patricia Carlin, Elizabeth Gaffney, David Gates, Tim Griffin, Shelley Jackson, Zia Jaffrey, Suzannah Lessard, Greil Marcus, Sigrid Nunez, René Steinke, Sam Tanenhaus, Lynne Tillman, Linda Tvrdy, Paul Violi.

An Affirmative Action/Equal Opportunity Institution

Absence of Mind

MARILYNNE ROBINSON

"A much needed cerebral pick-me-up. The Orange Prize-winning author of *Home* presents a collection of philosophical writings pitting science against religion, and finding science wanting." —*The Sunday Telegraph*

"Robinson's argument is prophetic, profound, eloquent, succinct powerful and timely."—Karen Armstrong, *The Guardian*

176pp. £16.99

What Ever Happened to Modernism?

GABRIEL JOSIPOVICI

In this agile and passionate book—a personal, penetrating and polemical account of what Modernism is—novelist and critic Gabriel Josipovici explores the literature, fine art and music that it has inspired—and how contemporary literary writing has failed it. The result is both a strident call to arms and a tour de force of literary, artistic and philosophical explication.

224pp. 6 b/w illus. £18.99

On Evil

TERRY EAGLETON

"Terry Eagleton, in his jaunty and surprisingly entertaining book on the subject, takes the unfashionable view that such a thing as evil does exist . . . His argument is subtle, intricate, provocative and limpidly expressed . . . A valuable contribution to a debate as old as Adam and Eve and as contemporary as 9/11 and Abu Ghraib."—John Banville, *Irish Times*

192pp. £18.99

www.yalebooks.co.uk **yale**

CONTENTS

PUT YOUR IMAGINATION TO WORK

PHOTOGRAPH BY MARY ELLEN MARK, *ACROBATS REHEARSING THEIR ACT AT GREAT GOLDEN CIRCUS,* AHMEDABAD, 1989

Develop your creativity, tell your stories, and gain skills essential for personal and professional development in the **FICTION WRITING DEPARTMENT** AT COLUMBIA COLLEGE CHICAGO.

FICTION WRITING & PLAYWRITING DEGREE PROGRAMS

- **BA in Fiction Writing**
- **BFA in Fiction Writing**
- **BA in Playwriting**
- **BFA in Playwriting**
- **MFA in Creative Writing – Fiction**
- **MA in the Teaching of Writing**
- **Combined MFA/MA**

Our renowned Story Workshop® approach emphasizes voice, imagery, audience, and positive reinforcement of your strengths as a writer. Check out **colum.edu/fiction**, or call **312 369 7611** for info on our diverse study programs, extensive course listings, award-winning student anthology *Hair Trigger*, and visiting writers series.

create...

YOUR STORIES.
YOUR FUTURE.

LEILA IN THE WILDERNESS

Nadeem Aslam

AYAZ JOKHIO
Mother and Child, 2008
Acrylic on canvas, gold frame. 1.1 x 1.5cm
© Ayaz Jokhio

And my soul is a woman before you . . .

– Rilke

I

In the beginning, the great river was believed to flow out of a lion's mouth, its size reflected in its ancient name – *Sindhu*, an ocean. The river was older than the Himalayas; the Greeks had called it *Sinthus*, the Romans *Sindus*, the Chinese *Sintow*, but it was Pliny who had given it the name *Indus*. One night under the vast silence of a perfect half-moon and six stars, a mosque appeared on a wooded island in the river, and Leila was woken by the call to prayer issuing from its minaret just before sunrise. It was the day she was to be blessed with a son.

As she knew there was no mosque within hearing distance, her initial impression was that the air itself was singing. Leila manoeuvred herself out of bed and went towards the door, making sure not to disturb her mother-in-law who had taken to sleeping in the same room as her in these last days before the birth. The servant girl appointed outside the door had fallen asleep, and as Leila moved past, a bad dream caused the girl to release a cry of fear.

Leila was fourteen years old, thin-framed with grey, glass-like eyes and a nervous flame always burning just beneath her pale skin. She pursued the song of faith drifting in the fifty-roomed mansion that had been in her husband's family for several generations. The river with its boats and blind freshwater dolphins and drowned lovers was half a mile away, and there was nothing but rocky desert and thick date orchards between the riverbank and the mansion.

Long after the voice withdrew, she continued her search for its origins, now and then placing an ear against a wall. Earlier in the night she'd heard momentary fragments of other songs from the men's side of the mansion, where her husband was celebrating the imminent arrival of his first son in the company of musicians and prostitutes. No doubt they were all asleep by now.

The windows in the women's section of the house were

inaccessible, nudged up against the ceiling, so the light poured in but not enough air. Leila was looking up at one of them when she heard someone come in behind her.

'You shouldn't be down here,' Razia, her mother-in-law, said, unable to conceal her alarm. 'If you needed something you should have asked one of the servants.' Her attenuated face was wheat-coloured and pitted with smallpox scars. She had long white hair and every other year a doctor would inject liquid gold into her bones and joints to counter the ravages of time. 'You should be resting,' she said. It was the tone she had employed a year earlier when Leila came to the mansion as a bride, a tone suitable for the child that Leila had been back then. Someone who longed for her dolls and frequently misplaced her veil. But as soon as she became pregnant there was no end to Razia's devotion and love. Along with the abundant care came the vigilance, an ever-present awareness that the girl was not mature enough to know the importance of the asset taking form inside her body.

Razia summoned the servants and they led Leila back up to her room.

'I don't mean to be harsh with you,' Razia said mildly, accompanying them up the staircase. 'If only you knew about the behaviour of my own mother-in-law and husband towards me. When I failed to conceive within the first few months of marriage, I was marked for days from the beating I received. But Allah heard my cries and granted me my son Timur.'

'I went downstairs because I heard a voice, a call to prayer,' Leila said as she settled on the bed and the servant girls began making her comfortable with pillows and cushions. 'Somewhere not too far.'

'You did,' Razia answered. 'I heard it too. I have just been talking to Timur, and he says that a mosque has appeared on the island in the river.'

The air in the room changed.

'Who was the muezzin?'

'No one knows. People woke at his call and followed the sound to the bank. There was the mosque, with a green dome visible through the trees and the mist of the river. But they say that when they rowed across to the building they found it empty.'

With great tenderness Razia neatened a stray lock of hair on Leila's forehead and kissed her on the temple. 'These are very auspicious hours. This miracle augurs great things for the boy about to be born.'

Leila had been told about the day Timur, her husband, was born. How Razia had been given one hundred and one gold necklaces, five hundred and one finger rings, and one thousand and one pairs of earrings. It was declared that if you could see the smoke of the cooking fires, no matter how far away you were, you should consider yourself invited to the feast – the festivities lasted an entire month. And similar things would no doubt occur after the birth today, though Leila knew she would not be allowed to wear any of the ornaments presented to her. Ten years ago, Razia had taken the oath that the women of the family would strictly abstain from jewellery until the daughters of Kashmir and Palestine were free of their Indian and Israeli oppressors.

Razia motioned to the shelf where an oversized book bound in green moss-like velvet lay, and two servant girls carried it to her. Since they were Christian, the girls could not touch the sacred volume and so carried it slung on a shawl between them. They placed it on a table and stepped back. It was the family *Book of Omens*. An image was painted on each of its right-hand pages, with the explanatory text occurring on the opposite page. During the previous weeks, Razia had asked Leila to open the book at random several times. And on each occasion the day that was just dawning was revealed to be the day of her grandson's entrance into the world.

Now once again she brought the book to Leila and it opened on a portrait of Muhammad. He had been painted in a robe of dark blue brocade, with a white turban and crimson boots that curled at the tips, his face unseen behind a veil. He was raising his hand to split the moon in half, the text on the opposite page reading:

O augury user! Know that the star of your ascendant has come out of malevolence, and your enemies have been disgraced and made contemptible by the grace of the Purest of Men. All your difficulties cease forever from today.

To others the augury might have appeared cryptic; but according to Razia's personal logic, there could no longer be any uncertainty about the day of the birth. A retinue of servant girls was installed in Leila's room. The midwife arrived, and brought with her fresh news of the river-island mosque, how the faithful were crowding the one available boat, a few throwing themselves into the waves to swim towards the work of angels, each swimmer wishing to be the one who would say the second call to prayer from the minaret.

As the morning progressed, excitement heightened in the mansion. A desiccated Flower of Mary, brought back from the pilgrimage to Saudi Arabia, had been placed in a bowl of water: a tight knot of wooden tendrils, grasping itself to itself, it opened slowly in the water and was believed to absorb the pain of the mother into itself during birth.

By the time of the noon prayers, however, when they heard again the call from the minaret, Leila still hadn't given birth. And Timur's child had not been born by the time of the afternoon prayers either. Leila, with a dreamlike expression, contemplated every nuance of the muezzin's call both times, but it wasn't the same voice as at dawn.

With the sun moving towards the west, the mother-in-law became acutely anxious, an anxiety that proved baseless because Leila's pains began, at last, just as the evening prayers approached – the hour every Thursday when the dead visited the living.

Timur was being kept informed via a mobile phone that a servant girl operated for Razia. Initially he stayed in the men's section of the mansion, but as time passed he came closer and closer to Leila's room, until eventually he was just on the other side of the door. He was a man of exact speech who seldom smiled even when alone, and he had carried Leila away from her village a year ago to be his bride, her eyes seeming to cast a brief spell on him. Like his father and grandfather before him, and the fathers and grandfathers before them, he would have needed time to think if asked how many people he had killed or caused to die.

That evening he was exhausted because he had slept very little during the previous seventy-two hours. In addition to the revelries for the upcoming birth, during the last three nights he had been supervising a group of workers as they secretly built the mosque on the island owned by his rival landowner. Lushly fertile, it was prime terrain and Timur had always been envious of it, always looking for a way to claim it as his own. The mosque was the ideal method to begin depriving the enemy of it. The masons and labourers had to work with minimum light, overcoming fear of snakes, djinns and scorpions. Only once did they think they were about to be discovered – when a truck broke down close to the riverbank and its driver and passengers got out to repair it, their voices reaching the island, the truck's headlights visible. But they were members of a jihadi organization returning from Faisalabad, the city full of textile factories from whose markets chemicals used in explosives could be bought in bulk without raising suspicion. That was the sole incident. And the plan seemed to be working. Timur had sent word to surrounding villages about the miracle of angels, and the arriving crowds were threatening to tear his rival and his men to pieces if they pulled down the sacred structure, or hindered anyone's access to it.

Timur heard a cry from Leila's room a few minutes before the call to the fifth and final prayer of the day sounded. He was at the door and the midwife emerging from the room in great panic ran into him. She stumbled to her knees and then, repeatedly begging his and his family's forgiveness, receded towards the staircase, her bloody hands leaving smears on the floor. The servant girls were the next to come out, and they too fled. Finally, with a look of utter devastation on her face, his mother appeared. Timur went into the room where he saw Leila dead on the bed sheets, the crying newborn by her side. He knew she was dead, but then she made a movement and raised her eyelids to look at him. He approached and grabbed her by the hair and, lifting his free hand as high as he could, he struck her face.

The minutes-old baby on the bed was a girl.

II

N ever ever has a girl been born in this family,' Razia said, an hour after the birth, tears running down her cheeks.

No verification was required, as it was a fact known throughout the province. Nevertheless, and half-heartedly, because a part of her was unable to accept the calamity that had befallen her son, she opened her Quran and scrutinized the family tree inscribed on the endpapers. The book was once owned by the founder of the dynasty, who was believed to have arrived in the region in the train of Emperor Babur. Along with the ancient dagger with which the umbilical cord was traditionally cut, she had kept the Quran within reach in anticipation of Timur's son, for his name and date of birth to be added on to the tree, in royal-blue ink if born during the day, in black if during the night.

Razia knew her son would inevitably vent his grief at Leila for daring to transform his seed into a female child. She had to make sure it was not excessive: for a few minutes, while he was in there with Leila, she stood outside the door with an implacable expression on her face, her heart breaking at his immense sorrow, and then she went in. Timur's temper when roused was ungovernable, but he always maintained the careful good manners of a son in the presence of his mother. 'She has learned her lesson, I am sure,' she said, shielding Leila from him. 'Forgive her now.'

Timur left the room and paced the grounds of the mansion until midnight, the moon and stars motionless above him. His mobile phone sounded three times in quick succession: twice it was friends calling from the celebrations wondering where he'd got to, and the third time one of those unsolicited texts reading: *The prisoners of Guantanamo are crying out for a saviour, forward this SMS to 10 others*. The air was briefly scored with a luminous arc as he hurled the instrument against a tree trunk. His child, his firstborn, was a female. His breast seethed with the fact, and he felt upon him the contempt and ridicule of his ancestors, of his friends and companions. Of the entire male population of the province, and of the women too. Sunk in darkest despair, he sat on the steps of a pavilion with his head held tightly in his hands. Lowering himself on to the pavilion floor, Timur fell asleep, waking up several hours later covered in dew. As one possessed of a sudden realization, he stood up with a jolt and went towards the house in long strides.

His mother was on a balcony, facing the direction of the miraculous mosque and mouthing a prayer. She had hung her thousand-bead rosary around her neck, looping the length of it on to her right wrist several times. She heard him come into the room behind her. But when she went in she only caught a glimpse of him leaving: the gun cabinet was open, the glass doors swinging on their hinges. She shouted his name in alarmed distress, and although Timur heard her he did not stop as he hurried towards Leila's room, taking the stairs two at a time.

Leila, half asleep on the bed, tried to sit up when she saw her husband enter.

'Who is he?' he asked her, approaching and pressing the barrel of the gun under her jaw. 'The child can't be mine. The only explanation is that you have another man, someone inferior.' He lifted the gun to the wall behind her and pulled the trigger, bringing the barrel back on to her after the explosion of stone-dust. 'Who is he?'

Just then Razia entered, out of breath, and she grabbed the barrel, pulling it off Leila's neck. 'She is at fault but you must stop behaving like a madman,' she said as she led Timur towards the door. 'She has wronged you, but you can win merit from Allah by forgiving her. And I know just the remedies that will correct her internal mechanisms. There are a hundred ways to make her insides obey you.'

'I remember a story that there was a tunnel under this house, so its inhabitants could escape in case of enemy attack,' Timur said, almost to himself. 'He could have got in that way.'

They were nearly out of the room when Leila asked in a hollow voice, 'Where is she?'

Timur didn't turn round. It was his mother who spoke.

'Where is who?'

Leila placed an arm across her eyes and began to weep.

Razia – staying Timur with a touch of her hand – told her in a reasonable tone, 'The bloodline has never seen an affront of this nature. It has been decided that the child cannot be accepted into the family. She has been sent away. It's the best thing for all concerned.'

Leila seemed unable to stop weeping. Razia sat down and took her into her arms. She waved a hand towards Timur who was staring at Leila with vehement hatred. 'Leave us now. She will make it up to you within ten months.'

At dawn a public declaration let everyone know that Timur's son was born dead, and a period of mourning was declared throughout the 687 villages and hamlets owned by the family.

The tragedy had been thoroughly unforeseen. It was only in the morning that Razia remembered the midwife and servant girls who had been present at the birth, and how they could not be allowed to reveal the abomination. They had to be intimidated into silence. But their own fears were even greater, because they all seemed to disappear from their homes.

Over the next month Razia supervised Leila's diet with the greatest of care, hastening the day the girl would be robust enough to begin receiving nightly visits from Timur.

'It takes one hundred drops of milk to make one drop of blood,' she told Leila. 'And it takes one hundred drops of blood to make one drop of semen. So you must not waste or misuse again something that takes so much out of my son.'

She asked Timur to concentrate solely on the glorification of the mosque. 'I heard that Nadir Shah's men have scuffled with ours.'

Timur nodded. 'He says it was all my doing. That the miracle isn't genuine.'

'What have we to do with the mosque?' Razia asked in indignation. 'He thinks we are out to swindle him at every turn, but to doubt a happening as hallowed as this, to reduce Allah's work to human battles, makes him an infidel.'

She didn't know that the imam and his aides, and every other mosque attendant, were Timur's men and employees.

He said, 'According to him the angels would have built a more perfect structure. Not just one small, rudimentary room with a dome and minaret.'

Razia read a verse against the influence of Satan, and said, 'Praise be to Allah that my son, unlike Nadir Shah, recognizes holy signs.'

'I am encouraging more and more people to come, and I will be expanding the mosque. Bringing in boats for an easier crossing. Tents. Free food. Building shops on the riverbank.'

And they were arriving in number: along the roads, the bridges, the streets, came the lepers and the terminally ill, the destitute and the helpless, the lame and the blind and the mute, asking the mosque to end their ordeals as they kissed its walls and floors for minutes at a time.

Every few days one of the new arrivals would detach himself from the crowd moving towards the mosque and make his way towards Timur's mansion. This person would be in possession of a jar containing dried leaves or blossoms. Others brought sacred pebbles, or butter churned from the milk of cows pastured in Paradise, or handwritten manuscripts of magic spells dictated by the djinns of Mount Kaaf. All these Razia had summoned from the farthest reaches of the province to ensure that Leila's next child would be a boy. She pretended that these remedies were either for a distant relative or were to darken the unsettling grey colour of Leila's eyes.

One treatment required Leila's entire upper body to be covered in gold leaf for a day. She looked as though she had acquired the torso of an idol. A goddess in a breastplate. Later, as the servant girls were gently rubbing off the thin metal, the skin above her heart refused to let go of it. An oval patch on her left breast would not come off no matter how hard they tried – Razia gasped in disbelief. One of the girls then revealed that whenever she had bathed Leila, her bangle had become lightly magnetized to Leila's heart and would have to be pulled free of the attraction. She was made to demonstrate it and the bangle fastened on to the gold-covered patch on Leila's skin.

'I was right,' Timur said, when he was called urgently by his mother. 'She is thinking of someone.'

Razia nodded. 'It does seem like longing. She's summoning someone.'

But there was no reaction from Leila, no matter how firmly they questioned her.

'Maybe it's nothing at all,' Razia said eventually. 'Just a side effect of all the medicines.' She led Timur out of the room. 'We have to wait and see.' Outside the door were the servant girls, who had been sent out so they could speak privately. As they made their way down the stairs, Razia asked about the mosque. Timur told her that Nadir Shah was trying to get the government involved, hoping the mosque would be declared officially illegal.

'The government would do it gladly, of course,' Razia said, 'to prove their enlightenment to their Western masters.' She gave a sigh. 'My Allah, to think that mosques are being torn down in a Muslim country.'

'He won't succeed. We too have influence in the government.'

'Find a way to get the Saudi Arabians involved,' Razia advised. 'Win the patronage of an Arab prince for the mosque. They are a blessed race.'

The months passed and the longed-for day arrived. The Flower of Mary opened in the bowl of water once again, to float there like a wooden snowflake. Talismans obtained from the mausoleums of various saints were tied with different coloured strings around Leila's thighs. But the umbilical cord still hadn't been cut when Razia locked her bony fingers around Leila's throat. 'You little witch!

Why must you ridicule and torment my son like this?'

Timur had taken precautions this time: three stern giant-like figures appeared outside the room, materializing as though out of the shadows, to intercept the midwife and the servant girls. One of the girls attempted to run away but a blow lifted her off her feet and threw her against a wall. 'Come with us,' they were told firmly. Downstairs, the women were made to watch as one of their number was beaten senseless, and then their entire families were banished from the province and their homes razed to the ground.

A few hours later a group of children running after dragonflies on the edge of a pond discovered the body of a newborn girl floating in dark red water. Suspecting that it was the jettisoned fruit of a sinful union, the holy men and women refused to allow it to be buried in the graveyard proper. Its resting place was to be the patch of adjacent ground reserved for those wives, mothers, sisters and daughters who had disgraced their families by running away from home.

The divide wasn't just on the surface: an 'underground wall' – delving to the depth of fifteen feet – kept the dishonourable corpses separate from the honourable ones.

III

Wamaq and his brother Qes were travelling towards the mosque on their motorbike when they ran out of petrol.

Qes, riding pillion, and the more daring of the two, hopped backwards on to the ground before the machine had come to a halt. He was sixteen years old, his hair long and disorderly, and he had a mole above the right corner of his mouth that was considered lucky or unlucky, depending on the part of the country. Wamaq was a year older but no taller. He wore a green cap embroidered with tiny orange beads and dozens of circular mirror pieces, fragments of the world sliding in and out of them as he moved. There was a faint but permanent welt under his jaw. He had acquired it at the age of eleven when, to make him confess to the theft of a wristwatch, a policeman had put a noose around his neck and made him stand out in the open on a block of ice, the sun and the warmth of his own body strangling him slowly as they melted the ice.

Wamaq got down and lowered the battered 50cc motorbike on to the ground, leaving it there for a minute. The dregs in the petrol tank could be made to flow into the carburettor that way, good for another kilometre or so.

The last time they were in the area the brothers had found work on a crew constructing the river-island mosque. Having heard Qes's singing voice during the daylight hours, the other workers had insisted he make the first ever call to prayer from the mosque. He made believable every song he sang, as though he'd written it himself. You could hear his life in his voice. Afterwards Wamaq and Qes and the others were told to move on and to stay away for a period. The brothers were returning after about twenty months.

As he stood beside the horizontal motorbike, Wamaq wiped his sweat-covered face on his sleeve and looked around. Qes had taken a small music box from his rucksack and was turning its crank: the inch-long steel drum began to rotate, its pins catching against a metal comb – and the air filled with a melody of the purest notes. Qes had made the device himself and the music too was his own invention.

These brothers were what they appeared at first glance: two of the millions of youths who did menial work across the land – almost invisible, poor but resourceful, the lines on the palms of their hands shifting and realigning hourly. Their mother had had tuberculosis, and their father was an imam who had been cast out of his mosque for drinking alcohol, swaying a little while making the call to prayer, taking quick mouthfuls from a bottle of sugar-cane liquor before giving his brilliant and far-famed Friday sermons, saying he needed it for inspiration and eloquence. When their parents died, the boys continued to drift on their own.

As Wamaq got the motorbike running again, Qes walked to the edge of the path and positioned the music box on a large stone. 'Do you think it can be seen?' he asked his brother without turning around.

'Yes, I am sure someone will find it. Let's go.'

They resumed their journey. Qes had lost count of the number of music boxes he'd dispersed around the province, all issuing the same song when operated.

'We are hoping to find work,' Wamaq said to the man on the bicycle who was going in the same direction as them. He had reduced the speed of the motorbike to be able to converse with the stranger.

'There aren't many good jobs here,' the man replied, adding, 'You are young – try Dubai. Or a Western country, if you can get in.'

They were gliding side by side. Wamaq and Qes introduced themselves and after being silent for a while the man asked, 'What kind of a name is Wamaq?'

'I was named after a poet.'

'A poet?' The man looked at him.

'*At night my lost memory of you returned.*'

'That's a film song.'

'It's a poem of his turned into a song for a film, yes.'

The man gave a frown. 'I am sure I heard somewhere that he was a . . .' He struggled to recall the word. '. . . a socialist. Allah annihilate them.'

Wamaq didn't know what a socialist was but he felt compelled to defend his name. 'So what if a person is a socialist? As long as he keeps the promises he makes.'

The man did not respond and soon went down a side path, raising a hand in farewell.

The brothers were taken aback by the transformation the mosque had brought to the riverbank. It was a combination of a small bazaar and a circus of holy attractions. Things were being weighed and measured with a view to profit in either this life or the next. There were twenty boats for pilgrims wishing to cross the water. The mosque itself had been expanded and was large enough to be clearly visible from the bank, almost occupying the entire middle of the oval-shaped island – a handsome marble facade attached to a wide complex of prayer rooms and verandas, and courtyards that incorporated many of the ancient banyan trees. The original dome, a fibreglass replica of the one on Muhammad's mausoleum, which had been ferried across with difficulty on the last night of construction, had now been replaced with several varicoloured tiled domes, all with milk-white doves sitting on them.

The ascetic as well as the ambitious; men of genuine piety as well as those who just hoped to rub up against women and good-looking boys; gentle mendicants as well as jihadis who fantasized about nothing but what they'd do to the American president if ever they got hold of him. Wamaq and Qes explored the throng on the riverbank, drinking chilled Pepsi-Colas and sharing a packet of savoury cumin biscuits. The precarious wandering life had instilled in them a reluctance to interfere, and so they didn't say anything when they learned that the mosque was believed to be the work of angels.

Within the hour they had both found jobs – Wamaq as a boatman, rowing back and forth between the riverbank and the island, and Qes as a manual worker, digging and lifting. They rented bedding and sleeping space at the caravanserai and were given a locker for their rucksacks, and a safe space at the back to park the motorbike. As they were having their lunch at a roadside restaurant, a little girl appeared and stood grinning at them. Wamaq looked at her. 'What is it?'

She gave a shy nod in Qes's direction. 'Is it true?'

'You're famous already,' he said to Qes.

Qes smiled at her, lifted the spoon from the bowl of lentils before him and licked it clean. The girl laughed with thrilled delight when he held it to his heart and it remained hanging there.

She went away merrily and he detached the spoon from his body and put it back in the bowl.

'How far away is the place where you'd be working?' Wamaq asked.

'It's a big house half a mile away. They must be adding an extension.'

'It'll be hard work. You can take the motorbike if you want.'

'No one ever drowned in sweat.' He drank from his glass and said, 'And I know I can take the motorbike if I want.'

'Stay below thirty.'

Qes sighed.

'And don't fight with them and get yourself fired again.'

'I did not fight the last time. He tricked me into reading a sentence in a newspaper.' Most factory owners preferred, and some openly advertised for, an illiterate workforce, fearing arguments from even the most basically educated employees.

The small kit of implements with which he made his music boxes was the only personal possession Qes cared about, and he spent the rest of the afternoon bending steel nails into cranks, cutting strips of metal into eighteen-note combs and then screwing them in place against the rotating drum. By the time they went to bed that night he'd almost completed a new one.

How was work?' Wamaq asked him the next evening. They were among the doves on the mosque roof, having climbed a tree and gone along one of its sturdy branches.

'Don't ask!' Qes gave a small laugh. He was right at the top of one of the domes, sitting with his arms and legs loosely wrapped around the six-foot finial – looking downriver and wearing a garland of red roses like a wreath around his head. 'We won't be building any extensions. The people who own the house think a secret tunnel leads into it. So we were told to dig holes around the house at random – just pick a spot and start digging, stop after five or six feet. Then fill the hole up and start again somewhere else.'

'Too much money makes you mad,' Wamaq said from the base of the dome, where he was resting his back against the arabesques. In the distance, a train crossed the steel bridge put up during the days of the British, its mighty criss-crossing girders made in Sheffield.

'I wonder if he's looking for treasure,' said Qes.

The next day, in a secluded section at the back of the mansion, he saw a lion looking out at him through a broken windowpane. It was some moments before he realized it was a mounted specimen. He went closer and looked in. The large dusty room was filled with leopards and cheetahs, falcons and deer of several kinds, a black bear on its hind legs with a great V of white fur on its chest. A hundred inert eyes watched him as he climbed in and moved through the room, dozens of delicate cages hanging on long chains from the ceiling above him, containing lifeless bulbuls, golden orioles, hoopoes. He unlatched the door at the far end and went part way down the corridor. Returning, he took the music box from his pocket and worked the crank, the notes detaching themselves from the comb to begin drifting among the static creatures.

The next day he went back and saw that the music box he'd left balanced on the head of a white heron was missing. When he told Wamaq about the room, Wamaq asked him if the following day they could exchange jobs so that he too could see it.

He was feeling the softness of the fur on the neck of a mounted saluki, whose collar read: *This hound saved her owner from a wolf attack, 1912*, when he heard someone speak his name.

'Wamaq.'

She stood leaning against the door frame.

'Leila.'

'I heard music two days ago . . .' she said dazedly. 'I went towards it through the house but it stopped before I could find where it was coming from.'

He moved towards her.

'No, don't come near me,' she said, raising a hand in his direction. 'Where is Qes?'

'He is here. He's been looking for you ever since your family married you off. We have been making our way through the province. He thinks I don't know, but when he is sure you aren't in the vicinity, he gets himself into a fight and we have to move on, to look for you elsewhere.'

'I found the music box yesterday.'

'He's left hundreds of them. Everywhere. He was convinced you'd either find one or hear it being played, that you would remember the song he made up just for you.' Wamaq reached out his arm towards her. 'Shall I take you to him?'

'I can't.'

'What happened there? The bruise on your throat.'

She said nothing and would not look at him.

He felt he was being suffocated. 'I'll make him pay for it,' he whispered.

She seemed to come alive. 'Don't even think about it. Go away – both of you. You don't know what these people are capable of.' She came forward and pressed the music box into Wamaq's hand. Then she turned and left the room, shutting the door behind her. He heard the bolt being secured.

Three times that evening on the mosque roof Qes asked him in irritation, 'What?' and only then did Wamaq realize that he'd been staring at his brother while sunk deep in thought, following his movements. He quickly pretended to look elsewhere – the worshippers appeared doll-like on their prayer mats on the verandas far below, the great scarlet flame of the sunset before him – but soon he repeated the affront. Qes walked off in the end, muttering. Wamaq found him in the backyard of the caravanserai, cleaning the motorbike.

'Stop doing that. I have something to tell you,' Wamaq said, removing his mirror-embroidered cap. He was looking down but he could see Qes in the circular pieces shining in his hands. 'Before I tell you, I want to make sure you won't react stupidly. Are you going to pay attention and stay calm and do as I say?'

There was no answer. He looked up – Qes had gone so still that Wamaq felt a deep coldness in his own body.

'You know where Leila is,' his brother said. 'You've seen her . . . No, you've *met* her, at the big house. She heard my music two days ago . . .' He seemed to be putting the pieces of a story together. 'She . . . she ran around the house looking for the source of the music. But I stopped playing and she didn't know which way to turn.'

Wamaq was looking down on all the small images of Qes in his hands. Qes had made him promise that if he died, one of his music boxes would be buried with him, so he could continue his search for Leila in the next world.

After a while Wamaq asked, 'What are you going to do?'

Qes looked at him.

Deep in the night a few hours later, Qes got up from beside Wamaq, walked the motorbike out of the caravanserai and began his journey towards the mansion. He climbed the boundary wall and then, not allowing himself to be detected by the guard, entered the room at the back. Lowering himself on to the floor among the creatures, he began to wait.

IV

Leila picked up the shirt made of thin white paper and examined it with care. It rustled softly and was meant to represent the garment worn by Joseph, contact with which had restored sight to his father's eyes. Minutely inscribed with Quranic verses and prayers, as well as talismanic letters and their numerological equivalents, it was to be worn by Leila under her clothes as protection against misfortune, evil forces and enemies. She studied the writing and floral decorations that covered every part of the garment's surface like a page from an illuminated book, and had to struggle not to reveal her distress when she failed to locate the secret message she was expecting.

The midwife who had disappeared after the birth of the first child had contacted her a week ago, sending a letter through one of the people who brought remedies to the house. In the letter she promised that she would reveal to Leila the truth about her daughters. This was the reason Leila had refused to go to Qes. First she needed to learn where her children were.

But there had been no further word from the midwife.

She fought her tears. She had given birth to another daughter two months ago and had recently fallen pregnant again.

Razia came into the room and sat down on the deerskin she used as a prayer mat. The five prayers of the day were more or less the only times Leila was not under the mother-in-law's vigilance. Since talking to Wamaq the day before, she had tried not to think of the room with the animals and birds, but now she went down the corridors towards it, as fast as she could. Fortunately the noon prayers were the second longest of the day.

She stood before the closed door.

She could hear someone breathing on the other side. She raised her hand to undo the latch but then lowered it slowly.

'Leila.'

She imagined him standing there with the mute creatures. In there was the tiger that had headed the wedding procession when Timur came to marry her – claws blunted and mouth sewn shut for safety. It was shot a month later when the wounds festered.

'Leila. Let me see you.'

After a while he said, 'Are you weeping? Leila, open this door.'

He gave it a push and she withdrew down the corridor, having suddenly seen Timur holding a person underwater on the edge of the river and stabbing through the shallows with a knife, the murky water turning red.

Razia was still on the prayer mat, looped about with her thousand-bead rosary. She finished and pursed her lips to blow a gentle breath in Leila's direction, blessing her with the air still fresh from communion with Allah.

The servant girls brought them the *Book of Omens*, and Leila distractedly opened it for Razia.

'Where are my daughters?' she asked the woman suddenly.

'You know you are not to mention them,' Razia said, taken aback. She looked towards the door. 'What if the servants hear?'

'I want to see them,' Leila said, raising her voice, drawing strength from Qes's nearby presence.

'I will not discuss this,' Razia said sharply, putting the *Book of Omens* aside. 'Every few months you raise this accursed subject, just when I am about to forget it. Why are you intent on destroying this family? Because of you – the continued rebellion of your body – we are all suffering.'

Leila glared at her. 'I will run away.'

'That's enough, you child of adultery! My son picked you up from a hovel in a godforsaken village and installed you in this palace – and this is the thanks we get? You unspeakable interior organ of a swine!'

With no father or mother, Leila's bone-poor relatives were only too glad to be rid of her, telling her on the wedding day, 'Don't come back. If you can't have your husband's love, find sustenance in his hatred.'

'We are feeding you and giving you shelter,' said Razia, 'and yet you want to run away. Don't you know how dangerous and depraved life is on the outside for a woman on her own?'

Leila buried her face in her hands, in pain as though a hundred needles had pierced her skull from the inside.

She was still a small child when her father died, leaving behind a debt of 1,000 rupees. The council of the wise and the powerful argued late into the night and decided that, to make up for the loss, the men of the moneylender's family could possess the debtor's widow one hundred times.

At dawn the men took their boats and went on to the lake where Leila's mother was collecting lotus leaves somewhere in the rising sunlit mist. They returned an hour later with words nobody could accept as true – words about wings that suddenly appeared, about flight. Everyone believed they had drowned her in their ineptness and collective arousal. But as she grew older, Leila imagined her mother, a quarter of a mile from the lake's edge, the mist roaming the water like a soft supple fire around her. The seven boats that converged on her bore a total of thirty men, silhouetted in the fine-grained vapour. Some of them leaped over the water like panthers even before the boats connected. She fought them, surrounded, numbed by shock but with her eyes screaming the outrage of her solitude. The only escape was upwards and that was what she had chosen, willing the wings into existence upon her body, the emptiness of mist closing behind her as she rose.

The council of the wise and the powerful decided that the moneylenders must wait for Leila to grow up to be compensated – with the interest on the original debt accumulating annually till then.

As the years passed, her aunts warned her against wandering too far from home. One day when she was thirteen she did; and the men, connecting with each other through mobile phones, had recognized their opportunity. She was running from them, having managed to elude them for the time being, when she was seen by Timur, who was on a hunting expedition on the outskirts of the village. They were married within ten days.

When her anger had somewhat subsided, Razia turned to the *Book of Omens* and began to study the page Leila had opened earlier, a Chinaman wearing a bright red coat. It was in fact the poet Saadi, travelling through China disguised as a monk, spying on temples dedicated to false gods.

O augury seeker! she read aloud, *know that there is loss in mingling with those who are not of your sort, but you are aware of their deceit and will triumph over them, but to remain safe you must not take off your amulets.*

She walked to her bed and lay down with her eyes closed. She didn't move for an hour. According to the complex architecture of faith in her head, the *Book of Omens* seemed to be advising that she and Leila spend the next ten days in continuous silent prayer at the mosque on the river island.

'Is it absolutely necessary?' Timur said when she spoke to him.

'Yes, my son, it is Allah's will,' she replied. 'With remedies and prayers and fasts, I am making sure that it will be a boy this time, and we must proceed according to what He tells me to do through the *Book of Omens*. Three days ago, He told me to make Leila wear a Shirt of Joseph, to keep the boy safe from harm, and I have done that. Now you must immediately make a generous donation to the mosque and have a private room cleared for our use.'

Nadir Shah, aware that the island was irrevocably gone from him, wanted the next best thing, which was control over the mosque. Knowing the enemy would try force, Timur had recently decreed that nobody with weapons should be allowed on to the island. Almost all of the donations to the mosque found their way to Timur, and they were no longer just a few rupees offered by everyday people – word had been spreading and thousands upon thousands were being sent by rich industrialists, businessmen, local and national politicians. An Arabian prince had sent a silk carpet, another a hundred rosaries of black Gulf pearls, and in the imam's Quran, each of the 77,701 sacred words was outlined in crushed rubies, each of the 1,015,030 consonant dots in crushed emeralds. Things that had been free in the early days – food, shelter, the river crossings – now had to be paid for by pilgrims. All this had to be defended.

But Timur could not reveal any of this to his mother, and so in the end he agreed with her wishes.

'I am not going,' Leila said when Razia told her the plan.

She had decided: she hadn't heard from the midwife, and these people were unwilling to lead her to her daughters – so Qes was the only remaining hope. She knew she must wait until Razia sat down on the prayer mat again and then slip away to talk to him. That he was still there on the other side of the door was not something she doubted.

'You will do as you are told,' Razia said firmly. 'We have been lenient with you so far but that ends now. I am warning you, if the three acts of injustice against my blameless son are repeated at the next birth, neither he nor I will be responsible for the consequences. Like all good and honest people, my son has enemies, forever waiting for an opportunity to strike. They'll take everything away from him if he doesn't have sons to stand beside him in later years.'

A black air-conditioned jeep with tinted windows took them from the mansion to the riverbank, from where they crossed the waters of the Indus on a boat. Both Leila and Razia were entirely veiled, and a path was cleared for them through the crowd. A man selling a soap-bubble-making device for children was told to stop demonstrating lest the bubbles come into contact with the two women. Four servant girls accompanied them, three Muslims and one Christian. Philomena, the Christian, was to remain in the unconsecrated area until required to assist, and then approach either on tiptoe or on the outer edges of her feet to minimize contact with the sacred building.

It was a long white room off the main prayer hall, featureless but comfortable, and as Timur turned to go he saw Philomena try to pass an envelope into Leila's hand. Leila didn't seem to notice it and so Philomena quickly pulled it back into the folds of her veil. From the door he asked Philomena to come back to the mansion because more things were needed for the room.

Two men with Kalashnikovs under their blankets were positioned outside the room, pretending to say the rosary beads, and when he told them just before leaving, 'Be on your guard,' one of them grinned in response.

'It'll be easier for a man to fetch a bowl of lioness milk than to get past us.'

Timur took Philomena back to the mansion, re-emerging an hour later and driving back to the mosque. He had managed to make her talk just in time.

Upon entering the prayer hall he saw three women in conversation with the guards. When they saw Timur, one of the guards said, 'This woman says she is a midwife and has been summoned.'

She turned round and saw Timur.

'She *is* a midwife,' Timur said, smiling.

Her voice echoing off the high dome, the midwife said, 'In Allah's house today I am going to reveal the truth about you to everyone.' A few of the worshippers sitting around the prayer hall became interested and looked up. However, one man, without raising his eyes from his Quran, said, 'Yes, this is Allah's house, so would the lady kindly allow us some silence and peace?'

Timur addressed the hall. 'I apologize, but this dire matter concerns all Muslims. This woman was a midwife employed by me for the birth of my first child. When my son was born, she – a Christian – strangled him.' A few cries went up uncontrollably around the prayer hall at this. 'Yes, she was a Muslim but has secretly converted to Christianity, and is now conspiring against us genuine Muslims.'

'Liar!' the woman shouted, but she became intimidated when the imam of the mosque appeared, gazing in displeasure at the scene. She said in a lowered voice, 'Allah is still my Lord. And I am walking out of here with that poor girl.' All around were constant murmurs and sounds of agitation from the worshippers.

'She disappeared immediately after killing my unfortunate newborn son, and has reappeared today. Earlier this afternoon she bribed a Christian servant girl from my household who agreed to help her. She has brought with her these other women – schoolteachers and members of a foreign organization that preaches vulgarity to our pious womenfolk in the name of liberation. They have come here to this blessed place – which, as everyone knows, was built by angels at Allah's own command – to kidnap my wife. Go in and see how the Christian servant has drugged my Allah-loving mother by putting something in her drinking water.'

People were now standing up, their voices louder, one man nodding to himself and saying, 'The influence of the West has been the biggest calamity to befall the planet since Noah's flood.'

'I returned because I lived in guilt for all these years and months,' the midwife said. 'There was nothing I could have done back then but I should have done *something*. You did not have a son, you had a daughter –'

'That's enough. You are an apostate and a blasphemer.'

'I am a Muslim!'

'Then how do you explain this?' Timur said. A man had appeared and handed him a small cloth bundle. 'This is yours? We found it a minute ago in the boat you have hired to take away my wife.'

'Yes, it is mine.'

Timur pulled out a crucifix on a chain. 'I will not untie the bundle but those of you who need further proof will find a desecrated copy of our beloved Quran in it.'

There were wails and sounds of deepest genuine anguish from everyone. The three accused protested their innocence but their voices were drowned out as a number of men and women moved forwards and began to beat them, pulling them to the floor by their hair and clothes. They were screaming desolately as a pack of policemen arrived and took them away, the worshippers striking them constantly, a few spitting on them. Timur handed over the evidence to a policeman, who kissed the bundle repeatedly before pressing it to his heart, and held the swinging crucifix at arm's length as though carrying a dead rat by the tail. Apostasy was punishable by death, as was blasphemy, but it was possible the case would not reach the courts – the women would be murdered within the next few days in the police cells, either by their fellow criminals or by the policemen, so repugnant were the crimes they were accused of.

As the people returned to their worship, Timur went into the white room. His mother lay on the mattress at the far end, conscious but with her eyes half shut. The servant girls were massaging her feet and head. Philomena had administered nothing but a mild sedative but Razia thought she was dying.

'Tell them not to bury me in the public cemetery,' she said, 'or the grave robbers will dig me up to get at all the gold in my bones.'

Leila stood just a few feet from Timur. 'I had no knowledge of any of it,' she said, trembling.

'You'd better be telling the truth,' he said. He had discovered nothing to implicate her: the envelope Philomena had tried to pass on had contained just one sentence from the midwife, telling her she would be free before nightfall. He leaned towards her and added in a lowered voice, 'And you'd better give me a son this time, because if it's a girl again, I'll drown you in the river out there.'

It was almost a whisper but the boatman whom Timur had hired to come in and carry his mother out, and who was just entering the room, heard it clearly. It was Wamaq. He did not react – either to the words or to suddenly finding himself face to face with Leila again. The old woman had revived and was saying that they would not be returning to the mansion, that she intended to carry out Allah's wish and stay in the mosque for ten days. Timur waved his hand in Wamaq's direction and he nodded and left the room.

V

Finishing work an hour later, Wamaq walked to the caravanserai and saw the motorbike leaning on its kickstand in its usual place. Qes had decided to return from the mansion. He found him outside the barbershop, reading the rates for a bath painted on the glass front. He went and stood beside him.

PLAIN WATER: 5 RUPEES.
WITH LIFEBUOY SOAP: 8 RUPEES.
WITH LUX BEAUTY SOAP: 12 RUPEES.

Qes didn't acknowledge his brother, moving around him to enter the shop. Wamaq went in after him. Later, in clean clothes, their wet hair and sparse moustaches retaining the furrows of the comb they had run through them, Wamaq followed Qes wordlessly to a food shop situated under a large mulberry tree. There the older brother ordered their meal, with sweet cardamom tea to follow, while the younger went to sit on the bench chained to the tree trunk.

'She wouldn't see me or even talk to me,' Qes said at last, quietly, eyes averted. His face was drained from hunger and lack of sleep. 'All I heard were her tears.'

Wamaq then recounted how he'd seen Leila at the mosque, telling him also the exact words of Timur's threat to her. They were both silent after he finished speaking, then Qes said, 'We have to get her away from here.'

'I know,' Wamaq said. 'We'll do it while she's on the island.'

Qes was nodding his head. 'Everyone says this family always

has sons. So obviously they are unhappy that she has had girls.' He looked at his brother. 'I won't allow it to continue, any of it.'

'Me neither.'

They sat listening to the river and the insect song floating above it, now and then looking at the mosque, Wamaq examining Qes's face openly for a few moments and Qes allowing it. After they had told Qes that Leila was getting married, they had had to hold him down and he had torn himself out of his clothes. They locked him in a room. When he broke free a week later it was on her wedding day and the havoc he wrought in the bazaar, lunging at possible weapons, made many people think the wedding procession tiger had slipped its leash.

Wamaq said, 'And I don't like the feeling I get when I think of the animals and birds in that room. What kind of a world is it where you aren't free even after death?'

The waiter brought them their food and by way of making conversation said, 'Those things are a mystery to me.' A man in denim jeans had just gone by.

'Don't tell me, Uncle,' Qes said. 'I tried on a pair of Western trousers once. Didn't know how to walk.'

'Which way is the bus station?' Wamaq asked the man.

'The bus station? Where do you want to go? My brother has a car you can hire instead.' Just then his mobile phone rang – the ringtone was a recitation of verses from the Quran – and he walked away, to the relief of Wamaq and Qes who would have preferred not to have awakened his curiosity. Not for nothing were roadside food places known as 'newspapers made of brick'.

After eating they rode to the train station instead, stopping wordlessly for a minute at a bend in the road to watch a church in the distance being consumed by a powerful fire, the rioters clustered around it.

At the ticket window, they asked the name of the farthest destination it was possible to travel to from that station, making a note especially of the non-stop services over the next twenty-four hours. Coming back to the river they crossed over to the island and said their prayers at the mosque, Wamaq's furtive nod indicating Leila's room to Qes. The two guards were still there.

After the prayers, they left the building and walked away along the rim of the island, flocks of water birds stirring in the reeds or hovering in the air with piercing screams. There was the smell of leaves decaying in the earth. In places upriver – the mosque out of sight behind monolithic banyans and Persian lilacs – other birds had hollowed countless nest-holes in the vertical walls of the mudbanks, making them look like giant sponges.

'We'll come here with her,' said Wamaq. 'We have to get a boat and hide it here in advance. We'll use it to cross over to the riverbank.' He pointed to the secluded spot on the other side of the river. 'Hardly anyone goes there. The motorbike will be waiting – you and Leila will use it to go to the station, get on the train and leave. I'll follow later.'

It was getting dark but the pure white shell of an egg fallen to the ground below a nest-hole drew Wamaq's attention. He went to pick it up to put it back in the nest, but it had cracked. The sound of astonishment he gave upon discovering a rifle bullet inside the egg brought Qes to him. Qes put his hand in a nest and removed an intact egg, pale indigo in colour. Breaking the shell at the tip he turned it upside down, and the metal bullet slipped out on to the palm of his hand along with the living albumen.

They walked along the perforated wall of earth, counting: each nest held at least half a dozen eggs and there were hundreds of nests.

'And here are the black serpents waiting to feed on what comes out of those eggs,' Qes said when they found large wooden crates hidden among the reeds and opened one of them. It was full of guns.

Just then they heard voices and moved deeper into the reeds, from where they saw a group of men arrive and begin to drag the crates out into the open. The weapons were distributed and then they went towards the wall of nests. They all wore prayer caps and had been among the worshippers earlier. The route Wamaq and Qes were planning to use – to take Leila off the island – was exactly the route that had been used to smuggle the weapons on to it.

The brothers emerged after the men were gone, and as they looked into the empty nests they heard bursts of gunfire from the mosque. They hurried towards it but it was difficult for them to enter because the panicked worshippers were trying to flee in the opposite direction, shouting and screaming, trampling each other underfoot. Someone told them that the imam of the mosque and all of his aides had been assassinated, the entire staff being replaced by Nadir Shah's men.

When at last they managed to get in, they found the prayer hall empty. The bodies of the two guards lay outside Leila's room. Wamaq and Qes moved towards it and looked in. The old woman was sitting on a deerskin on the floor – undisturbed at her prayer. It was as though the gunfire – which began again outside at that moment – did not penetrate her ears while she communed with Allah.

Two servant girls crouched fearfully on the other side of the bed. 'All this is Nadir Shah's doing, isn't it?' one of them whimpered.

The other shook her head, looking with undisguised contempt towards the old woman. 'It's the wrath of Allah.'

Wamaq asked, 'Where's Leila?' but there was no answer. He and Qes went out and began looking for her separately among the people running towards the boats on the water's edge. Half an hour later, Qes was walking by an upstairs room when he came to a standstill. He entered and quietly spoke her name.

A few small hexagons of light were coming in from outside, scattered on the walls and floor like ghosts of diamonds. She called to him from the far corner. It was perhaps a room meant for scholars because there seemed to be books everywhere, ink pots and pens, and nibs that rang musically when they poured themselves on to the floor, his elbow nudging the box.

'You sound like paper,' he said as he touched her.

'It's the Shirt of Joseph.' Putting her arms around his neck, she added, 'But I feel like I am almost blind. I want to see you clearly.'

'We can't put on the light just yet,' he replied. 'I'll go and find Wamaq and then we'll leave. Lock the door from the inside.'

'My husband will be here any moment,' she said.

'I know. With a hundred armed men of his own.'

There was no human noise as he descended the outdoor staircase and crossed the large half-lit courtyard. He was walking towards the main entrance of the mosque when he met Wamaq. He told him he had found Leila and the two brothers were heading towards the water's edge, wondering about a boat, when suddenly Timur appeared ahead of them and said, 'Halt.' They stopped just where the darkness met the light.

'What's the situation on this side?' Timur asked. Ten or so of his men were behind him.

Qes shook his head. 'We don't know what's going on.'

'Where are you coming from?' Timur tried to look into the darkness behind them. He recognized Wamaq. 'Didn't I see you earlier today – the boatman?' Then he turned to Qes and seemed to become transfixed. Qes feared his thoughts were being read.

Timur seemed to be in disbelief over something, even shock. He took a step towards Qes and said, 'Where is my wife?'

'I don't know what you mean.'

'Move forward just an inch into the light,' he said, walking towards Qes without taking his eyes off him, the gun raised. He did not stop as he neared and for a second Qes thought he would walk right through him. But then he stopped and reached out his hand to lift the metal nib stuck to Qes's heart.

He turned the small shining object in his hand, light coming off it in shards.

He tossed it gently at Qes's breast. Just to make sure it would stick again.

Wamaq raised his hand to stop it from arriving and attaching itself to his brother. The sudden movement caused Timur to turn the gun instinctively towards Wamaq and pull the trigger. In the trace of sound that the bullet left in the atmosphere, Qes watched the blood emerging from his brother's stomach. First there was a thin line that fell through the air in an intact curve, breaking up just above the ground to land as a chorus of drops. Then, as he was being thrown on to his back, a large glowing spurt came out.

Wamaq fell backwards into the darkness and lay shaking and Timur fired a second and a third bullet into him without looking. Just then there was a deafening burst of gunfire from somewhere nearby that claimed Timur's attention. It was a matter of perhaps two or three seconds, but it was enough for Qes to turn round and start to run. They must have followed him but he could neither see nor hear anything any more.

When he regained his senses he was in the ten-foot reeds behind the mosque. The sound of gunfire came in short bursts and from various parts of the building, now near, now distant, like a flock of swallows circling the area very fast. When he remembered, he climbed out into the courtyard and Wamaq was still there, alone, his eyes open and his breathing shallow. Qes half lifted, half dragged him into the light and touched the wounds. Each bullet hole was less than an inch in width, but from the amount of blood it was as though the stomach had been torn open by claws and giant fangs. It was his death – the invisible beast eating into the body.

'Qes.'

He lowered his ear to his brother's ice-cold lips. 'Yes?'

'Qes, it hurts.'

'I know. Open your eyes. Stay awake. Someone has just gone to get a doctor. You'll be all right.'

He felt a sudden, quickly subsiding wave of terror and in its wake he was filled with an immense love, for his brother and their life together, and for the world in which they had had that life. He got up and went towards the boats, but gunfire forced him back. Upstairs, the door stood open and the light had been switched on in the scholars' room when he got there. He called to Leila several times but received no sound in return.

In the courtyard, Wamaq's body was folded up like that of an unborn child.

'Qes.'

He took his brother's head in his lap. 'Yes?'

'Isn't the doctor here yet?'

'You always were strange. I told you about the doctor just one second ago. He's not going to fly here, is he?'

'Did you? It feels much longer.'

'You'll be all right.'

'Qes, I'm thirsty.'

Qes went to the river and entered the reeds, taking off his shirt when he got to the current that broke and swirled into dangerous eddies. Soaking the shirt in the water, he brought it back dripping, and gently squeezed a little from the sleeve into Wamaq's mouth.

'Qes, it hurts so much.'

Their father had told them once in his cane-liquor eloquence, 'The strength with which a molar holds on to the jaw when you have it extracted is as nothing to the strength with which the soul is attached to the body. When they begin to tear away from each other, the torment is unbearable.'

Qes lowered his own forehead on to Wamaq's and wept silently, the roots of Wamaq's hair smelling of the bitter Lifebuoy soap from the bath a few hours earlier. He got up and went into the night again, trying to find a way off the island. By the time he came back, Wamaq's heart had stopped beating. The eyes had lifted so that the whites beneath the irises showed – an unmoving stare, transfixed by whatever it was that the dead could see but could not convey.

The fingers of his right hand were still closed around the nib.

VI

One morning ten months later, the black air-conditioned jeep with the tinted windows left the mansion, carrying Razia and Leila, two servant girls, the driver and a bodyguard who was the size he was because he injected himself with cattle steroids. Leila was being taken to a desert shrine to receive a blessing, a two-day journey from the mansion and the Indus.

Nothing lay around the 300-year-old shrine except low, cactus-covered hills and sand dunes, and ancient time. Shaken by the ferocity and organization of Nadir Shah's raid – unsuccessful though it proved in the end – and to try another path towards a male child, Timur had married again. The marriage took place within weeks of the attack. At twenty-one, the new bride was five years older than Leila. She lived at the mansion with them and was expecting a child any day. The *Book of Omens* predicted it to be a boy. Timur continued to demand from Leila what she owed him, however; insisting she make up for the years of torture to which she had subjected him.

The saint who lay buried at the shrine had had control of certain female djinns – those that guarded the souls of dead warriors, conducting them safely from the battlefield to Paradise. The she-djinns also guided the souls of those women who had died giving birth to boys, for having sacrificed their lives to provide future warriors.

A group of nine sacred men resided there now, renowned throughout the country – and throughout the Pakistani immigrant communities around the planet – for helping women to have male children. Prior to lying down with her husband with the intention of conceiving, the woman would spend one whole week in strict seclusion with the nine exalted personages, praying, meditating and eating the simple food they cooked. Afterwards, the woman would speak of holy visitations, of intense dreams and hallucinations. She would have no recollection of entire hours of the seven-day period. If she failed to have a male child, she would return to beg forgiveness from the saint and the nine men, for not having cleansed her mind and soul of impurities thoroughly enough, for having trespassed on and squandered their valuable time.

Just before midnight Razia brought Leila to the room where she was to spend the week with the holy personages. They walked to the wooden bed in the far corner and she made Leila lie down on her right side, so she could face Mecca. One of the servant girls was carrying a box of one-inch iron nails and a hammer, and, working slowly all around Leila, Razia nailed her clothes to the bed. This didn't have anything to do with the nine holy men. This precaution was taken at the mansion too: it was the result of her leaving the mosque's white room on the night of Nadir Shah's raid. Whenever possible, if she was to be in a place for longer than a few minutes, Razia had her clothes fixed to the walls or floor.

Razia and the servant girls would be sleeping in rooms on the other side of the shrine, and they left after they had secured her, leaving behind the nails and hammer so the holy men could resecure Leila after she attended to her toilet.

Leila, with the thirty spikes holding her immobile, waited anxiously for the men to come to her room. When they entered they brought with them a cool serene scent of violets. They did not approach her, arranging themselves on the other side of the room instead, eyes closed in prayer. Now and then one of them would come, mouthing sacred words as he walked, and after blowing those words softly along the length of her body, he would withdraw.

She fell asleep as the hours passed, listening to the sandstorm outside the window. Her body woke her in the middle of the night and she saw that all nine men were approaching the bed. They came and surrounded her, their hands in contact with the intimate places of her body. She fought against the nails in her clothes but didn't have enough strength to uproot herself, wanted to shout out but found her tongue paralysed. She felt terror and then a rage and grief the size of the sky, the rage of the damned and the abandoned, and she imagined once again her mother on the dawn lake, struggling powerlessly in the mist with her assailants. She clearly saw the wings emerge from her body, their movement leaving a scribble of clarity in the gold and silver vapour of the lake.

The desert shrine was roused a few minutes later by the confusion and shouts of the nine exalted men. Razia went into the room and saw how the window had had its panels shattered and was now open to the violent sandstorm. The empty bed where Leila had been lying was covered with syllables and smears in a radiant silver liquid.

The nails that outlined her body had small pinches of fabric and fine threads attached to them, like tiny brilliant feathers, shaking in that great wind from the broken window.

'I suspected right from the beginning that this girl was not real,' one of the nine men said. 'So much beauty cannot be human.'

The sandstorm continued to howl past dawn, and in the morning when the air and sky cleared at last they spread out on to the dunes. There was so much static from the storm that sheets and jagged fibres of bright blue electricity danced on the ground all around them, climbing silently up their bodies as they walked. They found marks on the sand indicating the recent presence of jackals, gazelles, snakes and beetles, but there was no sign of her in any direction. And then, almost a mile away, her tracks suddenly began, halfway up the low incline of a dune. The footprints were enclosed within two lightly scored continuous lines, as though she had been dragging two sticks behind her. It was early but already the sun was baring its teeth, the heat intense. Her tracks disappeared into a large flock of demoiselle cranes in the distance and they found her at the centre of it, lying face down, exhausted from thirst and the sun.

They brought her back. Razia didn't know what to do when she saw her, in despair at the provocations Leila continued to throw at her son.

'That scan at the hospital five months ago didn't reveal anything of this,' she said as she stared at the wings on Leila's back. She had disapproved of Leila having the ultrasound scan to determine the sex of the foetus, because Muhammad had said that no one but Allah held the answers to such mysteries as the country of a person's death and whether the child growing in a woman's belly was a boy or a girl. But Timur, saying that these were modern times and that the world was moving on, had insisted – so that the foetus could be aborted if female. To the joy of everyone, the scan showed the fourth child to be male, but when the time came Leila had given birth to a girl yet again. Razia saw it as a punishment from Allah for doubting Muhammad's word.

And now there was this new difficulty.

The wings were gently alive, the feathers giving a slow hypnotic shake as the desert sand fell out of them. They were large and white and they were beautiful like those of the woman-headed steed that had taken Muhammad to Paradise from the minaret in Jerusalem.

'It's a miracle,' a servant girl said.

Razia lost her temper. 'A miracle? The mosque appearing on the river island was a miracle. This is an illusion, some example of the arts of the black realms.'

'Yes,' the bodyguard nodded, thinking. 'It must be some trick.'

Razia muttered to herself, 'A miracle! Why would Allah waste His attentions on a wife who allows her body to continue disobeying her husband and in-laws? On a Muslim who rejects the company of men as supremely spiritual as these nine?'

She sent for their sharpest scissors but all they could find was a large rusty pair the shrine-keepers used on thorn bushes. With them she tried to cut back the flight feathers a few at a time. They proved to be composed of too resistant a material, and it was noon by the time she managed to reduce each wing to just the bony outer ridge, the ceiling of the room covered with down and the segmented feathers – they had all floated upwards on becoming free. 'There is an explanation for everything,' Razia said as she watched them rising all around her. 'It must be due to the static electricity.'

To prove that the wings were indeed an illusion, and weren't connected in any meaningful way with Leila's body, she summoned the butcher.

With an array of knives and cleavers beside him, the butcher positioned Leila on her side on the courtyard floor, held the tattered remains of the wings firmly in place by squatting on them, and made the first quick incision close to the shoulder blades. Leila didn't feel anything, and for Razia it was a vindication. She reached out her finger and touched the wound and it was then that a trickle of blood appeared and Leila cried out in pain. She struggled to sit up, her violent movements causing the cut to become elongated and tear. They overpowered her, and with the pain making her scream to Allah and all of His 124,000 prophets for help, the butcher detached them with several swings of the cleaver. There was so much blood from the two appendages that it looked like a small massacre, and everyone and everything close by was freckled with red. Barely conscious, Leila sobbed and attempted to crawl away. But she was like a maimed animal. The servant girls struggled to hold her down again as the wounds were stitched up with shoemakers' twine.

A journalist who happened to be present at the crumbling seventeenth-century shrine, to write an article lamenting the decrepit condition of Pakistan's historical buildings and monuments, witnessed the entire procedure and immediately sat down on the veranda to write the story of the wings. Razia had noticed him earlier, looking horrified as he watched. Now she stopped on the veranda for a moment on her way indoors and said, 'There was no need for you to be so upset, son. But then you men don't understand anything about women's bodies – we can take more pain than you.'

Inside, she said to Leila, 'I hope you won't take too long to heal.' She was dusting the wounds with the ash of a reed prayer mat she had had burned for the purpose. 'When we get home you will be ready to receive Timur again. The new wife is going to give him a son very soon, and yours too is bound to be a boy next time. It'll be your fifth pregnancy and five is a fundamental number of our glorious religion. There are five prayers in the day, and Islam has five pillars.' She gained eloquence as she talked. 'Taste, smell, sight, touch and hearing. Allah in His wisdom gave us five external senses, and five internal – common sense, estimation, recollection, reflection and imagination.'

She spoke to the nine exalted personages to see if they would honour Leila with the favour of their continued presence. They not only refused, but also asked them to leave immediately. The men appeared afraid of the shrine itself now, looking stricken at the merest noise – three of them wondering if the she-djinns of the legend had returned to the building, two of them fleeing even before Razia and Leila had left.

Passing through a city on the return journey, Razia had the driver stop at a hospital so a doctor could examine Leila's wounds. A commotion broke out while they were there. A woman who had just given birth began shouting that her newborn male had been exchanged with a female, refusing to accept that she had produced a girl, labelling the hospital staff liars and criminals and sinners, and calling down Allah's fury on them. When the exasperated doctors said that if she did not relent they would carry out a DNA test immediately, she stopped protesting and agreed that, yes, the girl baby was hers. Her postman husband had warned her that she would be thrown out on to the streets if she brought home a seventh daughter.

'I have heard that nurses and doctors at hospitals can be bribed to exchange female newborns with male ones,' a woman whispered to Razia, and Razia shuddered, grateful that Allah had given her the foresight to keep her own daughters-in-law at home.

The black jeep arrived back at the mansion at dawn. Everything was silent. In the men's section the party in anticipation of Timur's son had ended some hours ago, a few revellers asleep among the rose bushes. Leila's grey-glass eyes had remained closed throughout the journey, with a weak sigh escaping her lips now and then, and she was carried up to the bedroom. Razia stood by the bed hesitatingly for a few moments, but then went out to get the hammer and nails.

Leila opened her eyes and sat up carefully, shivering and trying not to weep. She looked at the picture hanging directly above the bed – a man and a woman in a flowering grove, a peacock on a bough near them, the tail exquisite, the feet dry and gnarled. She had concealed a knife behind it the previous week, considering it the easiest place to reach during Timur's upcoming night visits to her.

From her waistband she took the music box she had come across at the hospital – an orderly said he had found it on the stump of a jacaranda tree some years ago and that she could have it. Sitting there with her raw shredded shoulders, she began to turn the crank.

Hundreds of miles away in the city of Lahore, he placed the glass of water on the aluminium table in front of him and became very still. He had just finished work and was having a meal on the street named after the slave girl Anarkali, whom Emperor Akbar had had walled up alive for having an affair with the Crown prince. He worked as a driver for a printing press, delivering bundles of newspapers to various corners of the city before the sun rose. He had very few long-term memories and at times he was doubtful even of the most basic facts about himself. *Had that happened? Who was she and where is she now? Who was he?* During the previous months there had been hours that had come at him like spears, at different angles – sometimes it was his body that was in pain, at others his mind. Everyone believed him to be mute, a few even mad.

He got up and walked towards the motorbike, the sky glistening with light above him. Mynahs and crows that had been sitting without trepidation in the middle of the empty roads lifted themselves into the air briefly to let him pass. At the train station there was an unbroken beeping from the metal detectors that had been installed since the jihadi attacks began, but they were unmanned and everyone and everything was getting through, setting them off. He bought a ticket, indicating the destination by pointing to the chart on the wall. It was almost involuntary: it felt like falling, or like rising in a dream. The motorbike had to travel in the goods carriage and when they asked him for his name, to be put on the receipt, he spoke for the first time since the day he'd buried his brother.

'My name is Leila.'

The train began its journey and he sat looking out of the window, the dead memory stirring as he went through the land he knew, past the basement snooker clubs full of teenagers, past the mosque whose mullah had decreed polio vaccination a Western conspiracy but had then made announcements in its favour after his own little daughter was taken by the disease, past the house of a dying man whose five children could not come to his deathbed because they had sought asylum in Western countries, past the policeman who stopped by the roadside to take a deep drag from a hashish smoker's cigarette, past cart donkeys no bigger than goats who were pulling monumental loads along thoroughfares where humans were being beaten and abused in prisons, madhouses, schools and orphanages, past the words on the back of a rickshaw that playfully warned the driver behind it: *Don't come too near or love will result*, past the dark-skinned woman who had used so much skin-bleaching cream that although she was now pale, she bruised at the merest of touches, past the college boy reading a novel in which the only detailed descriptions occurred during sex and torture or during sexual torture, past the beggars whose bodies had been devoured by hunger, past the green ponds above which insects the size of tin-openers were flying, past the towns and cities and villages of his immense homeland of heartbreaking beauty, containing saints and sinners and a gentle religion, kind mothers and dutiful fathers who indulged their obedient children, its crimson dawns and its blue-smoke dusks, and its unforgivable cruelty, its jasmine flowers that lived as briefly as bursts of laughter and its minarets from where Allah was pleaded with to send the monsoon rains, and from where Allah was pleaded with to *end* the monsoon rains, and its unforgivable dishonesty, its rich for whom the poor died shallower deaths, its poor to whom only stories about hunger seemed true, its snow-blind mountains and sunburned deserts and beehives producing honey as sweet as the sound of Urdu, and its unforgivable brutality, and its unforgivable dishonesty, and its unforgivable cruelty, past the boy sending a text message to the girl he loved, past the two shopkeepers arguing about cricket, past the clerk who was having to go and work abroad ('I love Pakistan but Pakistan doesn't love me back and is forcing me to leave!'), past the government-run schools where the teachers taught only the barest minimum so the pupils would be forced to hire them for private tuition, past the girl pasting a new picture into her Aishwarya Rai scrapbook, past the crossroads decorated with giant fibreglass replicas of the mountain under which Pakistan's nuclear bombs were tested, past the men unworthy of the

rights their women conferred on them, past the trucks painted with
the colours of jewels, past the six-year-olds selling Made in China
prayer mats at traffic lights, past the ten-year-olds working in steel
foundries, past the poet who was a voice in everyone's head telling
them what they already knew, past the narrow alleys of the bazaars
where it was possible to get caught in human traffic jams and stand
immobile for half an hour, past the fields of sorghum and sugar cane
and pearl millet, past the most beautiful, surpassingly generous and
honest people under the sky, past the mausoleum of a saint who
arrived on a visit and was murdered because the people knew his
grave would bring pilgrims and trade to their village, past the men
and women for whom it was impossible to believe that there was no
God and that He wasn't looking after them, because how else could
they have been spared the poverty, destruction and random violence
that lay all around them?

Getting off the train he rode to the Indus on the motorbike and
on towards the mansion. *Why had he gone so far away from here?*
Because he had to take Wamaq's body to Lahore, because Wamaq had
always said he would be buried in the same cemetery as his namesake
poet. Walking away from his brother's grave, his mind had stumbled
into the void from which it was only now emerging.

It was fully dark by the time he climbed the mansion's boundary
wall and entered the room at the back. As he crossed it he felt the
presence of the animals and birds in the darkness around him, the
stags with antlers weighing a third of their bodies, the glittering Gilgit
butterflies under their glass dome, the cheetah whose spots made it
look as though it had come in out of a black rain. Silent, he stopped
in front of the door.

She undid the latch on the other side and blindly reached out her
hand to take his, the absence of light so complete around them that
their strongest glances were absorbed and utterly disappeared. He
led her to where he knew there was a divan covered in a dust sheet.

They undressed and in the glow of the gold attached to her skin
they saw each other for the first time since becoming separated all

those years ago. Gently they touched each other, he mindful of her torn back, she kissing his mouth and throat and chest, the parts of his body he used for singing. No one – not even they themselves – knew the origins of their attachment. Perhaps the earliest incident had been the mullah beating Qes for not having memorized his Quranic lessons, and bruises appearing on Leila's body.

As they picked up their clothes afterwards, he noticed the small rips and tears in various locations on her garments. But she was smiling with happiness just to be near him. Dressed, they were once again in the darkness.

'I need something from my room before I go.'

'All right.' There was no fear or hesitation in the voice. They stepped into the corridor and with complete self-possession walked towards her room, entering a hall and going up a flight of stairs. He saw her wooden bed with the many nails driven into it, making outlines of her body. She went to the picture above the bed. Throwing aside the knife she took from behind it, she opened the frame and removed the picture. On its back she had written down the secret names that she had given to her four missing daughters.

They were descending the stairs when they saw Timur in the large hall. They stopped.

He was looking at one of the doors that opened on to the hall – it led to the suite of rooms occupied by the new wife. They watched as a devastated Razia opened the door and fell into his arms. 'It's not a boy,' she said, weeping. In her right hand was the ancient dagger with which the umbilical cords were always cut.

Timur separated himself from his mother and stood looking at the floor in a dazed state. Picking up the table that held a vase of plastic lilies, he hurled it against the wall with an immense roar. Leila moved backwards on to a higher step but Qes remained where he was. Razia was weeping, her eyes shut.

As the moments passed and they waited for Timur to look up and discover them, Leila came back down and stood beside Qes.

At that moment, a dozen of Timur's men entered the hall, all of them armed.

'What do you want?' Timur turned to them and bellowed.

One of them came forward and prepared to speak up. He was wearing black clothes and only when red spots materialized on the floor below him did it become obvious that he was bleeding. 'Nadir Shah is on the island. He has complete control.'

'Why is Allah punishing us good Muslims?' Razia exclaimed.

'That fucking island!' Timur shouted. 'Set fire to it – the building and everything in it, the trees and every last blade of grass. Burn even the water around it!'

The old woman let out a cry of horror. 'What are you saying, Timur?'

The man in black said, 'We can't get near it. They have rocket-propelled grenades and there are landmines all along the edge of the island. We don't know where they got them from. He and his sons must have developed links with the jihadis.'

'I don't care. Take every bandit and son of a whore in this house and go and burn it all to the ground.'

Razia grabbed his arm. 'You can drive him off another way. Allah is on our side, remember.'

'Where is your Allah and how many cannons does he have?' Timur said. 'Stay out of it, it doesn't concern you.' Then he turned squarely to her. 'And it's your fault that I am alone against him and his sons – why didn't you perform your duty as a woman and give me brothers?'

Razia raised the hand with the dagger to her mouth and bit her knuckles, the long dazzling blade with the verses of the Quran etched on to it jutting from her fist. She stepped away from him, the eyes ringed with white lashes wide with surprise, the head lowered as she seemed to recover and, with a fixed empty smile, said, 'The fate of the mosque does concern me. It concerns me as a Muslim. Angels sent by Allah Himself built that mosque . . .'

Leila tightened her grip on Qes as Timur struck the old woman hard on the face, knocking her to the ground, the elegant dagger rattling to the other end of the hall. 'I am sick of all this,' Timur said and he bent down and grabbed hold of the thousand-bead rosary and tore it to pieces, sending the little black spheres flying in all directions. Some of them even slipped under the door to the new wife's rooms. He straightened and turned to his men.

'What are you still doing here? Didn't you hear my orders?'

'Call them back, in the name of Allah,' Razia pleaded as she wept on the floor.

He stood above her with his loud breathing and then walked over to the dagger. He picked it up, went to the door behind which the birth had just taken place and kicked it open with his foot. Screams and cries went up in the room, the sounds of panic. Leila attempted to stop Qes but he stayed her gently and went down the staircase at great speed, she following a few steps behind.

'For the last time, don't do that to the mosque,' Razia was saying wretchedly, scrabbling around for her rosary beads with her fingers, as Qes and Leila went past her. They heard Timur give a great enraged shout and then an immense silence descended on the world.

Leila and Qes entered the room and saw that the new mother, with her hands red and an expression of crazed hatred on her face, was standing above Timur, who lay on the floor, his mouth still open from that shout. The woman stepped back as he pulled the dagger out of his breast and, the instinct for force still undamaged within the confused and dying mind, stabbed his own stomach with it, once, twice, driving the blade most of the way in each time as the blood welled out of his mouth through gritted teeth. He plunged it blindly into his thigh and groin, and into his face below the right eye, and lastly into the house itself, stabbing the granite floor beside him. Against the walls stood the motionless servant girls, and the midwife clutching the minutes-old human being. She came forward and handed the baby to its mother.

Timur's blood roamed the floor. Razia, having finally gathered the remains of her rosary from the hall, entered and slowly began to pick the beads off the bedroom floor, each new one bringing her deeper into the room, and closer to Timur's body. Many of them she collected out of his blood. One lay near his hand – the hand that held the dagger embedded up to the hilt in the stone floor. Only then did she seem to see him.

Brushing against the stationary animals in the darkness, Qes and Leila crossed the room and went out into the night. They stood looking at the sky, taking the galaxies on to their faces, the tide of scents from night flowers. But a minute later he brought her back to the room and switched on the lights. He opened all the windows one by one and began to move the animals so that they faced the door to the outside. When she understood, she lifted the glass dome off the emerald butterflies and carried them to a windowsill. He climbed on to the shoulders of the tiger and raised his hand to unhook the opening of the cage in which a paradise flycatcher sat, bound to its swing with thin wire. He moved towards the tiger's haunches and opened the cage of the blossom-headed parakeet. Without touching the ground he stepped on to the table and then on to the back of the lioness and on to the blue antelope, opening all the cages suspended from the ceiling that was painted like a garden. When they left they made sure both panels of the door were open behind them, each cage swinging on its long chain.

The next song he'd make up for her would be about a lamp in a room where two lovers met – so engrossed did the flame become in watching them that it continued to burn when the oil finished. ∎

PK 754

The city glitters
and in some dim light you, too, are sleeping.
From these heights
the moon's surface is closer.
But, no –
no one knows
whether the air is swift or cold here,
whether this is a floating smoke of clouds
or the dust of companionship.
Is this the quivering wave of the final call
or the unsteady vessel of flight
or the lurching earth below?

Who was it went to sleep holding sand in his fists
became distant even to imagination and dream
disappeared in the tangled hair of straying night?
Are the stars moving with me?
What regret is it that has not yet been soothed?
Heights, separations
even intimations of death have not eased it.
Fellow traveller of depths
of altitudes
tell me –
on earth
in the air

the path that never took shape
what came of it?
Tell me
what kind of sleep is it
that can cross the wall of night
and transform into morning?

What kind of dream?
Tell me, what is this cry of pain in the air?
What is this restlessness?
The journey is coming to an end
and the noise is deafening.

Translated by Waqas Khwaja

National Theatre

Autumn 2010 Season

Danton's Death

by Georg Büchner
in a new version by Howard Brenton

★★★★★
Sunday Telegraph

'Thrilling... Toby Stephens
is in splendid form.'
Daily Telegraph

Until 14 October

Supported by
Laura Pels Foundation

Sponsored by

Media Partner
THE TIMES

Blood and Gifts

a new play by J T Rogers

This epic political thriller, shot
through with mad humour,
sweeps from refugee camps
to the corridors of power
in Washington DC.

From 7 September

Blood and Gifts
was commissioned by
Lincoln Center Theater,
New York City

A short version of the
play was presented at
the Tricycle Theatre
in 2009 as part of
The Great Game

Hamlet

by William Shakespeare

Following his series of celebrated
performances at the National,
Rory Kinnear plays Hamlet.

From 30 September

Sponsored by
Travelex

Media Partner
THE TIMES

Men Should Weep

by Ena Lamont Stewart

A moving and funny portrayal of
impoverished 1930s Glasgow. This raw
salute to the human spirit was voted
one of the top hundred plays of the
last century in the NT millennium poll.

From 18 October

020 7452 3000 no booking fee

Supported by
ARTS COUNCIL
ENGLAND

nationaltheatre.org.uk

Photos © (Toby Stephens) Hugo Glendinning; Mauricio Lima/AFP/Getty Images; (Rory Kinnear) Ela Hawes; Barbara Orton

GRANTA

PORTRAIT OF JINNAH

Jane Perlez

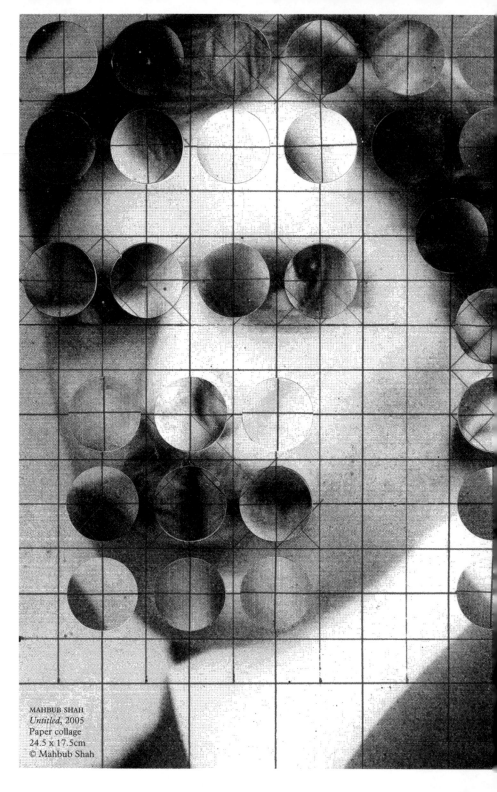

MAHBUB SHAH
Untitled, 2005
Paper collage
24.5 x 17.5cm
© Mahbub Shah

When a Pakistani friend won a promotion to a powerful job in Peshawar I went to congratulate him on his new sinecure. He is a cultivated man with a beautiful home from the British colonial era and tentacles all across Pakistan's tormented tribal region, where he once served as a political agent – the all-purpose government official who is supposed to act as lord and regent over the fractious tribes and the inexorably rising tide of the Taliban.

As always, my friend wore a starched and pressed white shalwar kameez. While we talked he carefully untied the green ribbons on stacks of well-worn cardboard folders, signed the government papers stacked inside with a fountain pen, and then tossed the retied folders on to the floor. Every half-hour, a clerk appeared and carried away the piles of completed paperwork.

Government offices are important symbols in Pakistan – size, furniture, scope of retinue. This one was handsome, a large room set off a broad veranda in the ersatz Moghul-era quadrangle of pink stucco. A white mantelpiece signalled the dignity of the office holder. Above it hung a portrait, more a sketch in dingy brown, of Pakistan's founding father, Muhammad Ali Jinnah. The face was gaunt and elderly – an aquiline nose, sunken cheeks, unforgiving mouth. A peaked cap high off his forehead and a plain coat buttoned to the neck with a high collar gave the aura of a religious man. The picture reminded me of the first image I had ever seen of Jinnah: a mysterious, dark oil painting covered with glass hung high on a wall of the formal reception room at the Pakistani High Commission in London.

A few months later I returned to see my friend. Same signing of documents, same clerk, different portrait above the mantel. The new visage showed a serious young man with a full head of dark hair, an Edwardian white shirt, black jacket and tie, alert dark eyes. What happened? I asked.

'I would like to see Jinnah brimming with life,' my friend said. He did not want to be reminded of the clerical image that is now considered politically correct in many places throughout Pakistan. An Anglophile acquaintance of my friend's in Peshawar had found the more youthful, secular image of the founding father as a law student in England and had personally come to hang the replacement.

The question of Muhammad Ali Jinnah's portrait is no small matter in Pakistan. For a foreigner, the choice of portrait is one of the most telling signs of where you are, whom you are meeting. The style of portrait will give clues as to how your host interprets the intentions of the founder, a lonely, ascetic and, by all accounts, brilliant, British-educated lawyer.

In most nations, there is energetic debate about the philosophy of the founders; sometimes over who among a group of prominent men was the true maker. There is no doubt about who was responsible for the birth of Pakistan on 14 August 1947. It was Jinnah who had argued for Pakistan, and who stood beside Mountbatten in the new legislature in Karachi to accept a message from King George welcoming Pakistan to the Commonwealth as a new independent nation. But there is ceaseless argument over what the founder intended, and the identity of Pakistan – secular nation or Islamic state – has been in dispute among its citizens ever since.

What did Jinnah envision? Did he wish for a homeland for Muslims, a secular country where they could practise their religion without discrimination, and where others could too? Or did he want Pakistan to be an ideological state committed exclusively to the practice of Islam? Did he even want a separate country from Hindu-dominated India? Maybe not. As historians comb the archives, and a small but increasing number of Pakistanis watch with envy as India surges ahead, it has become fashionable to argue that Jinnah used the idea of Pakistan as a mere bargaining chip for Muslim majority rights within a loosely united post-colonial India.

An astute tactician, Jinnah never explicitly answered these vital questions. From 1938, he fought for Pakistan as a principle but provided few details, a tactic that allowed him to appeal to many kinds of Muslims – landlords, religious leaders, the urban elite, bureaucrats, villagers. There is little argument, however, that Jinnah was personally indifferent to his religion – he drank, smoked, ate pork. He was so unaware of the religious calendar that he planned the inauguration-day banquet for Pakistan as a luncheon even though it was Ramadan and the guests would be unable to eat. (It was eventually changed to a dinner.)

In his first speech to the newly independent country, Jinnah sounded the themes of a secular man. Like some upper-class Pakistanis today, he could not speak Urdu, the national language. In his patrician English accent, his voice ravaged by his daily habit of more than fifty Craven A cigarettes, Jinnah said: 'You are free. You are free to go to your temples, you are free to go to your mosques or to any other place of worship in this state of Pakistan. You may belong to any religion or caste or creed – that has nothing to do with the business of the state.'

When he took charge as Governor General in the new capital, the brutally hot seaside town of Karachi, he was terminally ill with tuberculosis and lung cancer. He died eleven months later aged seventy-one. He did not write an autobiography, and had few confidants. His wife had died of ill health ten years after they married. His constant companion, his sister Fatima, had little of substance to say during his life, although later she tried to keep the secular flame alive during a brief career as a politician.

The first year of Pakistan was marked by the staggering bloodletting that accompanied partition. The exchequer was empty. Experienced Muslim bureaucrats, some of whom had ruled large swathes of territory for the British in India and Burma in great style, arrived in Karachi to find not even desks and chairs for their makeshift offices.

Jinnah's physical decline prevented him from taking on the usual role of founding father: galvanizing the people. He spent his last weeks sequestered in the clear air of remote Baluchistan, his body a skeleton of less than eighty pounds. When his doctors agreed to fly him back to Karachi so he could die in dignity, Jinnah lay in the plane gasping for air from oxygen canisters. The ambulance that took him from the airport to Government House broke down, and Pakistan's founder nearly died, stranded on the roadside. He passed away a few hours later at Government House on 11 September 1948, his new country as frail as its founder.

Compared to Nehru, Gandhi and the never reticent Mountbatten, Jinnah remains a shadow in twentieth-century world history. Judging from the documents, books, expensive clothes, smart cars and stylish furniture assembled at the national mausoleum and museum in his birthplace, Karachi, he was a fastidious man with a taste for the best of everything. The museum curators' choices are remarkable for the absence of religious belongings: on show are the artefacts of a rich lawyer. There is a tasselled black silk dressing gown made in Marseilles, shoes from Lobb in London, black patent pumps with satin bows for his swearing in as Governor General, tortoiseshell-rimmed spectacles by E. B. Meyrowitz in Paris, several suits from among the two hundred Savile Row models that hung in his wardrobe at his death, a cream 1938 Packard convertible and a black 1947 Cadillac.

'The man had class in whatever he did,' said my companion at the museum, retired brigadier Javed Hussain, a former special forces officer. 'There was no barrister like him in Bombay. The judges would avoid him. He was so witty, so brilliant the judges felt inadequate in front of him.' The brigadier particularly liked the photo of Jinnah leaning into a pool table, cue stick in hand, cigar clenched between his teeth, taking aim.

Jinnah was born into a Shia mercantile family. After secondary school he sailed for London, practised law at Lincoln's Inn, attended parliamentary sessions at Westminster, and became a devotee of parliamentary procedure. He returned to India just before World War I, committed to Hindu–Muslim unity. His wife, a beautiful socialite, Ruttie Dinshaw, the daughter of Sir Dinshaw Manockjee Petit, the scion of one of Bombay's wealthiest families, was a Parsi.

The idea of an independent Muslim homeland on the subcontinent first surfaced in the nineteenth century, and was popularized in the 1930s by the poet Muhammad Iqbal, a national hero in Pakistan, whose portrait can also be found in offices and living rooms all over the country. In the same period, a Cambridge University student, Rahmat Ali, coined the word Pakistan from the initials: Punjab, Afghanistan, Kashmir and Sind; and from Baluchistan he added 'stan', meaning land.

These were the fragments that Jinnah built upon as he organized the Muslim League into a pre-eminent position among Muslim voters in the late 1930s. Key to the success of the League was Jinnah's pact with Sikandar Hayat Khan, a powerful landlord in the Muslim-majority Punjab who controlled the votes of the overwhelmingly rural electorate.

At the same time, Jinnah began using the rhetoric of Islam and adopted a slogan, 'Islam in Danger', for the Muslim League. In 1940, in the Lahore Resolution, Jinnah defined a two-nation theory, saying the Muslims were a 'nation by any definition'. Under Jinnah's direction, the League embraced *pirs* (spiritual leaders) and *ulema* (religious scholars) as a way of mobilizing the different ethnic and linguistic groups of the Muslim masses.

The big Muslim landlords who had thrown their weight behind him were not particularly religious but tolerated the use of religion as the path to greater power for themselves in their provinces. For political meetings, Jinnah shed his British suits and began wearing a high-collared, knee-length and tight-fitting jacket known as a sherwani that was favoured by educated Muslims. A portrait of him in these clothes hangs in the National Gallery in Islamabad. He was now referred to as Quaid-i-Azam, or 'Great Leader'.

Even so, the main religious party, Jamaat-e-Islami, opposed the new platform of the Muslim League, arguing that Islam was a world religion, not a religion of the state. To counteract this opposition, and to overcome the anti-Pakistan Jamiat-Ulema-e-Hind, Jinnah made sure a new Islamic party was created under a more compliant imam,

Maulana Shabbir Ahmad Usmani. By 1946, Jinnah had been so successful at transforming the Muslim League into a mass movement that the party won 75 per cent of the Muslim vote, a stunning leap from only 4.6 per cent of the Muslim vote in 1937.

There seems little argument that Jinnah was seeking political guarantees, not so much religious guarantees, for the Muslim minority within India. A group of historians led by Ayesha Jalal, the author of *The Sole Spokesman: Jinnah, the Muslim League and the Demand for Pakistan*, argue that if those guarantees had been entrenched in a strong federal state the Muslims would have stayed inside a unified India. They point out that in the rushed negotiations under Mountbatten, Jinnah was forced to accept what he called a 'moth-eaten' version of Pakistan. The new country was awarded only half of the vastly important Punjab and Bengal provinces and more Muslims were left behind in India than ended up in the new country.

To find out what the Islamists of Pakistan make of Jinnah, I travelled to the Darul Uloom Haqqania madrasa in Akora Khattack, not far from Peshawar. Some of Pakistan's most notorious militants have graduated from this place, including Jalaluddin Haqqani, the veteran Afghan Taliban commander allied with al-Qaeda. At a recent graduation ceremony at the madrasa, tens of thousands of Taliban fighters, organizers, funders and sympathizers turned up, all of them opposed to a secular Pakistan. I had visited Haqqania several times. The administrator, Maulana Yousaf Shah, is a friendly, gregarious preacher and politician. From time to time he welcomes Western journalists, and when journalists have been kidnapped in the tribal areas he has tried to help as an intermediary.

I turned up with my colleague Pir Zubair Shah, who is from south Waziristan, and a member of a prominent family of the Mehsud tribe. It was Friday, just before midday prayers at Haqqania, so we sat on the floor of the maulana's reception area, a grubby narrow room with a single bed, a row of cushions arrayed along one wall for the guests to recline on. A strip of neon light illuminated the dark space, and a clutch of red plastic flowers sprouted from a space on the wall. There was no image of Jinnah, or anyone else.

While the maulana delivered the sermon at the nearby mosque, we chatted with a barefooted, poorly dressed man who introduced himself as Juma Khan, a former member of Lashkar-e-Jhangvi, a militant group from the Punjab that is formally banned in Pakistan but seems unstoppable in its capacity to carry out terror attacks in major urban centres. He had been jailed a dozen times for speeches against the Shia, he said. Weary of jail, he had now retired from militant work to devote himself to hunting quail.

What did a foot soldier in one of Pakistan's myriad militant groups think of Jinnah? A dark look crossed his weathered face. 'He was a Shia. They are the worst infidels on earth,' he shot back. 'His past is not so good.' But was he not the founder of the nation? 'God made Pakistan, not Jinnah.'

The maulana, fresh from the pulpit, walked in wearing a dark turban and a fresh white shalwar kameez. Three of his children, two boys and a girl all under the age of seven, scampered in and out. One of them dutifully brought a tin spittoon and placed it on the floor by the bed where the maulana sat. Occasionally, he spat in it.

'I grew up in a very religious family; they didn't like Jinnah,' said the maulana. 'My forefathers were active in the referendum, and they supported Jinnah at every level at the formation of Pakistan. Then they complained: "You separated us from the Hindus but we do not have an Islamic state."'

In 1947, the expectations of the Islamists were high, the maulana said. The president of the new Islamic party, Maulana Usmani, raised the green-and-white Pakistani flag, decorated with a crescent moon and star, on Independence Day. That was a great accomplishment, a promising start for the Islamic cause. But ever since, he said, the foreign powers have worked against Pakistan becoming an Islamic state.

This is not exactly true. In the 1980s, the United States backed the Islamic military dictator Zia ul-Haq, who had overthrown and then hanged the democratically elected Zulfikar Ali Bhutto. Together, the United States and Pakistan supported the mujahideen fighters in their battle against the Soviets in Afghanistan. As the war raged inside Afghanistan, the United States looked the other way as Zia moved Pakistan towards becoming an Islamic state, one that ideologically matched the Islamic cause over the border in Afghanistan.

It was in this period that Jinnah was rewritten, redrawn, repackaged. The lawyer and astute politician was transformed into a proud Islamist. The school books were overhauled, and to this day retain the view of Zia and his Islamic ideologues. The language became stridently anti-Hindu, more fundamentalist. Some of the recasting verged on the comical as the curriculum mandarins tiptoed around uncomfortable facts. One passage in a social studies book reads: 'At the initial period of his political career, Jinnah had a conviction that the interests of the Hindus and those of the Muslims were not colliding, but with the passage of time he had to change his mind.' Jinnah is described as a 'true devotee of Islam'. Pakistan, the book says, is not merely a 'tract of land' but 'a laboratory for the implementation of Islamic injunctions'.

Jinnah, for all his secular habits, is partly to blame for this posthumous transformation. He often said one thing, but did another. He carved out his state on the basis of Islam and rallied the support of the Islamic religious leaders, but never intended that Pakistan would be a theocratic state. When he was garnering the support of the imams, photographs show Jinnah looking remarkably uncomfortable. In one shot he stands under a banner written in Urdu – 'Allah is Great' – looking terrified of the throngs of youth jostling around him.

The Jinnah portrait in the inner sanctum at the army headquarters in Rawalpindi – the room where Pakistan's top commanders meet each month around a long, oval, polished wood table – presumably reflects the Pakistani Army's verdict on Jinnah. A tall, lean, elegantly dressed Jinnah, in beige summer suit, white shirt and tie, sits in a 1940s art deco armchair, his right arm draped over the back of the chair, a cigarette in his fingers. He could be mistaken for an imperious, pre-World War II Hollywood producer. Outwardly, there is an eerie echo of the current army chief, the most powerful man in Pakistan, General Parvez Ashfaq Kiyani, in military fatigues, erect and handsome, who presides at the table in front of the Jinnah portrait chain-smoking cigarettes much as the founder did.

There seems little question that Jinnah would be shocked by Pakistan today. His daughter, Dina Wadia, now in her nineties and living in Manhattan, has told acquaintances that her father must be turning in his grave. On 11 September 2001, exactly fifty-three years to the day after his death, al-Qaeda showed the world how far Islamic extremists had eaten into the fabric of Pakistan.

A civilian government tarnished by the corruption and nepotism that Jinnah warned about in his inauguration-day speech is nominally in charge. But the army essentially runs the show. In July, the government granted General Kiyani an unprecedented three-year extension of his term, handing the military even more power. The military receives about 17 per cent of the total state budgetary expenditure, a precedent that Jinnah established when he devoted an overwhelming proportion of Pakistan's first budget to the army.

Today, the Pakistani Army is convinced that the India Jinnah left behind is the ultimate enemy. To offset what it sees as India's far greater economic and military strength, Pakistan uses Islamic militant groups to fight against Indian interests in Afghanistan and, on occasion, within India. Other militant groups have turned against Pakistan itself, and in the last year the army has fought against them. But the strategy of supporting some Islamic groups, and fighting others, further erodes the chance for secularism to have a dominant role in modern Pakistan. The Jihadistan that looms on the horizon as the future Pakistan, a likely compromise between extremist groups and the army, would not have a place for Jinnah today, regardless of how he portrayed himself. ■

Miami Book Fair International

Featuring... Dave Barry • Jaime Bayly • Ann Beattie • Sir Michael Caine • Susan Cheever
Pat Conroy • Michael Cunningham • Edwidge Danticat • Kate DiCamillo • Paquito D'Rivera
Nora Ephron • Harold Ford, Jr. • Jonathan Franzen • Ian Frazier • Carl Hiaasen • Susan Isaacs
Sebastian Junger • Greil Marcus • Sue Miller • Walter Mosley • Michele Norris
Eugene Robinson • Roger Rosenblatt • Salman Rushdie • Patti Smith • Gay Talese
Jorge Volpi • John Waters • Venus Williams • E.O. Wilson • Geoffrey Wolff ... and many more!

November 14-21, 2010 • Street Fair Nov. 19-21

www.miamibookfair.com

Florida Center for the Literary Arts at Miami Dade College

Miami Dade College
Wolfson Campus

Miami Book Fair International is a premier program of the Florida Center for the Literary Arts at Miami Dade College.

GRANTA

KASHMIR'S FOREVER WAR

Basharat Peer

On an early December morning in 2009, I was on a flight home to Kashmir. It doesn't matter how many times I come back, the frequency of arrival never diminishes the joy of homecoming – even when home is the beautiful, troubled, war-torn city of Srinagar. Frozen crusts of snow on mountain peaks brought the first intimation of the valley. Silhouettes of village houses and barren walnut trees appeared amid a sea of fog. On the chilly tarmac, my breath formed rings of smoke.

The sense of siege outside the airport was familiar. Olive-green military trucks with machine guns on their turrets, barbed wire circling the bunkers and check posts. Solemn-faced soldiers in overcoats patrolled with assault rifles at the ready, subdued by the bitter chill of Kashmiri winter. The streets were quiet, the naked rain-washed brick houses lining them seemed shrunken. Men and women walked quietly on the pavements, their pale faces reddened by the cold draughts.

In Kashmir, winter is a season of reflection, a time of reprieve. The guns fall silent and for a while one can forget the long war that has been raging since 1990. In the fragile peace that nature had imposed, I slipped into a routine of household chores: buying a new gas heater for Grandfather; picking up a suit from Father's tailor; lazy lunches of a lamb ribcage delicacy with reporter friends; teaching young cousins to make home videos on my computer. Yet I opened the morning papers with a sense of dread, a fear of seeing a headline printed in red, the colour in which they prefer to announce yet another death – the continuing cost of our troubled recent history.

Political discontent has simmered in the Indian-controlled sector of Kashmir since partition in 1947, when Hari Singh, the Hindu maharaja of the Muslim-majority state, joined India after a raid by tribals from Pakistan. The agreement of accession that Singh signed with India in October 1947 gave Kashmir much autonomy; India controlled only defence, foreign affairs and telecommunications. But, in later years, India began to erode Kashmir's autonomy by imprisoning popularly elected leaders and appointing quiescent puppet administrators who helped extend Indian jurisdiction. India and Pakistan have fought three wars over Kashmir since then. In 1987, the government in Indian-controlled Kashmir rigged a local election, after which Kashmiris lost the little faith they had in India and began a secessionist armed uprising with support from Pakistan. The Indian military presence rose to half a million and by the mid-nineties Islamist militants from Pakistan began to dominate the rebellion. The costs of war have been high: around 70,000 people have been killed since 1990; another 10,000 have gone missing after being arrested. Although there has been a decline in violence in the past few years and the number of active militants has reduced to around five hundred, more than half a million Indian troops remain in Kashmir, making it the most militarized place in the world. India and Pakistan have come dangerously close to war several times – once after the terrorist attacks on the Indian Parliament in 2001, and more recently after the attacks on Mumbai in November 2008.

And the attacks continue. A few weeks after I left Kashmir again, on the cold afternoon of 7 January, two young men walked through a crowd of shoppers in the Lal Chowk area in Srinagar. They passed bookshops, garment stores, hotels, and walked towards the Palladium Cinema, which once screened Bollywood movies and Hollywood hits such as *Saturday Night Fever*, and was now, like most theatres in Kashmir, occupied by Indian troops. As they neared the Palladium, the two men took out the Kalashnikovs they had been hiding and fired several shots in the air. One threw a grenade at a paramilitary bunker. Passers-by rushed into shops for safety; shopkeepers downed the shutters. Hundreds of armed policemen and soldiers drove from the military and police camps nearby, surrounded the hotel and began firing. The hotel caught fire.

The fighting continued for twenty-seven hours before the two militants were killed. The police announced that the militants were from the Pakistan-based terrorist group Lashkar-e-Taiba (the Army of the Pure), which had also been responsible for the November

2008 attacks on Mumbai. One of them was from Pakistan. Although most of the Kashmiri guerrillas who had started the war are either dead or have laid down their arms, the second militant, Manzoor Bhat, was a twenty-year-old from a village near the northern Kashmir town of Sopore. I was curious about what had led Bhat to join one of the most dangerous Islamist militant groups, many of whose members are from Pakistan.

I left my parents' house on a calm May morning of no news and began driving out of the city to Bhat's home. The village of Seer Jagir is a palette of apple trees and rice paddies, brown wood and brick houses. Old men smoked hookahs and chatted by shop fronts in the village market. Schoolboys in white-and-grey uniforms waited for the local bus. Everyone knew where Manzoor, the martyr, lived. On the outskirts of the village an old man and a boy sat by a cowshed. The sombre-faced boy in a blue *pheran* was Bhat's brother. He led me past the cowshed to an austere, double-storeyed house. His mother, Hafiza, a wiry woman in her late forties, joined us a few minutes later. She wore a floral suit and a loosely tied headscarf. 'I was feeding the cows,' she said in apology. Hafiza and her husband, Rasul Bhat, had three sons: an older one who worked in a car garage; the youngest son, the student who sat with us; and Manzoor, the dead militant. Though the Bhats lived amid a great expanse of fertile fields and orchards, they owned only a small patch of land, which produced barely enough rice to feed the family. Bhat gave up his studies after ninth grade and began work as an apprentice to a house painter. He learned fast and had in the past few years painted most of the houses in the neighbouring villages. 'He made around 8-9,000 rupees (US$200) a month,' Hafiza told me. 'He bought the spices, the rice, the oil, the soap. He ran the house.' She fell silent, her eyes fixed on a framed picture of Manzoor: a round, ruddy face, shiny black eyes and a trimmed beard. I was struck by the younger brother muttering something, repeating his words like a chant. 'He bought me clothes and shoes. He bought me clothes and shoes.'

On 1 September 2008, Bhat left home in the morning, ostensibly for work. He stopped in the courtyard and greeted his mother as usual. It was the first day of Ramadan. He didn't return in the evening. Hafiza and Rasul assumed their son had stayed with a friend. They got another friend of his to call the phone Bhat had recently purchased; it was switched off. They tried again the next morning; the phone was still off. 'We feared he might have been arrested by the military,' Hafiza said. Rasul went to a police station and filed a report about his missing son. Then he went to several military and paramilitary camps in the area, seeking information. A police officer told him that his son had joined the militants.

And here we have a familiar story. Two weeks before Bhat signed up, he had joined a pro-freedom march from the nearby town of Sopore towards the militarized Line of Control, the de facto border. The protests were provoked by a land dispute with the government and quickly morphed into a call for independence.

On 11 August, Bhat and his fellow protesters marched on the Jhelum Valley road which had connected Kashmir with the cities of Rawalpindi and Lahore prior to partition, before the Line of Control stopped all movement of people and goods between the two parts of Kashmir. When the protesters – riding on buses, trucks and tractors – reached the village of Chahal, fifteen miles from the Line of Control, Indian troops opened fire. Bhat saw unarmed fellow protesters being hit by bullets and falling on the mountainous road. Four were killed at Chahal, including a sixty-year-old separatist leader, Sheikh Abdul Aziz. In the months that followed, the scene in Chahal was repeated as hundreds of thousands of Kashmiris responded, marching in peaceful protests. They were often met with gunfire. By early September 2008, an estimated sixty protesters had been killed, and up to six hundred reported bullet injuries. Kashmir was silent and seething, crouching like a wildcat. Indian paramilitaries and police were everywhere, armed with automatic rifles and tear-gas guns.

Many of the injured from across Kashmir had been brought to the SMHS Hospital in central Srinagar. The hospital complex is surrounded by pharmacies and old buildings with rusted tin roofs. The surgical casualty ward has a strong phenyl smell, the cries of the sick and the wails of relatives echoing against its concrete walls. Here I met Dr Arshad Bhat (no relation to Manzoor), a thin, lanky man in his late twenties. The night before Manzoor Bhat, the would-be militant, saw protesters being shot near the Line of Control, Dr Bhat slept uneasily on a tiny hospital bed in the doctors' room. The next morning he walked into the surgical emergency room with five other surgeons at nine thirty. He and his colleagues were expecting an influx of wounded protesters. Within two hours, streams of them, hit by police fire, were pouring in. He summoned every team of surgeons in the hospital; some thirty doctors arrived and by the end of the day they had treated a few hundred people with grave bullet wounds. 'We might have saved more,' he told me, his voice full of regret, 'if they had not tear-gassed the operating theatre.'

Several young men I interviewed pointed to the killings during the protests of 1990 to explain their decision to join militant groups. Yasin Malik, then a wiry twenty-year-old from Srinagar, worked for the opposition during the rigged 1987 election campaign. After the election, many opposition activists, including Malik, were jailed and tortured. Malik and his friends decided to take up arms against Indian rule and cross over to Pakistan for training after their release. By the winter of 1990, Malik was leading the Jammu and Kashmir Liberation Front (JKLF), a guerrilla group that became the focus of overwhelming popular support.

'Self-determination is our birthright!' – all of Kashmir was on the streets shouting it. In those heady days, an independent Kashmir seemed eminently possible. But India deployed several hundred thousand troops to crush the rebellion; military and paramilitary camps and torture chambers sprang up across the region. Indian soldiers opened fire on pro-independence protesters so frequently that the latter lost count of the casualties. Before long, thousands of young Kashmiris were crossing into Pakistan-administered Kashmir for arms training, returning as militants carrying Kalashnikovs and rocket launchers supplied by Pakistan's Inter-Services Intelligence Agency (ISI). Assassinations of pro-India Muslim politicians and prominent figures from the small pro-India Hindu minority followed, leading to the exodus of over a hundred thousand Hindus to India.

Pakistan was wary of the JKLF's popularity, its demand for an independent Kashmir, and chose to support several pro-Pakistan militant groups who attacked and killed Malik's men. Indian troops killed many more. Malik spent a few years in prison in the early nineties; his body still carries the torture marks as reminders. In prison, he read works by Gandhi and Mandela. On his release in 1994, he abandoned violent politics, turned the JKLF into a peaceful political organization and joined a separatist coalition called the Hurriyat (Freedom) Conference, which pushed for a negotiated settlement of the Kashmir dispute.

By the time Malik came out of prison, however, a pro-Pakistan militant group called Hizbul Mujahideen dominated the fight against India. Its leader was Syed Salahuddin, a Kashmiri politician turned militant who had been a candidate for Kashmir's assembly in the 1987 elections. By the late nineties, most of Hizbul Mujahideen's Kashmiri fighters had either been killed in battles with Indian forces or arrested, or had spent time in Indian prisons and returned to civilian life, like Malik's men. Pakistan's ISI began backing jihadi groups like Lashkar-e-Taiba, which had no roots in Kashmir politics and were motivated by the idea of a pan-Islamist jihad. Hafiz Muhammad Saeed, a Lahore-based former university professor and veteran of the Afghan jihad, heads the Lashkar-e-Taiba. Most of Saeed's recruits came from the poverty-stricken areas of Pakistan's Punjab province. The jihadis from Pakistan introduced suicide bombings and took the war to major Indian cities – most dramatically with their attack on the Indian parliament in 2001, which brought India and Pakistan to the brink of full-scale confrontation.

Yet by late 2003, after vigorous American and British diplomatic intervention, a peace process between India and Pakistan was under way. The insurgency began to wane. Pakistan reduced its support to insurgent groups and India's long campaign of counter-insurgency appeared to be a success. However, Kashmir remains heavily militarized, and the abuse of civilians by Indian security forces continues, fuelling more rage and attracting recruits for Islamist radicals like Saeed.

The dead speak in Kashmir, often more forcefully than the living. Khurram Parvez, a thirty-two-year-old activist, is part of a Srinagar-based human rights advocacy group, the Jammu and Kashmir Coalition of Civil Society (JKCCS), which produced a report in 2009 exposing hundreds of unidentified graves in the Kashmiri countryside. We met in a garden café in Srinagar. Parvez, a tall, robust man with intense black eyes, walks with a slight limp. In the autumn of 2002, he was monitoring local elections in a village near the Line of Control. As he drove out of the village with a convoy of military trucks ahead of him, a group of militants hiding nearby detonated an improvised explosive device which blew up under his car. The driver and his friend and colleague, a young woman, Aasiya Jeelani, died in the attack. Parvez lost his right leg. Several months later, with the help of a German-made prosthetic, he began to walk again and returned to work. 'I couldn't give up,' he said softly. His engagement with the pursuit of justice in Kashmir has been personal from the beginning. His grandfather, a sixty-four-year-old trader, was one of the protesters killed by the Indian paramilitaries on the Gawkadal Bridge in January 1990. For months, Parvez had thought of taking up arms in revenge, but was persuaded to stay in school by his family. They lived on Gupkar Road, where the Indian security forces ran some of the most notorious detention and torture centres in Kashmir. Almost every other day, he saw desperate parents walking to the gates of the detention centres in his neighbourhood, looking for their missing sons.

Parvez's cousin and mentor, the lawyer Parvez Imroz, co-founded the Association of Parents of Disappeared Persons, along with a Srinagar housewife Parveena Ahangar, whose son, Javed, had been missing since early 1990, when he was seventeen, after being taken from their home in a night raid by the Indian Army. Ahangar and Imroz campaigned for information about the whereabouts of 10,000 people who had disappeared in Kashmir after being taken into custody by Indian troops and police. Parvez joined them full-time after graduating from college; by late 2005, when a devastating earthquake struck Kashmir's border areas, he was a veteran of civil rights activism. 'We were doing relief work in the earthquake-hit areas when we began hearing about mass graves of unidentified people,' he told me. His group placed several advertisements in Kashmiri papers requesting that people contact them with any information they had about the unidentified graves. Parvez, Imroz and a few other activists travelled widely, documenting this information. Their report, 'Buried Evidence', startled Kashmir.

At Kupwara in northern Kashmir, miles of lush green paddy fields spread out from the fringes of the run-down, cluttered town square. A short walk from the market, Shabir, a young shopkeeper, and I climbed up to a small plateau of walnut trees, willows and vegetable gardens, which was also one of the biggest graveyards described in the report Parvez's group had produced. Unmarked graves covered with wild grass stretched ahead of us in neat rows. Shabir and others from the neighbourhood had placed a tiny white plaque on each grave, with a number and the date of burial. The number on the latest grave read: 241. 'The police would bring the bodies and say they were militants killed in encounters or on the border,' Shabir told me. 'A lot of the faces would be disfigured. Some were mere teenagers, some older.' I had heard similar accounts on visits to other such sites in the area. 'We have no way of knowing who these people really are,' Shabir continued. Parvez had sent a copy of the report to the head of the Kashmir government. Nothing happened.

Civilians continue to be killed and described as terrorists. In April, a spokesman for the Indian Army announced that the troops had killed the 'oldest militant' operating in Kashmir. Aged seventy, Habibullah Khan was from the village of Devar on the slopes of a mountain range by the border in the Lolab Valley, an hour and a half from Kupwara town.

Khan had had a tiny patch of land, not enough to feed his entire family. He and his three sons worked as labourers and sold timber they gathered in the forest to make ends meet. In the early nineties, one of Khan's sons crossed the border into Pakistan and stayed there. In the summer of 1999, his oldest son, Ahmedullah, left to fetch wood in the forest; Indian troops patrolling there suspected he was a militant and shot him.

By 2003, Khan couldn't work any more because of ill health. In desperation, he took to begging in the nearby town of Sogam. 'I couldn't stop him,' his remaining son, Raj Mohammad, told me. On the morning of 11 April, Khan left for Sogam, where he would normally spend the day in the market, outside a mosque, returning in the evening with whatever generous strangers had given him. He never returned home.

On the fifth day of his father's absence, having made enquiries in the neighbouring villages, Raj Muhammad travelled to Kupwara. He heard talk about the army killing of a seventy-year-old militant in the forests of Handwara District, a couple of hours from his village. In a press release, the Indian Army claimed that they had shot him in a joint operation with the police and that an AK-47 rifle, four magazines and sixty-seven bullets were recovered.

Raj Mohammad went to the police station closest to the shooting. 'A police officer we met showed me a picture of the dead man on his cellphone screen,' he said. 'It was my father.' He was granted permission to exhume his father's body from the graveyard where he had been buried as an unidentified militant.

Two decades of insurgency and counter-insurgency have resulted in the creation of a state of affairs that provides incentives to troops and policemen to show 'kills'. Those involved in counter-insurgency in Kashmir receive fast-track promotions, as well as monetary and other rewards for getting results. In February, the Indian government awarded one of the highest civilian honours, the Padma Shri, to Ghulam Muhammad Mir, a notorious counter-insurgent who worked with the Indian troops in central Kashmir and has several murder and extortion charges still pending against him. One of India's top bureaucrats, Home Secretary G. K. Pillai, told a television channel, 'Mir had done yeoman's service for the national cause.'

Two highly controversial Indian laws, the Armed Forces Special Powers Act and the Disturbed Areas Act, which have been in operation for twenty years, give the troops stationed in Kashmir the power to shoot any person they suspect of being a threat, and guarantee impunity from prosecution. To bring a soldier before a civilian court, India's Home Ministry has to remove his immunity and grant the Kashmir government permission to prosecute him. More than 400 such cases are still waiting for that permission.

All this has taken its toll. Srinagar used to be a city of elegant latticed houses, mosques and temples on the banks of the river. Srinagar was people strolling on the wooden bridges and wandering into old bazaars or stepping with a prayer into a Sufi shrine with papier-mâché interiors. Now it is a city of bunkers, a medieval city dying in a modern war. One of the most prominent landmarks of war is the sprawling Martyrs' Graveyard in north-western Srinagar; several hundred Kashmiris killed in the early days of the conflict are buried here. Among them is a well-known politician and head cleric of Srinagar grand mosque, Moulvi Mohammad Farooq, who was assassinated by pro-Pakistan militants on 21 May 1990. More than sixty mourners were killed when Indian paramilitaries fired upon his funeral procession. The cleric's eighteen-year-old son, Omar Farooq, left school to inherit his father's mantle. He is now one of the best-known Kashmiri separatists, heading the

Hurriyat (Freedom) Conference coalition.

A few days before the twentieth anniversary of his father's assassination, I walked past the Martyrs' Graveyard to an old wooden mosque nearby, where Farooq was holding a meeting with his supporters. In an elegant brown lambskin cap and delicately embroidered beige gown, he deftly mixed his roles as a modern politician and the head cleric in Kashmir's Sufi tradition, leading his followers in a sing-song voice humming Kashmiri and Persian devotional songs and then moving effortlessly to the question of Kashmiri politics. He spoke of the memory of the thousands who had died in the battles for Kashmir, including his father. He spoke of preventing further deaths. And then the old Kashmiri slogans for independence followed. 'Kashmir is for Kashmiris!' Farooq shouted. 'We will decide our destiny!' the people replied. He was about to lead a march through the city. Outside, excited young supporters were revving up their motorbikes and raising flags on cars.

Over the years, Farooq has engaged with both India and Pakistan and sought to rally the Kashmiris towards a peaceful agreement, often at a high personal price. In 2004, after failed peace talks with India, pro-Pakistan militants assassinated his uncle. Farooq had become cautious but participated when the Indian and Pakistani governments started secret talks to find a way to resolve the Kashmiri crisis. 'I met both Pervez Musharraf and Manmohan Singh and argued for demilitarizing Kashmir. Musharraf was sympathetic to Kashmiri concerns and Manmohan Singh said most things were possible except redrawing the borders,' Farooq told me. India and Pakistan agreed to withdraw their troops from the region gradually, as violence declined. It would be a great leap for the two countries, who had been stuck with their competing, aggressive nationalisms for around sixty years. This framework for the resolution of the dispute was due to be announced in 2007. In the spring of that year, Farooq was preparing a campaign in Kashmir to build public support for the deal. 'It was supposed to be an interim arrangement for the next five or ten years and then the people of Kashmir, India and Pakistan could make a call and move towards a final arrangement,' Farooq said.

However, things fell apart as Musharraf lost power and Pakistan was bogged down in a series of bombings by the Taliban and the takeover of the Swat Valley in the North West Frontier Province. In November 2008, while India was struggling to curb the biggest wave of pro-independence protests since 1990, a group of terrorists from Lashkar-e-Taiba attacked Mumbai. The peace process came to an abrupt end. In the two years that followed, hundreds of lives were lost in Kashmir and the tales of repression and protest drowned any hope of settlement.

Since then, Kashmir's youngest generation has started a Palestinian-style intifada against Indian rule. Young Kashmiris, who are coming of age with war, cable television, mobile phones and the Internet and are exposed to political images from other conflicts, see echoes of the Israeli occupation of Hebron and Gaza in India's military control of Kashmir. Palestinian stone-throwers become their inspiration. The nucleus of the intifada is the vast square and maze of lanes around Srinagar's grand mosque, an elegant structure of fine brick and filigreed wooden columns which rises like a trapezium to meet its pagoda-like roof. Two summers ago, when the stone-pelting battles between Kashmiri teenagers and Indian paramilitaries and police were nascent, I spent a few days hanging out around the grand mosque. One Friday afternoon, after the faithful had left, and the shops had closed for prayers and remained closed, fearing *kani jung*, or the 'war of stones', I stood behind an arched gate. Paramilitaries and policemen carrying assault rifles, tear-gas guns and bulletproof shields stood in a semicircle staring down at the growing crowd of teenagers and young men in their early twenties, wearing jeans, stylish T-shirts, trainers and Palestinian scarves and masks, armed with lumps of brick and stones.

A sudden volley of bricks tore through the nervous silence and struck an armoured car that charged at the boys, firing a burst of shells. Pungent tear gas filled the square; the stone-throwers scampered for cover. The soldiers made a ferocious charge, waving batons and raising a roar. The stone-throwers had melted into the houses, alleys and nooks they knew by heart. Soon a barrage of rocks came flying from balconies and narrow lanes, sending the soldiers retreating to their earlier positions. Stones, tear gas, stones, tear gas. And so it went on. I stood there watching the clashes, until the sun was about to set and the police officer in charge called it a day. A celebratory roar rose from the rebellious crowd. In a brief moment of reprieve I had asked a police officer what he made of the stone-throwers. 'It is a blood sport; it gives them a big kick,' he said calmly. 'When they push the police back, they feel like they have pushed India out of Kashmir.'

These clashes have grown increasingly violent. Hundreds have been injured. Many have died, including bystanders. The police launched a serious crackdown earlier in the summer and arrested around three hundred stone-throwers between the ages of fifteen and eighteen. But the news of death is frequent in Kashmir and so are occasions of protest. Another generation of young Kashmiris is being consumed by war.

I met up with some of this new generation in a college not far from the grand mosque. Wary of police informers, they refused to talk in the college cafeteria and led me instead to an empty classroom. They sat on wooden chairs, in a semicircle facing me, textbooks jutting out of their bags. As we made small talk, a wisp of a boy with curly gelled hair, wearing a white linen shirt, blue denims and black Converse trainers, played with his mobile phone. 'He is the commander of our group,' one of them said, half joking. The boy smiled. 'You can write about us, but don't use our real names. We will be arrested if we are identified.' His voice was measured, grave. I agreed. 'Call me Shahbaaz,' he said. Shahbaaz – the falcon. The boys laughed.

A friend of Shahbaaz's passed me his phone. 'That's him in a protest after Wamiq was killed.' I had read about Wamiq Farooq, a fourteen-year-old student who was killed when troops fired at a crowd of boys after a clash in January. I looked at the picture on the phone: a masked boy lunging at a bulletproof police car with a stone in his right hand. The memory hardened Shahbaaz's face. 'I was very sad and very angry the day they killed Wamiq. If I had a gun that day, I would have . . .'

Shahbaaz was born in the autumn of 1988, a year before the war began, in downtown Srinagar in a middle-class home. His father, a bureaucrat, worked for the local government. In 1991, one of his uncles who had joined a militant group was killed by the military. He did not remember the uncle. His first memory of the war is coming back from school when he was in fourth grade and seeing a big protest pass by his house. The military fired. A boy from his neighbourhood was hit by bullets and died outside his door. 'That was the first time I saw someone being killed,' Shahbaaz said slowly. He remembered feeling angrier after an incident in the autumn of 2000, when he was preparing for his eighth-grade examinations at his maternal grandfather's house. Protesters fired at the paramilitary and killed a soldier and angry troops began house-to-house searches, barging into Shahbaaz's family home. 'A soldier pushed my aunt around and asked where she had hidden the militants. Another soldier began beating my grandfather and asking him questions.' His aunt and grandfather repeatedly told them that nobody had come into their house. A soldier grabbed Shahbaaz by the neck and put a dagger to his throat. 'Tell me where the militants are or I will kill him!' the soldier shouted. After a while, the soldiers left. Shahbaaz stood there shaking in fear and anger. 'I still remember the cold edge of that dagger,' he said, lighting a cigarette.

We left the classroom after a while and walked to Nohata Chowk, the square where Shahbaaz and his friends often clash with the soldiers. Every street corner was a reminder of a battle. 'Here I was hit by a tear-gas shell,' Shahbaaz said, pointing to a communal tap. 'Here I was almost arrested,' said one of his friends, pointing towards an alleyway. We passed the square near the grand mosque and Shahbaaz signalled at a crumbling, empty house by the road.

'This used to be a BSF [Border Security Force] camp,' he said. 'Two of my friends were taken there and tortured.' We crossed a small roundabout and the boys stopped and pointed at the plaque on a electricity pole: Martyr Muntazir Square. Date of martyrdom: 7 July 2007.

We walked through a labyrinth of lanes and reached an old bridge over the River Jhelum. Shahbaaz talked to me about a boy named Muntazir. 'I was with him when he was shot,' he said. 'We weren't close friends but that day we shared a cigarette before the fighting began.' He didn't remember what had led them to come out on the streets that day. Shahbaaz, Muntazir and a few others were leading the attack on a group of paramilitaries outside the grand mosque. The paramilitaries ran for cover and the boys followed them. Then police came out of an alley and fired. 'Muntazir was hit in the abdomen and shoulder and fell on the street,' Shahbaaz said. 'Two of us picked him up and ran back towards the rest of the boys. The police fired tear-gas shells. The other boy was hit and fell.' Shahbaaz carried Muntazir to the alley where their friends waited. 'I saw some boys run towards us and they took Muntazir. He was bleeding intensely, dying. I fainted.'

We sat on a *ghat* by the banks of the River Jhelum under the bridge. Beautiful old houses with ornate balconies and shingle roofs towered over the river. A lonely-looking soldier stared out of the box-like hole in a bunker on the bridge. Shahbaaz suddenly stopped talking and turned to his friends. 'Look at that!' They rose from the steps we were sitting on and walked closer to the bank. A brown stray dog was struggling to swim his way across the river. The boys debated his chances and stood there until the dog reached the bank. I stood behind them, watching, and hoped they wouldn't end up as plaques in a town square.

I asked about their fears. They could be killed, or arrested and put in a prison for a year or two, which would block most possibilities in the future. 'We too have dreams of a good life. I want to be a computer scientist, but we can't look away when we live under Indian occupation. We aren't fighting for money or personal gain.

We are fighting for Kashmir,' Shahbaaz said, looking directly at me. He insisted he was aware of the price he and his friends could pay. 'I was arrested last year. They beat me so hard in the police station that bones in both my legs fractured. I wore plaster and couldn't walk for a few months.' One of his friends, Daniyal, who had sat quietly all this while, spoke up. 'I was arrested after a clash with the CRPF [Central Reserve Police Force]. They took me into a bunker and . . .' He stopped mid-sentence, rolled up the sleeves of his shirt and held out his bare arms. He had been burned with heated iron rods; each arm had four lines of scarred flesh running across it.

Shahbaaz invited me to his house, a short walk away. A car was parked outside the double-storeyed building. We sat in his carpeted room while he switched on his computer and began clicking through a series of videos on the desktop. He played a video from the early nineties, showing the wreckage of the north Kashmir town of Sopore after its main market had been burned down by Indian soldiers; he played a video of a funeral with relatives crying over the body of a young man shot by the soldiers, and then he played a video of Kashmiri protesters being fired on in Chahal village in August 2008 (the protest that Manzoor Bhat, the house painter turned militant, had been part of). 'How can we forget this?' Shahbaaz said, his eyes on the screen. 'But do you think stone-throwing will make India leave Kashmir?' I asked. 'It makes a difference. We show them that we are not completely helpless,' he replied. Then he lit a cigarette, took a long puff and said, 'We are not using guns. When Kashmiris used guns, the Indians called us terrorists. Yes, the gun was from Pakistan, but the stones are our own. That is our only weapon against the occupation.' He wanted to show me something else and played a documentary about the life and death of Faris Oudeh, the fifteen-year-old Palestinian boy who was immortalized by an Associated Press photograph taken a few days before his death: a diminutive youth in a baggy sweater, slinging a stone at an Israeli tank some ten metres away. 'He was hit in his neck by an Israeli sniper when he bent to pick up a stone,'

Shahbaaz said. 'His friends couldn't get to him, he was so close to the Israeli tank.' As he spoke, Shahbaaz's voice was low and full of passion.

I returned to New York a week later. My thoughts would often drift back to Shahbaaz, as every other day Indian paramilitary and police fired at young boys like him. Each death brought out more protesters and the uniforms would shoot to kill. A friend wrote in a newspaper article, 'The ages of the boys killed in the past few days read like the scores of a batsman in very bad form . . . 17, 16, 15, 13, 9 . . .' In Srinagar, the troops attacked the funeral of a young protester. Photojournalists, several of whom were beaten, captured the moment. On a stretcher in the middle of a street is a young man killed by the troops as they went about crushing the protests. Behind his fallen corpse, angry soldiers and policemen assault the pall-bearers and mourners with guns and batons. The mourners run for safety, except for a man in his late fifties: the father trying to save his son's corpse from desecration, spreading himself over the boy, his arms stretched in a protective arc. By mid-August, fifty-eight boys had been killed by the troops, hundreds were injured, and Kashmir remained under curfew.

I called Shahbaaz several times from New York, but I couldn't reach him. His phone was always switched off. ■

Trying Tripe

Three months this man's been off the farm –
go back now, back to diesel, earth and pumps.
Sugar cane I planted has come to term,
and now I count the stalks, the germination.
One clump is a penny, one row,
running, I will sell it for one dollar,
this field buys an olive suit, numerous books
boxed and mailed back, a knife I saw and craved;
along these fields, maturing silver trees
become lunch one afternoon in Rome,
a sweating wine, the restaurant *Archimedes*
(I chose it for the name, the Screw
of Archimedes in Nefwazi's *Perfumed Garden*,
tantric afternoon of love, seeping,
like this cream afternoon of mine.)
Lunching alone, what to do but get soaked again
in memory. Riverine prodigal heart,
I have spent whole countries on a woman's youth –
England, where L. is everywhere, like ash at nightfall,
and all the towns, pirate torching youth.
In Rome, slightly drunk, I order tripe,
wash it down, furry, valved and strange.

GRANTA

ICE, MATING

Uzma Aslam Khan

NAIZA KHAN
Iron Clouds I, 2008
Charcoal conte and acrylic on Fabriano paper. 150cm x 124cm
Courtesy of the artist and gallery Davide Gallo, Berlin. Fabrizio and Marina Colonna Collection, Milan.

The hole had been shielded by wheat husks and walnut shells. In winter, the covering would be removed so the snow could collect over the two ice blocks – a male, a female. After five winters, the couple would begin to creep downhill, growing into a natural glacier, free of the cultivating hands of men. Freshwater children would spring from her womb providing the village with water to drink and to irrigate their fields.

We'd come as witnesses, Farhana and I. She wanted to know how they were chosen. I told her. The female ice was picked from a village where women were especially beautiful and, because that wasn't enough, talented. Talent meant knowledge of yak milk, butter, fertilizer and, of course, wool. From caps to sweaters and all the way down to socks, the questions were always the same. How delicately was the sheep's wool spun? And what about the *kubri* embroidery on the caps – was it colourful and fine? Most importantly, did all the women cooperate?

'And the male? I suppose beauty and cooperation aren't high on that list?'

He was picked from another village. One where men were strong and, because that wasn't enough, successful. Success meant knowledge of firewood, agriculture, trekking and herding. There was a fifth, bonus area, and this was yak hair. From this *some* men could spin *sharma*, a type of coarse rug. A glacier in a village with such men had to be male.

She laughed. 'So who does the picking?'

'Men like him.' I pointed to an old man stooped inside a grey woollen jacket. Perhaps the ice-bride had spun it, I thought, envisioning fingers of ice melting into a warp and weft. In a whisper both soft and commanding, the old man directed two younger men on how to lower the ice-bride and ice-groom from off their backs without hurting them.

We'd followed, at a distance. The marital bed – the hole covered in shells and husk – had been dug into the side of a cliff as carefully selected as the bride and groom. Only this side of the mountain attracted the right length of shadow for the snow to hold for ten months, 14,000 feet above sea level. The porters had heaved the ice on their backs the entire way. We were brought in a jeep.

To participate in the marriage procession, we'd sworn an oath of silence. There was a belief in these mountains that words corrupted the balance between lovers-in-transit. But now we'd reached the marital bed, Farhana and I could speak again.

They tossed the male in first. *Whooshoo! Whooshoo!* A loop of air seemed to dance right back up the hole and circle around again, inside my chest. The female was released on top, falling without a sound.

'So this is copulation,' said Farhana, her gloved fingers far from mine.

They say it's bad luck for other eyes to watch, I thought. Eyes from somewhere else. Karachi eyes. California eyes. I took out my camera and aimed.

Farhana was skipping down the hill, away from me.

She was not in our cabin that night.

I walked along the River Kunhar, thinking of Farhana. My way was lit by the moon and the rush of the current and the silhouettes of the trees and the hut down the way where we'd eaten trout before she left and I knew the others were asleep so I unlaced my boots and peeled off my jacket and stood buck-naked. I kneeled at the Kunhar's edge and took a sip of her noxious water.

An owl soared across the river. Flapping twice before circling back toward me, she came to rest on a giant walnut tree. There, looking directly down at me, she spoke. '*Shreet!*' The sour glacier water inside me froze and my fingers grew so stiff that when I reached for my clothes I simply poked at them, as though with sticks, under the gaze of those gleaming black eyes.

Before the owl swooped across the moon's reflection, I'd been thinking about that word, *Kunhar*, how *kun* sounded like *kus* which sounded like a cross between cunt and kiss. I held the bitter taste of glacier melt in my mouth as the moon eased deep into the river's skin and she scattered him in pieces. I gazed down the Kunhar's length. She cut through the valley for 160 kilometres. I'd been thinking of a long labia.

'*Shreet!*'

The thought scattered like moonseed.

How long before the bird shot up into the sky and flew in the direction of my cabin? I couldn't say. Eventually, I returned, still naked, and slid into bed. No Farhana. I would have been grateful for the heat she'd radiate under our sheets. I would have curled into her back and stroked her hair into a fan, a blanket to shelter in.

I met her soon after moving to the Bay Area from Tucson, two years ago, on my way to becoming a photographer. It was landscapes I excelled at, or wanted to. I left Tucson and spent the next two months making my way up the West Coast, occasionally veering back into the desert after hitching a ride.

I still have photos of them in my portfolio, those who stopped for me: pickup trucks, scuffed boots, silver belts glistening in the sun. There was old man prickly pear cactus all around and of course the Joshua trees as the wind blew in from the north-west and purple clouds draped us. When I tired of the rides, I walked into the desert and did what I knew I could spend my life doing. I really looked at cactus. I really looked at triumph. Blossoming in shocking gimcrack hues of scarlet and gold in a world that watched with arms crossed, if it watched at all. It reminded me of the festive dresses worn by women in Pakistan's desert borderlands and mountain valleys. The drier the land, the thirstier the spirit.

When I finally arrived in San Francisco, for no reason other than it was San Francisco, I had a stack of photographs of the Sonoran Desert, the Petrified Forest and Canyon de Chelly. I mailed off the best and waited for offers to pour in while renting an apartment with three other men. I had two interviews. The first went something like this:

'Why are you, Nadir Sheikh' – he said Nader Shake – 'wasting your time taking photographs of American landscapes when you have so much material at your own doorstep?'

'Excuse me?'

'This is a stock-photo agency. We sell photographs to magazines and sometimes directly to customers and sometimes for a lot of money. We might be interested in you, but not in your landscapes.'

'In what then?'

'Americans already know their trees.'

'Do they know their cactus?'

'Next time you go home, take some photographs.' When it was obvious I still didn't get it, he dumbed it down for me. 'Show us the dirt. The misery. Don't waste your time trying to be a nature photographer. Use your advantage.'

Back at the apartment, my housemate Matthew felt sorry for me. He said a former boyfriend knew a nice little Pakistani girl. I ate his nachos while he talked on the phone.

In the morning, my cabin was colder than the river last night. I lay under the sheets, listening for sounds next door. I registered Farhana's absence with dull panic, the fingers of one hand switching off an alarm while the other reached for a dream. I could hear Irfan and Zulekha. I thought of the ghostly owl; anything to help tune out the laughter. The bitter taste of the Kunhar – the cunt, the kiss – the walk back in the dark. I'd knocked my toe against something. A carcass, a gun. Under the sheets, I picked at blood-crust.

I arranged to meet her the afternoon of my second interview. This time I included in my portfolio a series of photographs taken on a previous return to Pakistan. It was a series of my mother's marble tabletop, which she'd inherited from her mother and which dated back to the 1800s. The swirling cream-and-rust pattern changed as I played with the light, sometimes slick as a sheet of silk, sometimes pillowing like a bowl of ice cream. A few frames were, if I say so myself, as sensuous as Linde Waidhofer's stones.

The second interview didn't go very differently from the first.

'Your photographs lack authenticity.'

'Authenticity?'

'Where are the beggars or anything that resembles your culture?'

'The marble is a real part of my family history. It's old, from 1800–'

He waved his hand. 'It seems to me that when a war's going on, a table is trivial.' I wished for the courage – or desire – to ask what images of what war he was looking for.

He stood up. 'I'm a busy man. Could've ignored you. Didn't. You know why? There's something there.' He leaned forward expectantly, so I thanked him for thinking there was something there.

I left the office and walked down the corridor to the stairs, passing the photographs that hung on the walls, photographs I loved with an ardour that stung. I'd recognized them all on my way in, of course. There were prints by Linde Waidhofer to taunt me, including one from her *Stone & Silence* series. A Waidhofer can be a nature photographer of the Wild West but a Sheikh must be a war photographer of the Wild East! He must wow the world not with the assurance of grace. He must wow the world with the assurance of horror.

I wound my way slowly through prints from Ansel Adams's *Yosemite* series – it was the wrong moment to view *Bridalveil Fall*, the sheer force of the torrent almost making me weep, and I found myself wishing, childishly, *if only the drop weren't so steep* – before halting, finally, at *Golden Gate Bridge from Baker Beach*.

The coincidence hadn't hit me on my way into the interview but it hit me now, as my eye swooped down from the whiteness of the clouds to admit the whiteness of the surf breaking on the shore. I was meeting Farhana on Baker Beach in one hour. It had been her idea, and she'd been very specific about where on the beach I'd find her. I stared at the photograph, surprised at the fluttering in my breast. It astonished me that I was hoping to find her on the exact same length of shore depicted in the frame. Worse, I believed that once there, perhaps without her knowing it, I'd look up and see the bridge from exactly the same perspective as I was seeing it now.

Did I want the picture to be a sign? Possibly. It happens this way when you have just been tossed down a roaring cataract. You grope for a raft, anywhere. You even tell yourself that you have found it.

An hour later, I walked barefoot in the sand, expecting to see a girl of Farhana's description – 'Look for a long braid, the longest on the beach, black, of course' – waiting at the edge of the sea as per her instructions, her back to me (showing off the braid), with Golden Gate Bridge looming to her right. Instead, I wound up in a volleyball game, with all the players entirely in the nude.

Was she among them? How was I to know?

There was a player with a dark braid, though she had two braids, not one, neither as long as I'd been led to believe. Leaping for the ball, she made a full-frontal turn, and my God, how astonishingly she was built! I gawked at the hair between her legs, wondering if this were a cruel joke. (Granted, not entirely cruel.) Matthew must have arranged it, getting 'Farhana' to lure me here. He was probably watching, laughing till he hurt. *Nice little Pakistani girl.* Funny, Matthew, *funny.* I stared at the volleyball player one last time – no, that couldn't be Farhana, please let it not be Farhana! Please let it *be* Farhana! – and turned to my right to scan the bathers on the shore.

Almost all naked, mostly men. Obscenely overdressed, I jogged in mild panic toward a cluster of rocks on the far side of a thick cypress grove. Along the way, I tried to hunt discreetly for a long braid slithering down a shapely back, but many figures lay *on* their backs, some on their *hair.* I could see the rocks now. She wasn't there. Two naked men were, one walking out to the water, hand on hip. Long cock, wide grin. I waded into the sea, my back safely to him, but the water was too cold for my taste. After a few minutes, I trundled closer to the boulders, trying to look-not-look.

She was sitting there, smiling. Her braid was pulled to the side, draping her left shoulder, and she waved it at me like a flag.

'We must have just missed each other!'

'I thought you told me to wait on the beach?'

'I'm sorry. I got late.'

I was on the verge of asking how she got all the way here without my noticing when I saw how her eyes sparkled. So I clambered up without another word, crossing a series of tide pools and a snug sandy enclosure between the boulders that sprawled in a V. I crouched down beside her and looked to her right: there loomed Golden Gate Bridge.

'Did you think you'd recognize me better with clothes on?' she giggled.

'Your clothes *are* on.'

'Are you disappointed?'

'I'm relieved.'

'How disappointing.'

So I learned this immediately about my Farhana. She was one of those people who liked to receive a reaction, and she didn't like to wait very long for it.

We stayed till sunset. I took several shots of the bridge, but none of her. She wouldn't let me photograph her that day. When we finally stood up to leave, I realized how tall she was. And how boyish.

She knew. 'I would have gone topless if I had breasts.' Again, she required a reaction.

I am not an eloquent man and am usually tongue-tied around directness, but directness attracts me. I looked at Farhana and took all of her in, all that she'd spent the afternoon telling me: her work with glaciers, her father in Berkeley, her mother's death, leaving Pakistan as a young child, her life in this city where she grew up. I took that in while absorbing her height, her leanness, the paleness of her skin, and the way her braid now wrapped around her in a diagonal curve that extended from left shoulder to right hip. I said she looked more like a calla lily than any woman I'd ever met.

'Not just any calla lily,' I added. 'Jeffrey Conley's calla lily. Have you seen it?'

She bowed her head, suddenly self-conscious. Turning her back to me, she took off her T-shirt. 'I'll see you tomorrow then.'

I scrambled off the rocks, glancing up a final time before turning toward my apartment. She'd twisted to one side so her long, deep spine was now perfectly aligned with the braid and both encircled her like an embrace.

I walked to Farhana's side of the bed. On her bedside table lay a map, with Kaghan Valley circled in red at the easternmost corner of the North West Frontier Province, on the edge of Kashmir. Before we'd left San Francisco, I told her that to see the Frontier, you had to imagine it as the profile of a buffalo's bust, facing west, with the capital Peshawar the nose, Chitral Valley the backward tilting horn, Swat Valley the eye and Kaghan Valley the ear. The Frontier listened to Kashmir at its back while facing Afghanistan ahead, and it listened with Kaghan.

I opened the door, listened to Kaghan. Around me rose rounded hills, scoops of velvet green on a brick-red floor. Like the mossy moistness of rain-kissed tailorbirds. It was for this that I'd come, not to fall into myself in an abandoned cabin. Around me the valley undulated like the River Kunhar that gave it shape, cupping nine lakes in its curves, sprouting thick forests of deodar and pine, towering over 4,000 metres before halting abruptly at the temples of the Himalayas and the Karakoram. The only way through the mountainous block was by snaking along hair-thin passes, as if by witchery. I'd known the witchery once. Now I had to relearn it.

In colonial times, the British considered it a pretty sort of wedge, this ear called Kaghan, nicely if incidentally squeezed between the more considerable Kashmir and the more incomprehensible, and feared, hill tribes of the west. And so they mostly left the valley alone. Today, nearly all of the hotels, restaurants and shops were run, though not owned, by Kashmiris and Sawatis. Even those who couldn't read, or didn't own a television, were keenly aware of what was going on, and where. They liked to say that the buffalo is as attuned to what lies behind as what lies ahead. Why else did shivers keep running up and down its spine? Why else did it keep sweeping its hide with the smack of a tail?

I'd noticed military convoys on our way to the valley. It was unusual here. I'd been too preoccupied to give this much thought. The trucks were as twitchy as buffalo tails, creeping up and down the valley's spine, seeing nothing, fearing the worst. The whole country was teeming with convoys of one kind or another. So what? We were here to enjoy the place, even if we couldn't enjoy the time.

A shadow flickered on the door frame. A lizard, sidling for a mate.

I courted Farhana with calla lilies. Nothing delighted me more than descending the hill into the Mission District where she lived with a potted plant in my arms. I knew the flower shops with the widest varieties, from white to mauve to yellow, some with funnels as long and slender as her wrists, slanting in the same way her braid embraced her spine that first time we met, and still embraced her each night as she torqued her body to undress. I longed to photograph that spine but she wouldn't let me. So instead, with my naked eye, I watched her fingers undo the knots of her braid.

Sometimes, she pulled me out of bed, to recline at her five-sided bay window. It pitched so far out into the street she claimed it was the one that caused the city to pass an ordinance limiting the projection of all bay windows. We'd sit there, nestled in glass in a purple house. Even by San Francisco's standards, the house was spectacular. Slender spiralling columns at the alcove, each with gold rings, like cufflinks on a white and crinkly sleeve. Halfway down the door of unfinished wood ran a tinted oval glass. *Mirror, mirror*, she'd giggle, the first few times I kissed her there. The bedroom balcony – with little gold-tipped minarets – is where I left her calla lilies, like an offering to the god of extravagance. Art-glass windowpanes under the roof.

At the window, we watched others on the street.

At the window, she asked, 'What's the most beautiful thing you ever witnessed? I mean, a moment.'

At the window, we played opposites. The Mission was once moist, fecund. In contrast, the stark, wind-swept Richmond where I lived was once a desolate bank of sand. We said she sprang from marsh, I from desert. She loved the damp closeness of curves, the rich debris of glaciers and deltas. She loved her gloves and her socks. I, though always cold, hated to cover my extremities. I preferred the exposed, violent beauty of the Pacific coast to the secret tides of the protected bays. We said 'opposites attract' and we were right. Converging is what divided us.

On her first birthday after we met, in one hand I held a calla lily with a lip pinker than hers, in the other, a bottle of champagne. She kissed me and said she knew what she wanted instead.

'What?'

'Let me show you.'

I shut my eyes, counted to ten, opened them. 'So where is it?'

'Not here, silly. Let's go for a walk. To *your* neighbourhood, the one you love to photograph, with all the cliffs and the cypresses.' She rolled her eyes as though cliffs and cypresses were toys for men.

It was an especially cold day in May and though I did love the bluffs, I'd been hoping for a more close-fitting day. Call it role reversal. I chilled the champagne and headed for the bay window to, well, anticipate some tidal advances. The last time we'd made love I'd teased that her needs were growing as strong as the tides rushing up the channels of a salt marsh, and inshallah they'd also be twice daily.

Well, it was not to be.

She'd planned the route. First, the Sutro Baths, which looked especially green and scummy that day, thick as a Karachi sewer.

We watched the pelicans. Dark hunkered shadows, sometimes in gangs of twenty or more, closing in on the fecund orgy at the microbe-gilded pools like evil clouds, like missiles. They launched headlong, scattering the seagulls and the swifts, dropping one after the other in a heavy, gut-wrenching fall. A rain of bombshells. The invasion mesmerized us.

From the pelicans I moved my camera to the austere silhouette of a cormorant. He seemed to be watching the assault of the pelicans with as little interest as God.

'Nadir, talk to me for a minute, without that.'

I didn't have to see through the lens to see her point to it. 'In a minute.'

The pelicans gone, the seagulls multiplied. I watched a pair land softly on the boulders along the shore. And the hummingbirds – how did they survive in this wind, and at this height? And the purple flowers with the bright white hearts! Here it was again: the tenacity of the small. What I'd seen in the Sonoran Desert and the valleys of the Himalayas.

'It's over a minute.' Her voice trembled. I put the camera in its case. She cleared her throat. 'Nadir, are you as happy with me as you are alone on your nightly walks?'

'I'm much happier.'

She looked away. I took my camera out again. She sometimes let me photograph her now, though still not often enough, and only when dressed. I got a beautiful profile of her gazing at the ruins as the mist rolled across the steps in the background.

'Happier than in the mountains of Pakistan?'

Perhaps I hesitated. 'Well, yes.'

'Why?'

'I'm happy anywhere with you.'

'Why?'

I was still photographing her. From behind the lens, I replied, 'Because you don't remind me of my past.' And as I stepped on to a lower wall to get more of the ruins behind her, I realized that this was exactly so. She wasn't like any of the women I knew in Karachi. Her energy was – different. It wasn't sultry, wasn't Eastern. She was walking away from me now, walking away from my lens, and I noticed that her walk was determined and – how can I put it? – unstudied. As if no aunt had ever told her that women walk with one foot before the other. It wasn't graceful but it was vigorous. There are men on the Pakistan Afghanistan border who can spot a foreign journalist hiding in a burqa by the way she moves. Farhana would never pass. She could, however, keep up with them on the mountains. Not many women from Karachi could. And yet – of course I didn't tell her this – they had more patience in bed. Farhana didn't like to linger, not over food, shopping or sex. The only thing I'd ever seen her linger over was her hair, and that was not with pleasure. All the languor was in her spine, the part she never let me put behind my lens. Everything else about her had the slightly lunatic energy of Nor Cal, uncomplicated and nervy. I mean, for heaven's sake, she was passionate about *glaciers*. How many Pakistani women know two things about them? It was Farhana who told me that Pakistan has more glaciers than anywhere outside the poles. And I've *seen* them! I've even seen them *fuck*!

She was sobbing. I saw it first through the lens. I saw it too late, after I'd taken the photograph of her wiping her nose with the back of her hand. She said it was the worst thing I could have said.

The seagulls hovered, teetering in the breeze. Before they touched the rock it was beginning to sink in, yet each time I approached a landing, the wind pulled me away again. We loved each other, Farhana and I, for precisely opposite reasons. If I loved her because she did not remind me of my past, Farhana loved me because she believed I was her past. That day I came close to understanding; by the time I fully understood, we were already in transit, immersed in separate rituals of silence.

I expected to keep to the coast to Point Lobos, but, taking a detour, she began following the signs for Fort Miley. I said nothing. I didn't know what to say. How could I apologize for all that drew me to her?

There were picnickers in the grass between the gun emplacements dating to before the First World War. A plaque read: *Although they never fired on an enemy, coastal batteries here and throughout the Bay Area stood ready – a strong deterrent to attack.*

'You had enemies back then, too?' I muttered, before catching myself. 'I didn't mean *you* you.'

She cut me a furious look. I bounced foolishly on my toes. She climbed the hill to where enormous guns had once pointed out to the Pacific, guarding all three approaches to Golden Gate. There was a sublime view of Ocean Beach, but I knew it wasn't for the view that she'd brought me here.

Without looking at me, she said, 'Take me back.'

I assumed she meant to her warm purple house in the Mission. 'Let's go.'

'Take me back to the places in Pakistan that you love.'

I was stunned. If she'd never seen them, why did she say *back*? And why now? And why ever?

When she said it a third time I understood that she presented her idea as a condition: take me back and I will keep loving you.

For always? I wanted to ask. No matter where?

I glanced at her boldly now, and she returned my stare. I was hoping she'd understand that this is what my eyes said. It was here that a man loved her, a man with whom she could spend an unknowable quantity of time doing just about anything: walking, fucking, going to the movies, eating sushi and Guatemalan tamales on the same day, gossiping about a father in Berkeley, a father I'd still not met – I didn't know whom she was protecting more, him or me – but who'd brought her to this country when she was three and stayed. I didn't understand why she didn't feel this was home. All I understood was that she didn't. She was at a time in her life when other women long for a child. Farhana longed for a country.

'You're going home this summer. I'm coming with you. That's what I want you to show me, for my birthday.'

I didn't want to return. With her, that is. Nor did I want to explain that for me it was a return, but I didn't think it was for her. Nor that, just as she took joy in showing me this corner of the world because I was new to it, I could only take joy in showing her mine if she acknowledged it was new to her. Not if she claimed it as her own. I'd spent months lingering over northern California and I'd freely admit there was much I didn't grasp. How many months was she prepared to linger over Pakistan? How many years? Would she have the patience to wait and yield till the geography really did begin to construct the person, the way the breakers beneath us construct the shore? Did she want to yield to it? Of course not. It was a country practically under siege. *We might be interested in you but not in your landscapes.* What images did she want to see and to which land did she want to return?

We'd been happy. I wanted to stay happy. 'I'm going for work.'

It wasn't a lie. I was going to travel to the Frontier and the Northern Areas with my old friends from school, Irfan and Zulekha, to take pictures. Was I hoping to sell them here? Hoping, yes. Expecting, no. I'd started working long hours at a brew pub a few blocks from my apartment and took whatever other work I could find, usually as a wedding photographer. I anticipated doing the same no matter how many rolls I shot of the Pakistani Himalayas or the American Southwest. Yet her reply stunned me.

'What's the point? You'll never sell any. At least I *know* glaciers.'

I stopped rolling on my toes.

'Perhaps you're going back for the wrong reason,' she kept on.

'And being your tour guide is the right reason?'

She bestowed me with an ice-black stare, the kind I was to receive soon enough from a very different creature, in a very different place. Behind Farhana, I could *see* the guns that once pointed to the minefields outside Golden Gate. How easy it is to envision enemies lurking in the tide. As I looked over her shoulder, imagining what shapes those phantoms had once taken, I couldn't have guessed that within two months she and I would be posted at our own separate lookouts, not on a headland overlooking the Pacific, but near a glacier overlooking Kashmir.

The bathroom sink in my cabin was clogged. I moved to the kitchen, cracking the window as I shaved. I heard voices. It was Irfan, Zulekha and a third voice, perhaps the restaurant cook, discussing the reasons for the heightened security in the valley. Shia–Sunni riots had erupted in Gilgit District to the north and Mansehra district to the south, particularly near the town of Balakot, where the martyr Syed Ahmad Barelvi lay buried. Barelvi had once called for jihad against the British and dreamed of an Islamic state ruled by Islamic laws. Nearly two hundred years later, his followers were still dreaming his dream. They had training camps and, according to the third voice, men from the camps had started harassing the villagers here, trying to recruit their sons.

On our way to the valley, Irfan had whispered, 'We carry a heavy responsibility, travelling with them.' He'd nudged his chin in the direction of Farhana and Wes.

'She wants to return,' I'd declared, refusing to say more, while he stared at me in disbelief.

'We'll need an armed guard,' he said at last.

'I know.'

'This isn't what we'd planned.'

'I know.'

'Something happens to them, international fiasco.'

'I know.'

'Something happens to us, so what.'

'I know.'

Never was a wind between teeth more exasperated.

In the weeks following our fight at the Fort, I returned to the coast often, always alone. A small part of me knew it was to cleanse my palate, as if to revive something that had been lost on that wild stretch of land when it included Farhana.

My eye was hungry. I photographed the Monterey pines and the valley Quercus. The agave that bloomed before death. The pups that replaced them. California buckeye. Desert five-spots. Star tulips, and bell-shaped pussy ears with stems as thin as saliva. Diogenes' lantern, the sweetest of flowers, yellow as the yawning sun.

I crawled back to her house. *Mirror, mirror,* I bayed at her glass. *Forgive the ugliest of them all!*

When she flung the door open there was a man behind her. Farhana introduced him as Wesley.

'Call me Wes,' he said.

'You're not a Wes,' she gazed at him.

I stepped inside.

'I think I'll leave you with your beau.'

'Oh, stay. You guys should talk.'

Why?

'Nadir, I can arrange for us to go!'

'What do you mean?'

'We've applied for funding. We'll get it.'

We?

'A month to study glaciers in the western Himalayas!'

Wes smacked my shoulder. 'I want to know how those locals manage their water supply. You know, through seeding ice.'

I glared at Farhana. 'You *will* get it or already have?'

She soared into my arms, flinging all three of us side to side.

Later that night, when we were alone, she let me photograph her naked spine for the first time.

'Why?' I asked. 'Why today?'

She peeled off her sweater, shirt, bra, still delirious with the joy of having skilfully engineered her *return.* And all this time I'd believed she was waiting for me to say yes. There was no consent involved. We were going.

'Why today?' I insisted.

She giggled. It was as if she were drunk and wanting to have sex with me after refusing when sober. It was her choice, yet I was having to make it.

'Come on, Nadir. Pick up your camera. I know you're dying to.'

'Actually, I'm not.'

'Sure about that?'

I hesitated. To say yes would mean choosing no. I said no.

I didn't enjoy it. I didn't want Farhana, neither behind my lens nor in the flesh. Even when she wound her braid around her, I couldn't see the calla lily. It was all too conscious, too rehearsed. And yet, and yet. As I put her through my lens and captured that twisting torso, her ribs protruding, a thought flickered in my mind. Was it her pleasure that was dulling mine? I shook the thought away. It wasn't even pleasure. More like victory. I could see it in her gaze. It had killed the wonder this moment was always meant to hold. As she adjusted her hips and I kept on snapping, I tried to conjure it up, this wonder, this thing which cannot always be there, which is entirely fleeting and numinous, which, like luck, or talent, or wealth, cannot be equally distributed between those who love, between those who mate. *Snap!* She was raising her chin so high. She was rising from the bed. She was turning off all the lights.

W hat's the most beautiful thing you ever witnessed?' she used to ask, when we lay curled together in her bay window, playing opposites. 'I mean, a moment.'

I always said it was the mating of glaciers. 'And you, what's yours?'

She never hesitated. 'The way you looked at me, the first time, standing down in the sand on Baker Beach in your trousers while I sat sunning myself on the rocks. You compared me to a calla lily. That was the moment.'

We played differently now.

T he month before we left, I heard her on the phone. I seemed to have come in at the end.

'. . . it boils down to. One person in the mood when the other isn't?'

There was a pause while, I assumed, the listener spoke. Farhana shook her head. 'I'm not only talking about sex. Sex is just a metaphor.'

I expected her to elaborate. A long silence instead.

Finally, she exhaled. 'Yep, that's what I mean. Uh-huh.'

What did she mean?

'I mean, that day on the beach.'

Now I feared I could guess.

It had happened the other way more. I mean, my wanting sex while she didn't. It had happened the other way most of my life. Like a forgiving puppy, I bounced back up again at the merest hint of encouragement. Until recently.

She was saying, 'Women still suppress it, I know, nothing worse than letting go just to fall on your face. Though letting him decide, you know, what's hot, maybe that's worse.' Silence. 'Sure, I have, many times.' Silence. 'Uh-uh.' Silence. 'No. He doesn't.'

I don't what? And then panic: it was me she was talking about?

'Wes? Oh sure, yeah. It bothers him a lot.'

What?

I slammed the door. The door to the house with the five-sided bay window where she now spent more time with her phone. The door in the alcove where the gold rings of the columns now looked prosthetic, like gold teeth on a poor man from Tajikistan.

Why wasn't I aroused by her lately?

Was it our departure? Ours. I told myself I was at peace with her coming too. More importantly, I was excited about what I'd do there, with or without her, and this had renewed interest in my work. I'd bought a Nikon digital camera to go with my beloved F4, bought a 300mm lens and 20mm extension tube. I spent my free time photographing small fry. A California poppy. Farhana's nipple. The rainbow in a dragonfly's wing.

I suppose the image of the magnified nipple and the blurred contours of the breast preoccupied me more than she did, but then, she wasn't in a very preoccupying state of mind. Always on the phone, always talking about him, her work, her return. Her breasts. She liked me photographing them. Breasts that had begun to stir me only in the frame. At least I didn't get off on images of other women.

That day on the beach? It excited her, seeing herself magnified. And colour-filtered. Image pre-processing, not to be confused with post-processing, to enhance maximum photorealism. To make the infeasible feasible. She lay on her stomach; I drizzled sand on the mound of her buttocks. It cascaded down her curves, featherlike, matching her skin tone. When we viewed the images together, the texture of the sandspill on her flesh made her wet. We were nestled between the same cluster of rocks where I'd found her the first time, on the far side of the cypress grove. There were others around, though none in our nest, or so we thought. She rolled back onto her stomach, raised her hips high into my groin. The sand scrubbed my erection. I heard the figure behind me, his breathing. I could feel it on my neck. I assumed she mistook it for mine or would have stopped. There was no way she could have seen his shadow on her spine.

Later, we both lay on our stomachs a long time. When we eventually got dressed, we didn't speak of it. *He came when I did.* Perhaps she hadn't noticed.

We still call it a fault line, here where the subcontinent conjoins with Asia. I told Farhana I'd seen glaciers mate once before, and I had. The first time, I'd been in love with a girl called Rida, which means inner peace. I gave her purple roses that left blood marks on our lips. By the end of the year, I'd no idea where she was, or what she was doing. By the following summer, I was thinking of her less, and the memory kept on receding, creeping downhill, like a carefully constructed secret.

I knew where Farhana was and what she was doing. She was in Wes's cabin and they were eating breakfast. It was their laughter I could hear. My cabin was only growing colder. Soon Irfan and Zulekha would knock on my door. It would be time to return to the ice-bride and ice-groom, to see how they were settling in their new home.

The night she left. She lay sprawled across the bed, her legs bare before me. I didn't stir. 'I hoped that might change,' she whispered. 'Here.'

Now I saw her draped across a different set of sheets. The memory was an extraordinarily happy one. It was a memory from before our troubles and it took place in a purple house and it began with legs. Hers were steep legs built by steepness. Mountain legs; San Francisco legs. The white, tennis-ball calves tapering tidily to the ankles against dark sheets. I traced their stocky slant with a fingertip and moved higher, to where her sartorius cut a ribbony dialogue on her flesh, snaking across a taut inner thigh. I called her my ice queen, whom I alone could melt. And we'd heard our ascent – the rush of wings, higher, higher, through a smooth, silvery sky! And our fall – deeper, deeper, down a silky, slippery skein. *Whooshoo! Whooshoo!*

Months later in a cabin in Kaghan it was the sheets, not her calves, that shone. Her legs receded in the dark.

W hen we got to a place from where we could look across the valley, Irfan asked the driver to stop. We walked to the edge of the road and climbed up a set of rocks. Our armed escort stayed in the jeep.

'Does this look familiar?' asked Zulekha.

I nodded. We were facing the hill we'd climbed seven years earlier, the first time I saw the mating of glaciers, that time with Rida. The two ice blocks we'd seen then were now one white smudge of triangle in a fountain of black gravel.

How quickly they grow, I thought. Seven years ago was five years before I met San Francisco, or Farhana.

On the slopes were scattered a few sheep and goats, and closer, juniper trees whose leaves were still burned by shamans on special occasions. The afternoon sun fell just at the lip of the glacier. As

I photographed it, I thought of one of the first things I'd learned about seeing through the lens: normalize the view. Which meant the right exposure on the area the human eye is most inclined to drift toward, which, at this moment, was that sliver of bright light at the edge of the white smudge.

'It looks young,' said Wes. 'It has to be sixty feet thick to be called a glacier.'

'It doesn't matter what you call it,' muttered Irfan. 'I'm glad the tradition of marrying glaciers is coming back.'

'Here winter temperatures are rising,' said Farhana. 'More snowfall, less melt. So, after seven years, that *could* be sixty feet.'

So she'd guessed that was the one.

'Seven years?' said Wes. 'Doubt it.'

'They've always made do without science,' said Zulekha.

Wes shrugged. 'How far are we from ours?'

Ours.

'Not far. But if we want to return before dark, we should leave.'

Farhana and I were left alone. I lowered my camera.

'That is the one, isn't it?' she asked.

'Yes,' I said.

Below us, a row of military trucks raced up the highway, slowing to examine our group. I could hear them call out to Irfan, asking questions, waving their guns as casually as cigarettes. I let Irfan tackle them.

Ahead, a farmer was watering his wheat field. The sun was creeping off the glacier's lip and onto the dark gravel. He stopped to enjoy the light, just as we did. A goat grazed at his feet, her bells chiming through the valley. Gradually, the black earth immediately before them ignited, as if the sun had chosen that precise point upon which to rest its fingers, enfolding the man and the goat. We kept at our lookouts, squinting into the glare, waiting for the sun to release the captives. From the corner of my eye, I noticed a rolling, as of a rain cloud. It was the glacier, sliding into shadow. ■

"Brilliant ... One of the most profound and devastating novels ever to come out of Vietnam—or any war."

—SEBASTIAN JUNGER, front page of
The New York Times Book Review

NEW YORK TIMES BESTSELLER

"Unforgettable . . . A beautifully crafted novel of unrivaled authenticity and power, filled with jungle heroism, crackerjack inventiveness, mud, blood, brotherhood, hatred, healing, terror, bureaucracy, politics, unfathomable waste, and unfathomable love."

MATTERHORN

A NOVEL OF
THE VIETNAM WAR

"A powerhouse: tense, brutal, honest." —*TIME*

KARL MARLANTES

"Powerful ...
Matterhorn will take your heart, and sometimes even your breath, away."
—ALAN CHEUSE,
San Francisco Chronicle

"I've laughed at *Catch-22* and wept at *The Thin Red Line*, but I've never encountered a war novel as stark, honest, and wrenching as *Matterhorn*. . . . I found it nearly impossible to stop reading."
—MICHAEL SCHAUB,
National Public Radio

"Here is storytelling so moving and so intense that there were times I wasn't sure I could stand to turn the page. . . . There has never been a more realistic portrait or eloquent tribute to the nobility of men under fire. Vladimir Nabokov once said that the greatest books are those you read not just with your heart or your mind but with your spine. This is one for the spine." —MARK BOWDEN, author of *Black Hawk Down*

Over 150,000 copies in print after seven printings
In Bookstores Now

 ATLANTIC MONTHLY PRESS
AN IMPRINT OF GROVE/ATLANTIC, INC.
DISTRIBUTED BY PUBLISHERS GROUP WEST

In association with
EL LEÓN LITERARY ARTS
www.groveatlantic.com

THE HOUSE BY THE GALLOWS

Intizar Hussain

TRANSLATED BY BASHARAT PEER

ABDULLAH M. I. SYED
Attention: At Ease, 2007
Lambda print mounted on aluminium. 41 x 5cm
Edition of 3
Photography: Maheen Zia © Abdullah M. I. Syed, 2007

General Zia ul-Haq had taken over Pakistan. Piety filled the air; there was much talk of religion: praying, fasting. The General threw a party to break the Ramadan fast at the house of his figurehead Prime Minister, Muhammad Khan Junejo. I was among the writers and journalists invited. We had broken the fast, were eating, when the muezzin gave the call to prayer. The General rose hastily, leaving his food, and walked off to the prayer room. Most of the invitees followed. I seemed to be the only one left behind. I looked around and found Ahmed Ali Khan, a newspaper editor, sitting under a tree in a far corner of the lawn. A few others joined us, while the pious dictator and his guests prayed.

The next evening we were back at the Prime Minister's house. Junejo had thrown his own fast-breaking party. The same crowd filled the lawns, all except the General. The muezzin gave the call for prayer. The Prime Minister promptly rose from his plate and left for the prayer room. I looked around: a few followed him but the majority stayed by their plates. Prayer is an obligation for Muslims, but it seemed who invited you to pray made a difference.

The General's call to Islam had the strongest effect. Before him, Prime Minister Zulfikar Ali Bhutto had attempted to raise the banner of Islam in Pakistan, but without much success. He decreed the Ahmadiyya sect non-Muslim, made Friday a public holiday, banned horse racing and alcohol. Bhutto wasn't a praying, fasting man, and his flirtations with Islamism remained suspect.

General Zia aggressively nourished the Islamism Bhutto had midwifed. Overnight, bureaucrats began showing up in mosques and rows of the faithful became a feature of the offices. At my newspaper, *Mashriq* (the East), there were a few devout men. The moment the call for afternoon prayer sounded, their pens would stop and they would leave for the nearby mosque. And now, the moment the editor appointed by the General stepped out of his cubicle, every reporter and editor would rise from his seat and head for the mosque. The madman stood with a razor on our necks.

Rumour had it that two lists were being made: those who prayed regularly would be considered for promotion; those who didn't . . .

The Arts Council of Lahore promoted theatre, painting, music and dance. Maharaj Ghulam Hussain, a maestro of the classical dance, Kathak, would waltz into the Arts Council building every evening, casually waving his stick. He would sit cross-legged in a small room, chew betel-nut leaf, and lord it over his small class of dancers.

News came that the dance class had been banned. The Islamists had been attacking the Arts Council. I was on the board and we had a meeting that week. 'Why have you banned the dance class?' I asked the chairman. 'We haven't banned it,' he said. 'We have moved the class to the basement, away from peering eyes.' The chairman paused. 'Don't write about that in your column. That would make us cancel the class.'

The General issued a proclamation: the word alcohol shall not be mentioned on the radio or the television. I was a regular on literary and cultural shows on Radio Pakistan. One day, as we were about to record a literary discussion, the producer, Shakoor Bedil, instructed, 'Please don't read any poem that refers to liquor.'

Liquor makes frequent appearances in Urdu poetry in the context of romantic love and longing. But intoxication refers often to the love of God and love of the Prophet in the Sufi tradition of Islam. The great Urdu poet-philosopher Sir Muhammad Iqbal, who is also Pakistan's national poet, has written extensively in that vein, including a stirring poem, 'Saaqi Nama' ('The Book of the Cupbearer'), which speaks about the transformative wine of political and social consciousness that makes the young lead the old.

I wanted to have a little fun. 'Can we speak about the wine of mysticism?' I asked the producer. He was in deep thought. 'Can you avoid it?' he pleaded. The subject demanded that I refer to Iqbal's 'Saaqi Naama'. 'Would that be all right?' I asked. The producer was torn between the General's orders and the moral authority of the national poet-philosopher, who had come up with the idea of a separate homeland for India's Muslims which eventually became Pakistan in 1947. The producer rose from his seat, brought his hands together desperately and cried, 'Have pity on me! I will lose my job.'

Along with religion, an unthinking nationalism had become the other god of Pakistan. I was back at Radio Pakistan to record a discussion on Islamic cultural heritage. At some point I referred to the Taj Mahal as one of the highest points in Islamic architecture. The producer was overcome by a bout of anxiety. He stopped the recording. 'Leave the Taj Mahal out! The authorities will object,' he said.

'Why?' I was irritated.

'Because the Taj is in India!' he replied.

I refused to leave the Taj out and abandoned the panel. The other panellist burst into a fit of rage and left the studio, hurling a torrent of abuse at the dictator and Radio Pakistan and the censors. I began to leave and the producer repeated his familiar gesture of helplessness: 'Have pity on me! I will lose my job.'

The producer was right. Wavering from the General's censorship regime would have cost him his job. I got a better sense of the absurdity and ruthlessness of the regime when I mentioned *bhutta*, or corn on the cob, in a radio feature. The script editor made a minor mistake and the censors mistook it as a reference to Bhutto, the Prime Minister, whom the General had overthrown in a July 1977 coup and hanged two years later, in April 1979. The producer was removed from that programme, despite several explanations.

The censors didn't change their ways, even under later democratic regimes following the General's death in 1988. When Benazir Bhutto ruled Pakistan in the mid-nineties as a democratically elected prime minister, intense ethnic violence between the natives and the *mohajirs* (the Indian Muslims who had migrated to the city after partition and the creation of Pakistan in 1947) scarred Karachi and several other places in Pakistan. Pakistan Television screened a play I had written that examined the ethnic violence. It stopped abruptly during the broadcast. Advertisements followed. And then another show aired.

Some time later, on an official's insistence, I gave the script of a play to state-run Pakistan Television. The play, *The Eighth Question*, was a fantasy based on the ancient legend of Hatim Tai, in which a rich and beautiful woman, Husn Bano, decides to marry the man who could answer seven questions she asked. I was told the play was very well-written, but it didn't run. Some bureaucrat thought that Husn Bano would remind people of the Prime Minister, Benazir Bhutto.

A change in management at Pakistan Television followed. A friend got the top job and I reminded him of *The Eighth Question*. He ran it a few weeks later. Husn Bano did not remind anyone of Benazir Bhutto. The bureaucrats who had been raised under General Zia's martial law had become so sensitive to any hint of offence or dissent that they outdid the censors with their own self-censorship.

What an era General Zia had brought to Pakistan! The echoes of prayer and the roar of public hangings. I lived by the Jail Road in Lahore. You could see the prison complex from my terrace. One morning as I walked about on the lawn I was struck by a group of labourers at work in the prison yard. I walked closer and saw they were nailing together planks of wood. By the afternoon, I realized they had been building a gallows. A sea of people swept towards the prison complex. Men went about searching for terraces and balconies that would have a good view of the hangings. Many eager onlookers eyed my terrace. They begged and pleaded with me. I insisted on refusing them the spectacle. The time for the hanging came. I looked out at my terrace. A group had found its way there anyhow. I stared at them. They were oblivious to me, lost, watching the hangings. I could not bring myself to look at the gallows. I stared, instead, at the spectators on my terrace. Three men were hanged that afternoon. Everyone was invited. ■

BUTT AND BHATTI

Mohammed Hanif

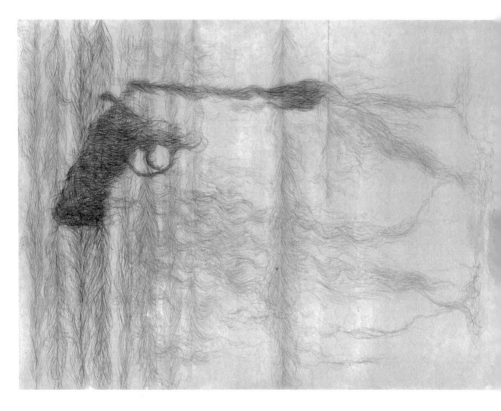

MUHAMMAD ZEESHAN
High Notes, 2005
Gouache on paper. 15 x 21cm
Courtesy of the Asal Collection, © Muhammad Zeeshan

Teddy has brought a Mauser to his declaration of love. He has brought a story about the moon as well but he is not sure where to start. The story is romantic in an old-fashioned kind of way; the Mauser has three bullets in it. He is hoping that the Mauser and the story about the moon will somehow come together to produce the kind of love song that makes old acquaintances run away together.

Before resorting to gunpoint poetry, Teddy Butt tries the traditional route to romancing a medical professional; he pretends to be sick and then, like a truly hopeless lover, starts believing that he is sick, recognizes all the little symptoms – sudden fevers, heart palpitations, lingering migraine, even mild depression. He cries while watching a documentary about a snow leopard stranded on a melting glacier.

He lurks around the Outpatients Department on a Sunday afternoon, when Sister Alice Bhatti is alone. She pretends to be busy counting syringes, boiling needles, polishing grimy surfaces, and only turns round when he coughs politely, like you are supposed to do when entering a respectable household so that women have the time to cover themselves. Sister Alice Bhatti doesn't understand this polite-cough protocol and stares at him as if telling him, See? This is what smoking does to your lungs.

Teddy Butt is too vain to bring up anything like stomach troubles or a skin rash, both conditions he frequently suffers from. Boldabolics play havoc with his digestion. His bodybuilder's weekly regime of waxing his body hair has left certain parts of his body looking like abstract kilim designs. For his first consultation with Sister Alice he has thought up something more romantic.

'I can't sleep.'

He says this sitting on a rickety little stool as Sister Alice takes notes in a khaki-coloured register. 'For how long have you not been able to sleep?' With any other patient Alice would have reached for the wrist to take the pulse, would have listened to their chest with a stethoscope, but she knows that Teddy is not that kind of patient.

'Since I have seen you,' is what Teddy wants to say but he hasn't rehearsed it, he is not ready yet.

'I do go to sleep. But then I have dreams and I wake up,' he says and feels relieved at having delivered a full sentence without falling off the stool.

Alice Bhatti wants to tell him to go to the OPD in Charya Ward, that is where they deal in dreams. The whole place is a bad dream. But she knows that he wants to be her patient and Senior Sister Hina Alvi has taught her that when a patient walks in with intent you listen to them, even if you know they are making up their symptoms.

She can also see the outline of a muzzle in the crotch of his yellow Adidas trousers. He looks like a freak with two cocks.

'What kind of dreams?'

Teddy has only ever had one dream, the one with a river and a kaftan-wearing God in it. The dream always ends badly as a drowning Teddy discovers that he can't walk on water even in his dream. God stands at the edge of a silvery, completely walkable river and shakes His head in disappointment as if saying, it's your dream, what do you expect me to do? But somehow bringing up God and His kaftan and His disapproval right now seems inappropriate. 'I see a river in my dream.' He conveniently leaves God out.

'A river?' Alice Bhatti taps the pen on the register without writing anything.

Teddy feels he is being told that his dream is not sick enough.

'It's a river of blood. Red.'

Sister Alice looks at him with interest. This Teddy boy might be a police tout but he has a poetic side to him, she thinks.

'Any boats in that river of yours?' she asks with an encouraging smile, as if urging him to go on sharing more of his dream with her, to go ahead and dream for her. Teddy accepts the challenge. 'It has bodies floating in it and severed heads, bobbing up and down.' He realizes that his dream doesn't sound very romantic. 'And some flowers also.'

'Do you recognize any of these people in the river? In your dream,

I mean.' Teddy shuts his eyes as if trying hard to recognize a face from the river. Teddy was hoping that somehow his midnight yearning for Alice and his insomnia would walk hand in hand and form a rhyming, soaring declaration of love that would reverberate through the corridors of the hospital. Instead he is stuck with embellishing details for a bad dream.

'I can't really stop your dreams but I can give you something that will ensure that you sleep well. And if you sleep well then you might start having better dreams.' She scribbles a prescription for Lexotanil then puts it aside. 'Actually I might have one here. An hour before you sleep. Never on an empty stomach. And no warm milk at night. Sometimes indigestion can give you bad dreams.'

Sister Alice gives him a curt smile, turns round and goes back to counting her syringes. She does it with such studied concentration that it seems the health of the nation depends on getting this count right.

Teddy Butt stumbles into the OPD the following morning, bleary-eyed, moving slowly. Even his voice seems to be coming from underwater. There is a sleepy calm about him. Even the muzzle of the gun in his trousers seems flaccid. 'I didn't have any dreams. What did you give me? What did you mix in that pill?' Teddy's words are accusatory but his tone is grateful.

'I didn't mix anything. It was a Glaxo original, supposed to help you sleep. Do you want more?' She reaches into her drawer and stops. She notices that he is wearing a little cross on a gold chain around his neck. She shows the slight, spontaneous irritation that natives feel when tourists try and dress up like them. 'What's that thing you are wearing?'

'A chain.' Teddy Butt says. 'A friend from Dubai got it for me.' The man whose neck Teddy snatched it from was indeed visiting from Dubai. One ear and the side of his face were blown off in an unfortunate accident during an interrogation. The man from Dubai had almost strangled Teddy with his handcuffs before Inspector Malangi put his Repeater near his left ear, shouted at Teddy, 'Knee on the left, *bhai*. Your left, not mine,' – and shot him. The chain with the cross was the reward Inspector Malangi gave him for keeping the man pinned down at that difficult moment. Teddy hadn't killed the man; he was only holding him down. It was his job. If he hadn't done it someone else would have. If he hadn't done this job he would definitely have to do some other job. And who knows what he might be required to do in that new job? He runs his forefinger along his chain and presses the cross into his chest with the satisfaction of someone who is lucky enough not to get the worst job in the city. He had felt the man's breath on his knee when he tried to bite him before getting shot.

For a moment Teddy wonders whether he can source a matching necklace for her.

'It's a cross, not jewellery. Why would a man want to wear jewellery anyway?' She scribbles a prescription for Lexotanil on her pad and turns away.

Teddy Butt is flummoxed and walks away without answering, without asking anything. He goes to his room in Al Aman apartments and sleeps the whole day. He doesn't have any dreams but after he wakes up and starts doing weights he watches a fascinating documentary about Komodo dragons who hypnotize their prey before going for the underside of their throat.

Teddy decides that he is going to tell Alice Bhatti everything but he will need her full attention. From what Teddy can tell, women are always distracted, trying to do too many things at the same time, always happy to go off on tangents; that's why they make good nurses and politicians but not good chefs and truck drivers. He realizes that he can't do it without his Mauser. He also realizes that he'll have to wait for the coming Sunday when there is only skeleton staff on duty.

Teddy is one of those people who are only articulate when they talk about cricket. The rest of the time they rely on a combination of grunts, hand gestures and repeat the snippets of what other people have just said to them. He also has very little experience of sharing his feelings.

He has been a customer of women and occasionally their tormentor but never a lover. He believes that being a lover is something that falls somewhere between paying them and slapping them around. Twice he has come close to conceding love. Once he gave a fifty-rupee tip to a prostitute who looked fourteen but claimed to be twenty-two. Encouraged by his generosity she also demanded a poster of Imran Khan and that put him off. Teddy promised to get it but never went back because he thought Imran Khan was a failed batsman pretending to be a bowler. On another occasion he only pretended to take his turn with a thirty-two-year-old Bangladeshi prisoner after a small police contingent had shuffled out of the room. He only sat there and played with her hair while she sobbed and cursed in Bengali. The only word he could understand was Allah. He had walked out adjusting his fly, pretending to be exhausted and satisfied, even joking with the policemen: it was like fucking an oil spill.

But Teddy Butt can be very articulate, even poetic, with a Mauser in his hand, and after much thought this is what he decides to do. He tries practising in front of the full-length mirror in his room. 'You live in my heart.' With every word he jabs the Mauser in the air like an underprepared lawyer trying to impress a judge. The gun might send the wrong signal but Teddy is convinced that he will be able to explain himself. People always listen and try their best to understand when their life depends on listening properly.

You can't go around in the Ortho Ward with that,' Alice Bhatti has emerged carrying a bedpan in one hand and a discarded, blood-smeared bandage in the other and starts admonishing him while walking away from him. 'Don't waste your bullets, this hospital will kill them all anyway.' Teddy feels the love of his life slipping from his hands, his plan falling apart at the very first hurdle. He grips the Mauser, stretches his arm and blocks her way.

Alice Bhatti looks confused for a moment and then irritated. 'What do you want to rob me of? This piss tray?'

With the Mauser extended, Teddy finds his tongue. 'I can't live like this. This life is too much.'

'Nobody can live like this.' Alice Bhatti is attentive now and sympathetic. 'If these cheap guns don't kill you, those Boldabolic pills will. Get a job as a PT master. Or come to think of it, you could get a nurse's diploma and work here. There is always work for a man nurse. There are parts of this place where even women doctors don't go. Charya Ward for example hasn't had a . . .'

Teddy doesn't listen to the whole thing, the word PT master triggers off a childhood memory that he had completely forgotten – a very tall, very fat PT teacher holds him by his ears, swings him round and then hurls him on the ground and walks away laughing. The other children run around him in a circle and decide to change his nickname from 'Nappy' to 'Yo-yo'. Teddy takes the gun to Alice Bhatti's temple and snarls in his high-pitched, sing-song voice.

'Give me one good reason why somebody wouldn't shoot in this hospital? Why shouldn't I shoot you right here and end all my troubles?'

'Mine too,' she wants to say but Teddy's hand holding the Mauser is trembling and one thing Sister Alice doesn't want in her life is a shoot-out in her workplace.

He orders Alice Bhatti to put her tray and bandages down, which she does. She has realized that Teddy is serious. Suicidal serious maybe, but he is the kind of suicidal serious who in the process of taking their own life would cause some grievous bodily harm to those around them.

Ortho Ward is unusually quiet at this time of day. No. 14, who is always shouting about an impending plague caused by computer screens is calm and only murmurs about the itch in his plastered leg. A ward boy enters the corridor carrying a water cooler on a wheelbarrow, and when he sees Alice and Teddy, he stops in his tracks. Embarrassed as if he has stumbled on to someone's private property and found the owners in a compromising position, he backtracks, taking the wheelbarrow with him. Sister Alice doesn't expect him to inform anyone.

'What do you want, Mr Butt?' Alice Bhatti tries to hide her fear behind a formal form of address. She has learned all the wrong things from Senior Sister Hina Alvi.

'You live in my heart,' Teddy Butt wants to say but only jabs the air with his Mauser, five times. In her limited experience with guns and madmen, Sister Alice Bhatti knows that when men are unable to talk you are in real trouble. She looks at him expectantly as if she has understood what his Mauser has just said, likes it and now wants to hear more.

Mixed-up couplets about her lips and hair, half-remembered speeches about a life together, names of their children, pledges of undying love, a story about the first time he saw her, what she wore, what she said, a half-sincere eulogy about her professionalism which he was sure she would appreciate, her shoulder blades, all these things rush through Teddy Butt's head and then he realizes that he has already delivered his opening line by pulling out a gun.

Now, he can start anywhere.

Alice Bhatti thinks that she should not do Sunday shifts any more and instead should help her dad with his woodwork. If she lives to see another Sunday, that is.

She looks beyond Teddy, outside the corridor; on the top of the stairs a man sits facing the sun like an ancient king waiting to receive his subjects. His legs amputated just above the knees, he sits on the floor, wearing full-length trousers that sometimes balloon up in the wind. He has a stack of large X-rays next to him. He picks them up one by one, holds them against the sun and looks at them for a long time as if contemplating old family pictures.

Teddy Butt decides to start with her garbage bin. 'I go through your garbage bin. I know everything about you. I see all the prayers you scribble on prescriptions. You never write your own name. But I can tell from the handwriting.' He sobs violently and holds the Mauser with both hands to steady himself. The muzzle of his gun slides down a degree like an erection flashbacking to a sad memory. Sister Alice sees it as a sign from God. Bless Our Lord who descended from the heavens. God accepts her gratitude with godlike indifference. And Teddy straightens his gun. He seems to have found his groove and starts to speak in paragraphs as if delivering the manifesto of a new political party which wants to eradicate poverty and pollution during its first term in power.

'The love that I feel for you is not the love I feel for any other human being. The world might think it's the love of your flesh. I can understand this world and their thinking. I have wondered about this and thought long and hard and realized that this is a world full of sinners so I do understand what they think but I don't think like that. When I think about you, do I think about these milk pots?' He waves his Mauser across her chest. Alice looks at his gun and feels nauseous and wonders if the peace and quiet of this corridor is worth preserving. 'I think of your eyes. I think of your eyes only.'

The octopus of fear that had clutched Sister Alice's head begins to relax its tentacles.

In her heart of hearts, Alice, who has seen people die choking on their own food, and survive after falling from a sixth floor on to a paved road, knows that Teddy means every word of what he has said. And he isn't finished yet.

'I was standing outside the hospital hoping to catch a glimpse of you. It was a full Rajab moon. Then I looked up at the balcony of Ortho Ward and saw you empty a garbage bin. I saw your face for a moment and then you disappeared. Then I looked up again and saw that the moon had disappeared too. I rubbed my eyes, I shut them, I opened them again. I stood and kept looking up for forty-five minutes. People gathered around me, I held them from their collars, made them look towards the sky and kept asking them where the moon had gone. And they said what moon? We have seen no moon. Did you just escape from the Charya Ward? And then I knew that I couldn't live without you.'

A thick March cloud has cloaked the sun outside. The perfect spring afternoon turns into its own wintry ghost. The man with the

X-rays is trying to shoo away a kite, which, confused by the sudden change in light, thinks it's dusk, and swoops down in a last desperate attempt to take something home.

The final bell rings in the neighbouring St Xavier's Primary School and eighteen hundred children suddenly start talking to each other in urgent voices like house sparrows at dusk.

Alice Bhatti bends down, picks the piss tray from the floor, holds it in front of her chest and speaks in measured tones. 'I know your type,' she says. 'That little gun doesn't scare me. Your tears don't fool me. You think that a woman, any woman, who wears a uniform, is just waiting for you to show up and she'll take it off. I wish you had just walked in and told me you want me to take this off. We could have had a conversation about that. At the end of which I would have told you what I am telling you now: fuck off and never show me your face again.'

Teddy Butt runs before she is finished. He runs past the legless man, now taking a nap with his face covered with an X-ray, past the ambulance drivers dissecting the evening newspapers, past the hopeful junkies waiting for the hospital accidentally to dispense its bounty.

As he emerges out of the hospital he raises his arm in the air, without thinking, without targeting anything, and shoots his Mauser.

The city stops moving for three days.

The bullet pierces the right shoulder of a truck driver who has just entered the city after a forty-eight-hour journey; his shoulder is almost leaning out of his driver's window, his right hand drumming the door, his fingers holding a finely rolled joint, licked on the side with his tongue for extra smoothness, a ritual treat that he has prepared for the end of the journey. He is annoyed with his own shoulder, he looks at it with suspicion. His shoulder feels as if it has been stung by a bee that travelled with him all the way from his village. His left hand grips the shoulder where it hurts and finds his shirt soaked in red gooey stuff. He jams the brake to the floor. A rickshaw trying to dodge the swerving truck gets entangled in its double-mounted Goodyear tyres and is dragged along for a few yards. Five children, all between seven and nine, in their pristine blue-and-white St Xavier's uniform become a writhing mess of fractured skulls, blood, crayons and Buffy the Vampire Slayer lunch boxes. The truck comes to a halt after gently nudging a cart and overturning a pyramid of the season's last guavas. A size-four shoe is stuck between two Goodyears.

School notebooks are looked at, pockets are searched for clues to the victims' identities, the mob slowly gathers around the truck, petrol is extracted from the tank and sprinkled over its cargo of three tonnes of raw peanuts. Teddy with his broken heart and the truck driver with his bleeding shoulder both realize what is coming even before the mob has made up its mind; they first mingle in the crowd and then start walking in opposite directions.

A lonely fire engine will turn up an hour later but will be pelted at and sent away. The truck and its cargo will smoulder for two days.

In a house twenty miles away a phone rings. A grandmother rushes on to the street beating her chest and wailing. Two motorcycles kick-start simultaneously. Half a dozen jerrycans full of kerosene are hauled into a rickety Suzuki pickup. A nineteen-year-old rummages under his pillow, cocks his TT pistol and runs on to the street screaming, promising to rape every Pathan mother in the land. A second-hand tyre shop owner tries to padlock his store but the boys are already there with their iron rods and bicycle chains. A policemobile switches on its emergency horn and rushes towards the police commissioner's house. A helicopter hovers over the beach as if defending the Arabian Sea against the burning rubber smell that is spreading through the city. An old colonel walking his dog in the Colonels' Colony asks his dog to hurry up and do its business. A bank teller is shot dead for smiling. Finding the streets deserted, groups of kites and crows descend from their perches and chase wild dogs that lift their faces to the sky and bark joyously. Five size-four coffins wait for three days as ambulance drivers are shot at and sent back to where they came from. Carcasses of burned buses, rickshaws, paan shops and at least one KFC joint seem to have a calming effect on the population. Newspapers start predicting 'Normalcy limping back to the city', as if normalcy had gone for a picnic and sprained an ankle.

During the three-day shutdown eleven more are killed; two of them turn up shot and tied together in one gunny bag dumped on a rubbish heap. Three billion rupees-worth of Suzukis, Toyotas and Hinopaks are burned down. During these days Alice Bhatti is actually not that busy. When people are killed while fixing their satellite dishes on their roofs, or their motorbikes are torched while going to buy a litre of milk, they tend to forget about their ailments, they learn to live without dialysis for their kidneys, home cures are found for minor injuries, prayers replace prescription drugs. Sister Alice has time to sit down between her chores, she has time to take a proper lunch and prayer breaks. Between cleaning gun wounds and mopping the A&E floor, Sister Alice has moments of calm and she finds herself thinking about that scared little man with the Mauser, his mad story about the disappearing moon. She wonders if he is caught up in these riots, if he is still having those dreams. She wonders if she has been in one of his dreams. ∎

The Pakistani Bride *Bapsi Sidhwa*

Born in Karachi and raised in Lahore, Bapsi Sidhwa has been widely celebrated as the finest novelist produced by her country. Her first book, originally published in 1983 and now back in print, tells the story of the conflict between adherence to tradition and the indomitable force of a woman's spirit as set in the wild, austere territories of northern Pakistan.

Milkweed Editions USD $14.00 | CDN $18 | PB

Ladies of the Field: Early Women Archaeologists and Their Search for Adventure *Amanda Adams*

Ladies of the Field tells the story of seven remarkable women, each a pioneering archaeologist, each headstrong, smart, and courageous, who burst into what was then a very young science. Amanda Adams reveals the dreams of these extraordinary women, and takes us with them as they unearth history.

Greystone Books USD $17.95 | CDN $21.95 | PB

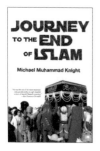

Journey to the End of Islam
Michael Muhammad Knight

'One of the most necessary and . . . hopeful writers of Barack Obama's America' (*San Francisco Chronicle*). Knight (author of *The Taqwacores*) visits holy sites throughout the Muslim world, attempting to reconcile the puritanical Islam promoted by Saudi globalization with its more popular folk incarnation, while ruminating on the possibilities for a personal connection to the faith.

Soft Skull Press USD $16.95 | CDN $22 | PB

White Masks *Elias Khoury*

A journalist investigating the death of a civil servant interviews his widow, a local engineer, a watchman, the garbage man who discovered him, the doctor who performed the autopsy, and a militiaman. Khoury, 'one of the most innovative novelists in the Arab world' (*Washington Post*), reveals the resilience of the Lebanese people with empathy and candour.

Archipelago Books USD $22.00 | CDN $18 | HB

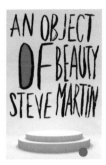

An Object of Beauty *Steve Martin*

'This very different novel will captivate your attention from start to finish.' – Joyce Carol Oates. An irresistible look at the glamour and subterfuge of New York's art world, from best-selling author and Hollywood star Steve Martin.

Read an extract at www.orionbooks.co.uk/object

Weidenfeld & Nicolson £16.99 | HB

Lights Out in Wonderland *DBC Pierre*

The spectacular third novel from DBC Pierre. Gabriel Brockwell, aesthete, poet, philosopher, disaffected twenty-something decadent, is thinking terminal. And his destination is Wonderland. On the back of Gabriel's voice – at once sceptical, idealistic, broken and optimistic – we are led on a remarkable global odyssey through London, Tokyo, Berlin and the Galapagos Islands and, along the way, see a character disintegrate and reshape before our eyes.

Faber & Faber £12.99 | PB

Where Three Dreams Cross

From the days when the first Indian-run photographic studios were established in the nineteenth century, this landmark book – and its accompanying exhibition – traces the development of photography in South Asia. Beginning at the crucial moment when the power to hold a camera and capture an image was no longer exclusively the preserve of colonial or European photographers, *Where Three Dreams Cross* gives an inside view of how modern India, Pakistan and Bangladesh have been shaped through the lens of their photographers.

Steidl & Partners £43.00 | PB

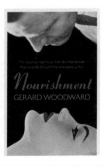

Nourishment *Gerard Woodward*

The new novel from the Man Booker Prize shortlisted author. With her children evacuated and her husband at the front, Tory Pace is grudgingly sharing the family home with her irascible mother. Her quiet life is thrown into turmoil, however, when her prisoner-of-war husband, Donald, makes an outrageous demand for sexual gratification. He wants a dirty letter, by return of post!

www.picador.com/nourishment

Picador | HB

HIGH NOON

Hari Kunzru

We hear a lot – perhaps too much – about 'identity' in relation to South Asian art. Whether it's national or personal, this elusive quality is often seen as the primary concern of South Asian writers and visual artists, to the exclusion of all other aesthetic categories. By contrast, those who can lay claim to sufficient whiteness or Western-ness are presumed to be the unreflective owners of secure but troublingly authoritarian identities whose dismantling is the proper task of progressive artistic practice. It's a formulation which has, after a generation or so of post-colonial criticism, become an orthodoxy.

High Noon, as the title suggests, stages a confrontation with this brittle identity politics and claims a kind of luminous clarity, where shadows and ambiguities disappear. Noon is when mad dogs and Englishmen are the only creatures out on the street. High NOON is also a punning physicist's term for certain states of quantum superposition, when particles exist in both of two possible states, so perhaps there's also a suggestion of *kairos* in the title, the 'time of chance', that suspended moment when decisive action may bring about great and significant change. Clearly, for Pakistan, such a time is at hand.

Whether Pakistani artists like it or not, the question of their identity now has geopolitical significance. Who are the inhabitants of this young country? What do they believe? Unmanned drones hover over the North West Frontier to mete out punishment to those who answer incorrectly, while men who have no time for representation of any kind, and who hate art for its advance into the territory of

religion, are waiting in the wings. As the confusion and carnage on Pakistan's northern border threatens to move southwards, the long-standing preoccupations of post-colonial cultural politics are pushed aside by more pressing concerns.

It may be that it's only possible to wage war on those whom one doesn't see fully, those whom one allows or forces oneself to view as less than human. This suggests that – seen now, in 2010 – the art in this collection has a particular urgency that exists as much in the desire to trace small, personal actions (getting dressed, drawing a line), as in overtly political gestures, such as the arresting opening image in which a woman hangs her blood-red washing out to dry on the wings of a decommissioned fighter plane. The machismo of the military, which has played such a decisive (and often disastrous) role in the history of Pakistan, is one factor at work in this time of chance. So is the public space of the street. What does it mean to turn private, domestic life (ironing, reading a newspaper) out on to the eerily empty roadways of Ramadan? What relationships do such actions have to the other uses of the street – as a place of protest, or commerce, or as the setting for an Independence Day parade? A wall stained with betel-spit is a modest testimony to the accretion of history, a guttural desi riposte to the vast canvases of Anselm Kiefer, with their caking of European ash and dust. Sometimes one feels the artists have internalized the categories of post-colonialism and are now doing what is expected of them as Pakistani artists, by reproducing them in the hope of critical approbation. Yet even the failure to represent oneself authentically, the impossibility of seeing oneself except as belated, constructed, supplicatory, is significant.

Right now we need more than news images, but representation of any kind feels inadequate in the face of the vast material forces driving the region towards conflict. The paradox is that the most fugitive, fleeting traces of humanity – melancholy petals painted in watercolour on a marble floor – may outlast those forces. The floor is in Kabul. The light falls across it, striating the painting with bars of shadow. What is pigment? What is light? Time is passing, quickly. ∎

HIGH NOON

In collaboration with
Green Cardamom

AYESHA JATOI
Clothesline, 2006

Pari Wania, 7.42 p.m., 22 August 2008, Ramadan, Karachi.

Ashish Sharma, 7.44 p.m., 23 August 2008, Ramadan, Karachi.

BANI ABIDI
Karachi Series 1, 2009

andra Acharya, 7.50 p.m., 30 August 2008, Ramadan, Karachi.

y Fernandez, 7.45 p.m., 21 August 2008, Ramadan, Karachi.

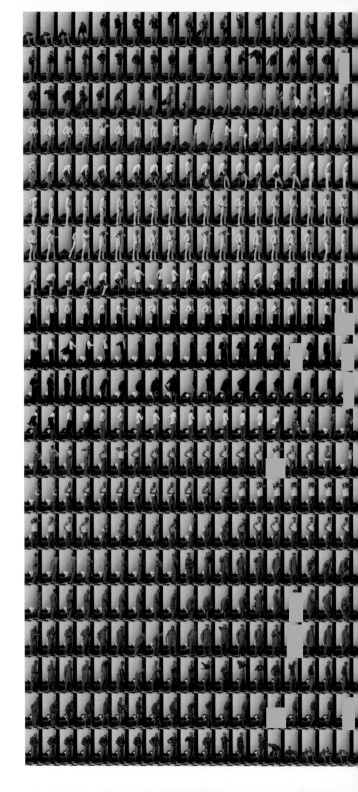

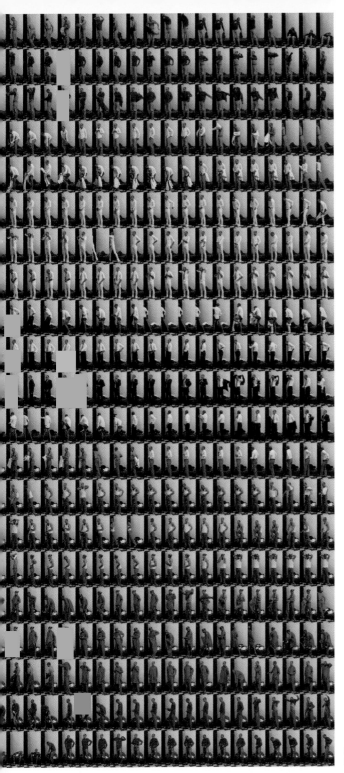

RASHID RANA
Identical Views II, 2004

AN QURESHI
he Changes, 2008

NUSRA LATIF QURESHI
Detail from *Did you come here to find history?*, 2009

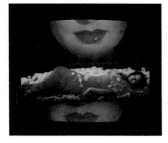

IFTIKHAR DADI
Urdu Film Series, 1990-2009

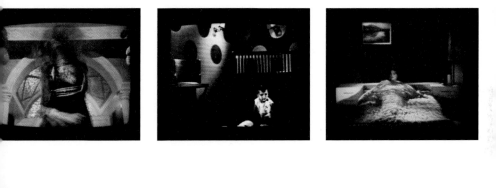

MANSUR SALIM
Sohni Mahiwal, 2003

MEHREEN MURTAZA
The Blowjob, from the series *An Anthology of Cosmic Snippets*, 2007

RASHID RANA
Detail from *I Love Miniatures*, 2002

NAEEM MOHAIEMEN
Kazi in NoMansland, 2008

MUHAMMAD ZEESHAN
Cityscapes, 2009

MED ALI MANGANHAR
itled, 2006

MOHAMMAD ALI TALPUR
Untitled (Machine Drawing), 2006

CAPTIONS

BANI ABIDI (IMAGE ON PAGE 135)

Edition of 5. Inkjet prints on archival paper, 28 x 18.5cm each (x9).
Loaded with cultural representation, this body of work deploys fiction to subvert meaning and destabilize dominant myths of national origin. A quixotic young man – ostensibly a young Christian convert to Islam – makes incongruous appearances in public places dressed as the Arab hero Mohammad bin Qasim. In this particular image he is photoshopped against the landmark 'Teen Talwar' (three swords) in Karachi, meant to represent 'Unity, Faith and Discipline', a secular motto atttributed to Muhammad Ali Jinnah.

AYESHA JATOI

Dyed garments on fighter jet, C-print, photograph of installation/performance. Image courtesy of the artist and Asif Khan.
Decommissioned aircraft and armaments – missile casings, old jets and once even a massive submarine – are frequently installed as public monuments, indicative of the presence of the military in the civic realm. In this performative act of resistance, the artist washed a load of red garments and then draped them across the aircraft to dry.

BANI ABIDI

Duratrans Lightbox, 50.8 x 76.2cm each.
At dusk during the month of Ramadan most Muslims in Karachi are breaking their fasts, leaving the streets eerily empty. Abidi imaginatively reclaims public space by allowing the streets to be occupied by ordinary citizens from religious minorities – Hindu, Parsi (Zoroastrian) and Christian – who are part of the shared history of the city, but increasingly less visible.

RASHID RANA

Edition of 10, C-print, Diasec, 194 x 197cm.
This is a composite image of photographs that could be from a video or a stop-motion animation. Frame by frame, the artist dresses himself, changing garb several times, reinventing his image. In the 'mirror' image the process is reversed, but does not correspond perfectly, creating a sense of dissonance.

IMRAN QURESHI

Site-specific installation, Qasr-e-Malika (Queen's Palace) Bagh-e-Babur, Kabul, Afghanistan. Emulsion and acrylics on marble floor and walls. Image courtesy of the artist and Turquoise Mountain, Afghanistan.
Qureshi uses the motif of foliage from traditional miniatures as a form, a weedy organic growth that seeps into architectural space. This installation in Kabul interacted with the play of light from the windows on the gallery floor, shifting the image with the passage of time.

NUSRA LATIF QURESHI

Digital print on transparent film, 65 x 870cm.
Qureshi's practice deals critically with the politics of representation, fragmenting dominant historical narratives. Borrowed images are reappropriated and transformed, obscuring or refusing their original meaning. This work is a combination of the artist's own ID photos, Moghul miniature portraits, early colonial photography and portraits by Venetian painters.

IFTIKHAR DADI

C-print Diasec, 64 x 52cm.
A suite of photographs of Urdu-language films shown on state-controlled television in the 1970s, examining television as a way of imagining and shaping collective ideas of 'success' or 'urban modernity' as exemplified by the interiors, fashion, personae and gestures of the films. Taken at slow shutter speeds, they capture scanning lines of the television screen and produce a grainy, blurred effect that suggests a dream or trance-like state, several steps removed from the 'reality' of the depicted scenes.

MANSUR SALIM
Oil on canvas, 81 x 122cm. Image courtesy of the artist and ArtChowk.
Mansur Salim's surreal subjects include landscapes on a fictional planet, a space loaded with magical symbolism, layered with nostalgic memories, art-historical references, vernacular mythology and mathematical riddles. Disrupting notions of time and the context of place, this work is named after the ill-fated lovers in the Punjabi tale, while the faces strongly resemble film stars from the 1970s.

MEHREEN MURTAZA
Archival C-prints, 38.1 x 38.1cm. Courtesy of the artist and Grey Noise.
From a series of a dozen digital collages in which Murtaza playfully examines the latent presence of technology in urban visual space, merging globalized modernity with local landscapes. Referencing old war films or sci-fi fantasies, she creates charged images with a lurking sense of the absurd.

RASHID RANA
Edition of 20. C-print, Diasec, gilt frame. 45 x 35cm. Image courtesy of the artist.
At first a conventional portrait of the Moghul emperor Shah Jehan, on closer inspection the image reveals itself to be composed of photographs of billboards from the streets of Lahore, challenging exalted cultural forms by reconstructing them with visuals collected from the everyday.

NAEEM MOHAIEMEN
Set of 5 digital prints, 6 x 61cm each. Installation of postage stamps from India, Pakistan and Bangladesh, sizes variable, displayed on white plinth. 30 x 30 x 100cm. Image courtesy of the artist and collection of Raffi Vartanian. Commissioned for *Lines of Control*, a Green Cardamom project.
STAMP INSTALLATION
Three sets of stamps, from India, Pakistan and Bangladesh, all bearing the image of Kazi Nazrul Islam, a revolutionary poet claimed by all three nations as a national symbol.
SET OF 5 DIGITAL PRINTS
The first four images are of the fierce, grimacing eyes of Nazrul as he was forced to pose for official photographs, unable to voice his refusal due to a mysterious disease which affected his speech and memory. The last image is of General Ziaur Rehman of Bangladesh at Nazrul's official funeral, which took place in Bangladesh against his own wishes and those of his family in India.

MUHAMMAD ZEESHAN
Digital print on canvas, 91.5 x 55.9cm.
A found urban image photographed by the artist, part of a series of abstract 'paintings' created by splatters of *peekh* on city streets, which are more visible on the footpaths and alleys in lower-income areas. *Peekh* is the spat-out juice of the paan leaf, commonly chewed with tobacco as a mild relaxant.

AHMED ALI MANGANHAR
Acrylic and oil on slate, 18 x 22.5cm each.
Slates and chalk are used widely in rural and lower-income government school environments as rudimentary writing materials. History, erasures, memory and nostalgia are all themes that the artist explores. The top figure is Seth Naomul Hotchund – a prominent Hindu trader rewarded by the British for his services to the Crown and considered a traitor by Muslim landlords and Talpur rulers of Sindh in the nineteenth century.

MOHAMMAD ALI TALPUR
Printer's ink on paper, 75 x 55cm.
Talpur used a mechanical printing press as an instrument to 'draw', varying the process to produce a series of works based on the form of the common exercise book. Although produced by a machine, the work registers a strong presence of the artist's hand and his desire to subvert the predictable. This particular piece combines the formats used to write in Urdu (upper half) and in English (lower half), reversing the linguistic and class order determined by access to education.

All images, unless otherwise specified, are courtesy of Green Cardamom and the copyright of the artist.

SUBSCRIBE NOW
RECEIVE FOUR ISSUES A YEAR
SAVE £22

UK
£34.95
(£29.95 Direct Debit)

Europe
£39.95

Rest of the world★
£45.95

Subscribe now at Granta.com/UK112
or by Freephone 0500 004 033
(Ref: UK112)

Excluding USA, Canada and Latin America

GRANTA.COM/UK112

ARITHMETIC ON THE FRONTIER

Declan Walsh

We rattled through the parched countryside, past fortress-like farmhouses and salt-flecked marshes, kicking up a cloud of dust. A village loomed. As our jeep slowed down, a gang of long-haired tribesmen stepped up, all turbans and curly whiskers, brandishing their Kalashnikovs with mobster panache. They seemed to be smiling. Then the firing started.

I crouched instinctively as three bullet bursts whipped over the jeep roof at a horribly low angle. My host, however, was entirely unperturbed. Anwar Kamal yanked his door open and strode purposefully into the gunfire, waving cheerily. His bodyguard, a strapping man with chipped teeth, trailed behind, cackling with delight as he, too, emptied his rifle into the sky.

It was January 2008, a fortnight before the last general election, and I had come to north-western Pakistan, along the troubled border with Afghanistan, to get a taste of the campaign among the Pashtun. Kamal, a local political veteran, was my guide. A burly sixty-one-year-old of martial bearing, Kamal was many things in life – lawyer and chieftain, landlord and warlord. Today, though, he was simply a candidate. Over thirty years in politics he had notched up six election victories, he said; now he was canvassing his rambunctious constituents for a seventh.

A whistle sounded, the shooting stopped and we were led into a courtyard where the elders, wrapped in wool shawls, were waiting. We sat down for an unusual variety show. The gunmen took to the floor to perform a traditional dance, whirling in a sort of shuffle-step waltz, rifles swinging wildly from their shoulders. I hoped they had engaged the safety catches; it seemed unlikely. Next up were the volleyball aficionados – teenagers in baggy pants (no shorts) who tossed around a child's pink ball that jolted violently when it hit the rutted ground, which was often. The crowd took the game seriously; when I overstepped a white scrawl in the soil, a gruff-looking man nudged me back with the barrel of his gun. 'Line,' he said.

Afterwards, Kamal, now garlanded with a Christmas-style

tinsel necklace, posed for team photos and addressed the villagers through a crackly speaker system. I could make out just a few words – 'electricity', 'money', 'America' – but the punters seemed to like it, chortling at the gags and clapping vigorously at the climax. Finally we were hustled into a long, low room where a feast had been spread out on a plastic floor mat – spicy chicken wings, chunks of juicy mango, spongy cake and sweet tea served in dainty china cups. As we kneeled, Kamal turned to me. 'I hope you're enjoying yourself?' he said. Of course I was.

Even by the rough-and-tumble standards of Pakistani politics, Kamal cuts a striking figure. Theatrical, loquacious and utterly unapologetic, he reminds me of a figure from another era – perhaps the Flashman historical novels. He is a commanding presence. His face is fleshy and pitted, dominated by a flamboyant moustache that sweeps from a centre part to sharply twirled ends. A lawyer by training, in public he articulates slowly and at length, speaking in a raspy baritone that swells on demand into a thunderous bellow, usually when addressing his fellow Marwat tribesmen. In private he is entertaining company, deploying a rascal's smile in the service of tales of skulduggery and derring-do. He has a maddening disregard for precision. 'You see that man over there?' he will say. 'He has killed six, seven, EIGHT men!' And he uses an idiosyncratic turn of phrase that would be charming if the ideas he was articulating weren't so alarming. 'You see,' he remarked casually during the electioneering, 'this murder and fighting business is very tricky.'

Murder and fighting, it turns out, are constant preoccupations in Lakki Marwat, an impoverished district in the southern reaches of Pakistan's Pashtun territories, wedged between the sluggish Indus River and the mountain wall of the tribal belt. I spent two days with Kamal on that trip, jammed into the back of his jeep. We splashed through ponds of mud and zoomed between stands of palm trees for a dizzy whirl of election rallies, sometimes three in an hour. I didn't see a single woman. Guns, on the other hand, were everywhere – Soviet-design Kalashnikovs, old British Lee–Enfields and imitation

Chinese pistols, often decorated with rainbow-coloured beads. 'Carrying guns is a common fashion around here,' Kamal told me as we bumped along. 'Like a woman wears her necklace, this is our jewellery.' Few were licensed, he added, but the authorities couldn't do much about it. He pointed to the rutted road. 'You see that strip of rubber? That is the only civilization around here. Either side of it, the government does not exist.'

Kamal sweetened his appeal with gifts – a wad of rupees here, an electricity transformer there – yet the people seemed genuinely to appreciate his swashbuckling style. 'All the wealth of Kabir Khan is not worth one hair from Anwar Kamal's moustache!' declared a village headman; Kamal grinned like the Cheshire cat. Haji Kabir Khan was his old nemesis, a rich businessman with more hard cash to splash around. They had once been allies. But if Khan had the voters' pockets, Kamal was confident of their hearts. In one place, villagers presented him with a jet-black turban wrapped with thick, luxuriant folds; for good measure they dropped one on my head too.

Nearly every building – houses, petrol stations, even mosques – was capped with a square tower, two or three storeys high and studded with loopholes. These medieval-style fortifications were called *burj*, Kamal said, and served as both home security and a marker of status. The richer a man, the higher his *burj*; poor families made do by punching a few holes in their living-room wall. But the feared enemy was not some invading army; more likely it was a vengeful cousin or an irate neighbour. Most Marwats were embroiled in blood feuds, he explained, and disputes dragged on for decades, handed from father to son like cherished heirlooms. 'You never forgive,' he said. 'You may wait twenty, thirty, fifty years – and then you take revenge.' I suddenly understood why, in some villages, Kamal held two rallies, often just a stone's throw apart: any larger gathering would have risked a shoot-out among the voters.

The second day of campaigning took us into the low, stubbly hills of southern Lakki District. 'Bandit country,' said Kamal. Criminals sheltered here, some resident in caves; one village, Shah Hassan

Khel, was filled with local Taliban sympathizers. We didn't stop there. 'We leave them alone. They don't touch us,' Kamal said. As the light faded we rolled up to a whitewashed compound buried deep in a valley. The setting had a serene quality: the first stars glittered overhead; a black camel stacked with reeds was tethered in the corner; the low wail of infants drifted from the women's quarters. The headman handed a wish list to Kamal, who laughed. They wanted a school, an electricity connection and, rather ambitiously, a hospital. 'These people actually come from that village,' he said, pointing to a cluster of buildings a mile distant, 'but they migrated years ago due to an enmity. There have been five, six murders on each side. So now no man dares go outside without his gun.'

Inevitably we were presented with food. My stomach clenched: it must have been our twentieth five-minute feast of the day; I couldn't face another bite. But the tribesmen were watching and Kamal, speaking under his normal voice, issued a soft rebuke. 'If you can eat, eat. If not, just touch it,' he muttered. 'These people get heavily annoyed if you don't take anything.' I reached for a chicken leg.

Roasting hospitality, smouldering pride, cold and clinical revenge – thus it has always been among the Pashtun. Down the centuries they have stirred poets, produced legendary warriors and frustrated mighty empires. From Alexander the Great to the Moghuls, from the British to the Soviet Union, all have swept through these lands, welcomed at first but ultimately hounded out, departing with the bitter-sweet sensation of having encountered men who do not compromise – at least, not for long.

The Pashtun homeland is a diagonal swathe of rock, soil and sand that straddles Pakistan's 1,600-mile-long border with Afghanistan. On the Pakistani side, it stretches from the searing red deserts of Baluchistan to the twinkling, snow-dusted peaks of Chitral in the Hindu Kush. British colonists in pith helmets and pressed shorts shaped the boundaries of this land more than a century ago; today they still exert a powerful – and often undue – influence over our understanding of the people who live there.

The Pashtun united in 1747 under Ahmad Shah Durrani, forming a powerful tribal confederacy headquartered in Kandahar; Victorian imperialists wrenched them apart. In 1893 the British, fretful about creeping Russian influence from the north, negotiated the Durand Line, a boundary that separated the northern territories of British India (now Pakistan) from Afghanistan and split the Pashtun in two. Other British legacies have also endured. The Frontier Corps, a paramilitary force drawn from the tribes and founded in 1907, is leading the fight against Taliban militants. The old railway still runs up to the Khyber Pass, although it has fallen into disuse. Then there is the literature.

Hardly a modern article on the frontier is complete without a reference to the fading diaries of some overheated officer dispensing bitter wisdom about the 'noble savages'. British ministers and American generals alike are fond of invoking Churchill, who as a young man served a few adventurous years on the frontier, or Kipling, whose poem 'Arithmetic on the Frontier' captured the savagery of battle against mountain warriors. Not all colonial writing revolved around bloodshed; some was written with a lyrical pen. In his oft-quoted book, *The Pathans*, the last British governor of the frontier, Sir Olaf Caroe, wrote:

> *The weft and warp of this tapestry is woven into the souls and bodies of the men who move before it. Much is harsh, but all is drawn in strong tones that catch the breath, and at times bring tears, almost of pain.*

These days, though, it is perhaps wiser to leave the misty-eyed colonials on the shelf. Things have changed too much in recent decades, mostly, alas, for the worse.

Pakistan's 'frontier', home to most of the country's 28 million Pashtun, is composed of two parts – Khyber-Pakhtunkhwa, the smallest of Pakistan's four provinces, which was called North West Frontier Province (NWFP) until early this year, and the tribal belt, a constellation of seven tribal agencies nestled along the Afghan border and known officially as the Federally Administered Tribal Areas (FATA). Incredibly, the FATA is still ruled under a draconian colonial-era instrument called the Frontier Crimes Regulations (FCR) which strips tribals of their constitutional rights and is repugnant to every tenet of modern governance.

Getting to the frontier is deceptively easy. The old route curled through Attock, where a 400-year-old Moghul fort towers over the swirling confluence of the Kabul and Indus rivers. These days the visitor sweeps in on a slick, six-lane motorway from Islamabad, two hours to the east. The provincial capital, Peshawar – thought to derive from the Sanskrit for 'city of men' – squats at the foot of the Khyber Pass, thrumming with nervous energy. Parts retain the romantic exoticism of Kipling's verse. Blind beggars roam the spice bazaars of the old city; veiled women dart between glittering jewellery shops; peacocks strut on the preened lawns of the governor's colonial-era mansion. Everywhere else, though, there are garish splashes of modernity – chromed plazas selling mobile phones; tacky American fast-food joints; giant billboards advertising remedies for male baldness; and 'slimming academies' for women. Cheap Chinese rickshaws swarm through the raucous traffic.

A pungent cloud of intrigue overlays everything. This is largely a legacy of the 1980s, when Peshawar was the cockpit of the 'jihad', the guerrilla war against the Soviet occupation of Afghanistan. The leaders of the mujahideen factions at the forefront of the resistance were based here; so were the American and Saudi spies who funded the war to the tune of at least $6 billion between 1979 and 1989.

These days the tempest of Taliban violence ripping across the frontier has shaken Peshawar to its core. Suicide bombers ravage bustling markets; politicians are gunned down outside their homes; trucks carrying Nato supplies are plundered as they trundle up the Khyber Pass towards Afghanistan. Nobody is safe, not even the

American spooks huddling inside their prison-like consulate, which was attacked last April. The violence has receded this year, following a tough army counteroffensive. But the city remains rattled. Cinemas and music halls are closed, police checkpoints clog the streets and factories are shuttered. Business is booming, however, in the smugglers' bazaar at the edge of the city, where thick-bearded traders offer stolen US uniforms, boxes of counterfeit Viagra (with pictures of topless women), and DVDs of the speeches of Osama bin Laden, who once lived in a pine-shaded house in the upmarket University Town neighbourhood and founded al-Qaeda here in 1988.

Still, there's fun to be had. One night I was invited to dinner with a group of Peshawar professionals – old university pals, now in their late thirties, working as bankers, aid workers and civil servants. We sat in a circle in a small garden in the old city. To my right was a pudgy *malik*, or tribal elder, from Dara Adam Khel, a lawless town about fifteen miles away famed for its gunsmiths and their knock-off AK-47s. To my left was a shy man with a long beard whom the others teasingly called 'Mullah Omar', after the Taliban leader. He was in charge of rolling the joints.

The promised meal never materialized; instead we drank and smoked. Bottles of cheap whisky circled in one direction; the hashish went in the other. The conversation was lively, full of politics and rude jokes, but after three hours I was having trouble keeping up. My head started to spin; then I felt something rub against my foot. The *malik* had nudged his foot close to mine and was stroking my toes. Unsure whether this was a sign of friendship or something more purposeful – jokes about Pashtun men and buggery are rife in Pakistan – I discreetly curled my toes inwards, safely out of stroking distance.

Finally, at half past midnight, the call went up – food. The group staggered out of the garden and into three small cars that made a dash for the city centre, the occupants roaring and cheering like teenage joyriders. In my car a small dashboard screen showed a bikini-clad dancer writhing to a roaring Bollywood sound track; veiled female shoppers blurred past in the street outside. It felt surreal. Reaching the restaurant, supper was consumed with a minimum of ceremony: my new friends wolfed down plates of chicken, said their farewells, and parted ways. Back in my guest house I flopped on to the bed, exhausted, inebriated and exhilarated.

The origins of the Pashtun are lost in a genealogical fog. Some consider themselves the 'lost Jews' – descendants of Qais, an Afghan convert to Islam who was descended from Saul, king of the Israelites. It is an odd theory, given the vicious anti-Semitism of many Pakistanis, but it has been embraced by Israel. In the 1950s, the country's second president, Yitzhak Ben-Zvi, publicly supported the notion that the Pashtun were among the 'ten lost tribes' of Israel. Scholars are sceptical of this link, though, and many Pashtun prefer to see their roots among the other ancient powers that have passed through: Arabs, Persians, Central Asians and Greeks. Simply being a Pashtun, however, is a less complicated matter. There are two requirements. The first is to speak Pashto, an ergative language considered trickier than Urdu. Two dialects are spoken – Pukhto, the hard-tongued variety of the Peshawar Valley, and Pashto, the softer version spoken south of an invisible line that runs between Kohat in Pakistan and Paktika in Afghanistan.

The second requirement is to observe *Pashtunwali* – literally, 'the way of the Pashtun' – the famous code of conduct. Its bedrock is *nang*, or honour. A Pashtun without *nang* is considered worthless; in fact he is no longer a Pashtun. Honour faces a multitude of threats – a murdered relative, a philandering wife, perhaps just a casual insult – but has one fail-safe remedy: *badal*, or revenge. Hence the profusion of blood feuds in places like Lakki Marwat. But bloodshed is not compulsory: *Pashtunwali* also has noble tenets that promote compassion and conciliation. Under *nanawatai*, the law of sanctuary, a man can go to his enemy's house and beg forgiveness. And *melmastia*, hospitality, is practised with great seriousness. After the devastating 2005 earthquake, I climbed for hours to a Pashtun village untouched by rescuers or aid. There I found families huddled in the rubble, their food stocks precariously low. Yet they insisted

I share a meal. 'You are our guest,' they said.

Educated Pashtun see the image of the trigger-happy tribal, tethered to tradition and blind belief in a bloodthirsty God, as a simplistic orientalist cliché. They have a point. Pashtun form the second-largest ethnic group in Pakistan's army and crowd the upper echelons of its powerful bureaucracy. There are Pashtun pilots and pop stars, sports icons and tycoons. Shahid Afridi, a showy batsman, until recently captained the national cricket team; Zebunnisa Bangash and Haniya Aslam, two Pashtun women, are among the country's hottest music acts. There have even been Pashtun dictators – General Ayub Khan, who seized power in 1958, hailed from Haripur.

Pashtunwali has been diluted in urban areas where the writ of the police is strong, which makes blood feuds trickier to prosecute. Anyway, educated Pashtun consider a shoot-out with the neighbours to be a drain on their time, and have much to lose from a tangle with the law. Consequently most disputes are entrusted to the courts, crooked as they may be.

Yet while urbanites have tailored *Pashtunwali* to the modern world, this is not true of everyone. Large swathes of the frontier are neither modern nor urban. Here, tradition retains its grip and people observe the laws of Islamabad more in the breach than in the observance – which, in turn, can place unusual demands on their elected representatives.

There are, by his own admission, two Anwar Kamals. One is the 'polished gent' of Peshawar, a leading member of the Pashtun elite with a taste for frontier bling. His pied-à-terre is a spacious house in Hayatabad, the city's best suburb, where he frequently dines with his three university-educated sons. He drives an imposing white Japanese jeep with dashboard television (and prayer counter for Islamic recitations), carries the latest mobile phone and, being a qualified pilot, keeps a small plane at the local aerodrome. Some years back he imported a pair of greyhounds from England for the purpose of hunting boar on the family lands. A fading portrait of a serious-looking man on his living-room wall is testimony to his rich political pedigree. Khan Habibullah Khan, Kamal's father, was a minor star in the early decades of Pakistan, serving as Home Minister in the 1960s and chairman of the Senate in the 1970s. At one point he was Acting President of the country. Kamal has had a less prominent, yet also distinguished, career in public service. He was a provincial minister twice and a national senator once; in 1990 he addressed the United Nations General Assembly in New York, during which time he lodged at the luxury Roosevelt Hotel in Manhattan.

The second Anwar Kamal emerges when he jumps into his jeep and heads for Lakki Marwat, a bumpy four-hour ride to the south. Lakki is his constituency, but also his land, his power, his identity. Here, Kamal sleeps with a rocket launcher under his wooden-framed bed, in a sprawling, draughty fortress guarded by dozens of tribesmen, spends his time in lengthy confabulation with bearded elders and generally acts in a manner that seems to contradict everything the other Anwar Kamal stands for.

The first time we met, in June 2007, we were sitting in his living room in Peshawar, which is adorned with pinkish, flowery wallpaper. On the table between us was a photo album, the sort that might contain snaps of foreign holidays or grinning grandchildren. Instead it was a gallery of war: dozens of images of fierce-looking tribesmen, bristling with weapons, against a harsh backdrop of arid hills. Kamal featured in several of the pictures; in one he sat at the controls of a long, menacing weapon. It was an ack-ack, he explained: a 12.8cm anti-aircraft gun of the kind used by the British to fend off German bombers during the Second World War. A most satisfying weapon, he added, recounting its most recent use.

'You see, we were being fired on from three sides by some individuals who were hiding in a *burj*,' he said in his gravelly voice. 'So I called up my driver, Akhtar' – a smiling young chap I'd met earlier – 'and I said, "Bastard! Get that ack-ack and fire back!" So he grabbed it and gave it a burst of seven or eight rounds. What a noise – the whole ground started shaking! The bullets went right through that *burj*, killing two of those individuals who were sitting there.'

He paused for effect, then chuckled.

'Within a split of a second there was absolute silence. Everyone was calm and cool.'

This dramatic exchange had taken place in 2004 at the height of some particular aggravation with the Bhittanis, the Marwats' nearest neighbours and oldest rivals. A row had erupted and for the next year hotheads from both sides engaged in the usual needle tactics – tit-for-tat shootings, kidnappings, hostage executions – when things got out of hand. In a brash upping of the ante, the Bhittanis snatched two Marwat women. Kamal was outraged. 'Now, kidnapping men we don't mind. That is usual. But taking our ladies – that was totally unprecedented!'

In retaliation, first the Marwats kidnapped six Bhittani women and three children. Then they roused a *lashkar* – a tribal fighting force – with the aim of sweeping into the Bhittani lair, retrieving the abducted damsels and teaching their insolent neighbours a sharp lesson. Kamal led from the front, binoculars in one hand and pistol in the other. It was, by several accounts, a messy affair. The Pakistan Army, which was conducting operations in the nearby tribal belt, mistook the tribesmen for al-Qaeda fugitives and fired a few artillery rounds at them. 'A genuine misunderstanding,' said Kamal.

Combat was sporadic. The most dramatic confrontation occurred when Kamal's guards shot dead a pair of Bhittanis racing towards them on a motorbike. 'Two hundred bullets in each!' he recalled with relish. And the hostages were less lucky. One of the abducted women was burned alive with lamp oil (some said it was suicide, others murder); the second was spirited deep into the tribal belt. When the matter was finally resolved a year later, an inter-tribal *jirga* ordered the Marwats to pay 16 million rupees – about $260,000 – in blood money. It was expensive, Kamal admitted as we polished off our tea, but worth every cent. 'It's not about money. The question is: "Did you restore your honour?" And we did.'

I stayed in Kamal's guest quarters that evening, rising early the following morning to travel to Lakki. I found him after dawn in his bedroom, alone, watching the National Geographic channel on television, an AK-47 propped against the bed. His wife, a hepatitis sufferer, had died in tragic circumstances a year earlier. They had travelled to China for a liver transplant, but she died of complications after the operation. Kamal flew home with her body. He spoke about the episode quietly and sparingly; it seemed to pain him.

After a breakfast of eggs and greasy paratha bread, we plunged into the belching Peshawar traffic and left the city. The road swept past Dara Adam Khel, the storied village of gunsmiths, then descended on to the rock-strewn plains of the southern frontier. Halting for tea at a grubby truckers' cafe, we sat outside on a cluster of rope beds. Kamal pointed to one of his bodyguards: Mina, a stocky fifty-five-year-old with creased skin and gleaming eyes, now contentedly slurping his tea. 'A complete and utter outlaw,' he said. He wasn't exaggerating. Eighteen years earlier, as part of a blood feud, Mina had chased a man across Sindh and Punjab provinces. He finally cornered his quarry after nine months in a dusty Punjabi backwater. Whipping out his pistol, he shot the man repeatedly – the *coup de grâce*, Kamal said, was a bullet to the temple – then picked up his bicycle and fled back to Lakki Marwat via the Indus (where he forced a boatman to carry him across). Some time later, Kamal gave him a job. He slapped my knee and chortled. 'We may have licensed weapons, but we don't have licensed individuals!' The guards laughed along.

Kamal might have been a diplomat. As a young graduate he was on the verge of being posted to the Netherlands in the late 1960s when his father called him home to study law and tend the family's political affairs. For the past two decades he's been a supporter of Nawaz Sharif, the current opposition leader. It seems an odd choice: Sharif's party is rooted in Punjab, Pakistan's most populous province, and enjoys little support among the Pashtun. But it makes sense to Kamal because the alternatives – Pashtun nationalists, liberals and mullahs – are not to his taste. Still, he can be sharply critical of Sharif.

'Honestly speaking, I find him to be a mediocrity,' he once confided. And his rustic, hip-shooting style doesn't always sit well with the slick Punjab-wallahs who dominate the party. 'Sometimes,' he told me in a moment of exasperation, 'I think I am the only straightforward man in my party.'

For all that, Kamal is fiercely loyal. He served a short jail stretch on political charges in 1993 (he was released due to a heart condition) and proved his mettle again in September 2007. As Sharif attempted to return from exile, in defiance of General Pervez Musharraf, Kamal led a posse of supporters to welcome him at Islamabad airport. It ended in fiasco. Sharif was turned back and Kamal's mob ran into a checkpoint twenty-five miles from the capital, where they clashed violently with police. The Marwats sacked the local constabulary, looted its contents and hauled seven police hostages back to Lakki. The authorities held Kamal responsible and charged him with seventeen crimes including kidnapping and dacoity. For months he could not visit Islamabad, fearing arrest. The charges were eventually dropped a year later when Sharif, now successfully returned from exile, won control of the Punjab government.

After four hours of driving, we reached Lakki Marwat, a scrubby, mustard-tinted plain with a line of hills in the distance. A reception committee was waiting on the roadside: a dozen tribesmen loitering by a pair of 1970s-model Datsun cars with red velvet curtains across their rear windows. Nearby, a sign peppered with buckshot read: *Karachi, 1,400 kilometres*. The tribesmen hugged Kamal warmly, served him a glass of soda and led the way into town, guns poking from the car windows.

The Marwat are not among the celebrated tribes of the frontier, such as the smuggler Afridi of Khyber or the Yusufzai of Swat. Farmers by nature, they migrated from Paktia in southern Afghanistan perhaps five hundred years ago. The British arrived in 1850, bringing bureaucracy and some development. Within half a century, Lakki had 52,000 inhabitants, a train station and colonial administrators who had grown fond of the locals. 'In person, they are tall and muscular; in bearing, frank and open. Almost every officer who has administered the District has left on record a favourable mention of them,' recorded the *Imperial Gazetteer* of 1909.

Today the population has swelled to 700,000 – as Kamal puts it, 'Sexual intercourse is appealing to everyone. Everyone!' – and the railway has been replaced by the Indus Highway, a battered ribbon of tarmac that stretches almost eight hundred miles from Karachi to the Khyber Pass. The town has a tumbleweed feel. Traders squat in boxy shops before gunny sacks of grain and sugar; camel-drawn carts slide down the main street. The local bigwigs, the Saifullah family, are among the richest people in Pakistan, with textile mills, power plants and city real estate. Most folk are dirt poor. A few thousand have jobs at a sprawling Saifullah cement factory; a few thousand more work at a secretive government uranium mine that extracts 'yellow cake', a raw material for the military's nuclear bombs. Otherwise there's farming, but the land is useless without irrigation, which is expensive and difficult (well-diggers often sink seven hundred feet before striking water). Their engagement with the state is weak. Nobody pays income tax, the roads are full of duty-free cars smuggled from Afghanistan, and everyone steals their electricity, which helps explain why the voltage is so feeble (it's hard to power even an electric iron). The state vigorously reciprocates their lack of enthusiasm, providing threadbare education and health services. Only 12 per cent of women can read and write – unsurprising, perhaps, considering how rarely they leave their houses – but even among men literacy rates are shockingly low. Kamal offered a dispiriting explanation. 'To his father, a crude man is an asset. You tell him to plough the land, or kill another man, and he will do it. But if the son is educated, he will say, "I am too good for that." And if he cannot find a job, he will get frustrated. So the father prefers a crude man.'

In this Bermuda Triangle of governance, the one constant is tradition. Kamal sits on *jirgas* that mediate disputes, often involving murder, through the payment of blood money. This may offend Western legal sensibilities but it chimes with the legal core of

Pashtunwali, which favours the satisfaction of the victim over the punishment of the aggressor. It's not cheap. The blood price is about $1,000 per death these days, and Kamal has seen poor families driven to the wall, hocking their houses or pawning their gold to end a feud. But there are loopholes: a guilty man may delay *jirga* justice until his enemies have knocked off an equal number of his own relatives, thereby evening up the score. This is what Kamal calls a 'trick of the trade'.

The preferred method of dispute resolution, however, is the donation of a daughter in marriage. This is good for the peace – such exchanges produce the most durable settlements, Kamal said – but bad for the women, who may be taken as second or third wives and treated little better than servants. Their opinion hardly matters, though. Once the deal has been struck, elders from both sides are enjoined to sit together, slaughter a sheep and swear their peace on the Quran. It's a system that puts Kamal in league with some rough characters.

We drove out to a shabby little village called Tajori to visit the home of Saadullah Khan, a famous local brigand. About ten men were waiting in a hot, sparsely furnished room (the electricity was off); rifles were propped against the wall. Several of our hosts, all brothers and cousins, were cross-eyed. 'A very dashing group,' Kamal whispered in my ear. 'They must have killed eighteen or nineteen people; five of their own have died. Very hot-headed, always in trouble.'

A gummy old man, folded into a chair in the corner, piped up. This was Saadullah Khan. Seventy-five years old with blazing eyes, he asked Kamal to arrange jobs for his sons as chowkidars – guards – at the local primary school. Kamal nodded. The police had been trying to arrest Saadullah for years, he said; on one occasion Saadullah's sons seized the cops' car only to return it days later, peppered with bullet holes.

That night, over supper in his gloomy dining room, I asked Kamal about the contradictions in his life. Was it not strange for an elected official to spend his time shielding outlaws, pardoning murder and instigating small wars? People often asked that, he replied. 'They say, "You are a law graduate. You consider yourself to be a polished man. So why do you act like a barbarian?" But that is not the point. Certain things are our compulsion. To me, my customs and traditions are more holy than the law of my country. You live with them and you die with them, whether you like it or not.' In other areas, the *khans* – Pashtun chieftains – had lost touch with their people, he added. But the Marwats, for all their desperate poverty, remained a 'compact' tribe. They would stick by him. In his hour of need, rogues like Saadullah Khan and his sons would be by his side.

As a religious man, he conceded, this was problematic. Islam did not sit well with *Pashtunwali*'s obligations to violent revenge. 'Belief relates to your heart, your prayers; *Pashtunwali* is about traditions, culture, life,' Kamal said. But, when the two clashed, *Pashtunwali* usually won. He posed a practical dilemma. 'Suppose your wife elopes with someone else: you are the most disgraced man in society. Can you leave it to Allah that the man will be punished at death? How can you live in society until then?' He shrugged. 'Pashtuns are Pashtuns.'

If the state was no competition for the magnetic draw of Pashtun tradition, a more potent force was rising in the tribal belt. The first sign came in early 2006. I was at home in Islamabad when a friend from Waziristan arrived with a video he had just bought in a Peshawar bazaar. 'You need to take a look at this,' he said.

It had been filmed a few months earlier in Miram Shah, the main town in north Waziristan tribal agency. In the opening scene, long-haired, turbaned tribesmen waving AK-47s stood triumphantly before three bodies hanging from electricity poles. A fourth body lay slumped on the ground, a whisky bottle perched in the man's lap and banknotes stuffed into his mouth – elementary symbols of decadence and disgrace. They had been executed, a fierce figure announced to the camera, for the crimes of kidnapping, banditry and 'forcing women to remove their veils'. Hundreds of people clustered around him, watching silently. The recording ended with a pickup truck dragging the battered corpses through the grimy streets, yahooing gunmen hanging out the back. 'This is reality, not fiction,' read the ticker. 'Come wage jihad or you will miss the caravan.'

I called the army spokesman, who tried to downplay the incident as an innocent 'local dispute'. But more sophisticated observers saw it for something else: the seeds of Pakistan's own home-grown Taliban movement.

The word *talib* means student; the original Taliban were born in the chaos of Afghanistan's civil war. In 1994, a group of righteous seminary students, many of them schooled in Pakistan, rose from the countryside around Kandahar to challenge the predatory warlords then ripping Afghanistan apart. They were led by Mullah Muhammad Omar, an enigmatic, one-eyed cleric who refused to be photographed. The Taliban's first act was to hang an accused rapist from the barrel of a tank; that mixture of theatrics and bloody retribution would become their hallmark as they fought their way to power in Kabul in 1996. Accused adulterers were executed, music and kite-flying were banned, and in 2001 the magnificent Buddha statues at Bamiyan were destroyed with rocketfire. They were quietly boosted behind the scenes by the Pakistan military's Inter-Services Intelligence spy agency, which viewed them as useful proxies for influence in Kabul.

Pakistan's Taliban, on the other hand, was born of the tumult that followed the September 2001 attacks in America. Under pressure from Washington, Pakistan's army deployed to the tribal belt to flush out hundreds of al-Qaeda militants sheltering there. This greatly irked the local Wazir and Mehsud tribesmen who vigorously defended their foreign guests. This was partly *nanawatai*, the obligation of sanctuary, but was also driven by more earthly considerations. Bin Laden's Arabs paid for their bed and breakfast with thick wads of US dollars.

By early 2006, when the Miram Shah execution video surfaced, the Taliban had set about establishing a religious mini-state. Militants torched video stores, threatened to kill barbers who shaved men's beards and patrolled the streets to ensure that shalwar trousers were worn at the appropriate height above the ankle. More profoundly, they attacked the established social order. Disputes were no longer settled in *jirgas* but in Saudi-style sharia courts; the *maliks* – pro-government elders who upheld the old social order – were assassinated or forced to flee. The Taliban justified their brutality by claiming to fight in the name of Islam.

Pashtun have always revered Islam, but until a few decades ago the mullahs enjoyed a tightly defined social standing. They officiated at weddings and funerals, ran small madrasas and were notorious for two things: their love of halwa, a soft dessert that floats in a pool of liquid sugar, and bedding young boys. (They're not the only ones. One alarming UN-sponsored study in 2001 found that 37 per cent of NWFP respondents felt that sex with boys was either a 'matter of pride' or a 'status symbol'.) Things had changed during the anti-Soviet guerrilla war of the 1980s, when madrasas turned into radicalization and recruitment centres; one US-funded textbook taught children that 'J is for jihad' and 'K is for Kalashnikov'.

The mullahs got another boost under the military ruler Pervez Musharraf. In the 2002 elections, ISI vote-riggers boosted to power a six-party alliance of religious parties known as the Muttahida Majlis-e-Amal (MMA) which won control of the NWFP government. For the first time in Pakistan's history, the mullahs had a province in their hands. In mid-2006, I went to see Muhammad Yousuf Qureshi, chief cleric of the Mohabbat Khan Mosque, a famous, virgin-white Moghul structure in the centre of Peshawar. A short, rather fat man with twinkling eyes and a henna-stained beard, Qureshi was famed for his venomous anti-Western sermons. He welcomed me with warm, pillowy hands and offered green tea sprinkled with cardamom. He was troubled: local cinemas wanted to show movies on the Prophet Muhammad's birthday. 'We told them, "If you show the films on that day, we will burn your cinemas,"' he explained. 'So they closed them.' Still, he liked some aspects of Western life: three of his sons lived in America, and until 9/11 he visited them regularly. Now, he complained, the US government refused to issue him a visa. He seemed rather hurt by the rejection.

As Taliban violence started to spill out of the tribal belt and into NWFP, the cleric-led MMA government did not directly aid the militants. But it did little to stop them. This failure was most starkly highlighted in the Swat Valley, a mountain idyll of fruit-laden orchards and gurgling brooks once dubbed 'the Switzerland of South Asia'. In 2007, a mullah named Fazlullah burst on to the scene and briefly turned it into the subcontinental Somalia. A thirty-something, baby-faced cleric, Fazlullah once made his living operating the chairlift that spanned the Swat River; after a stint fighting in Afghanistan he galloped back into the valley on a white steed. His popularity, however, came from pirate radio. A clerical shock-jock, Fazlullah used an illegal radio station to deliver fiery sermons that railed against girls' schooling and a polio vaccination drive, which he claimed was part of a Western conspiracy to sterilize Muslim children. Meanwhile, his foot soldiers – gangly youths waving Kalashnikovs – swaggered through the streets. The MMA's local administrator stood behind Fazlullah at Friday prayers.

When I visited in late 2007 the mosque was expanding, with construction workers swarming over bamboo scaffolding. Fazlullah's spokesman, Sirajuddin, a man with piercing cobalt eyes set in a thin face, told me the new mosque would cost $2.5 million. He apologized: his leader was unavailable because the army was chasing him. Besides, he wasn't keen on Westerners. As a young militant served goblets of Mountain Dew soda from a silver tray, Sirajuddin sketched out their programme. They would Islamize Swat, Pakistan, and then the world, he declared. 'We want Paradise on Earth,' he said. 'And the people want it too.' He was right: the Taliban's rhetoric had resonated powerfully with Swat's dispossessed. Fazlullah promised his poor fighters that he would divide the property of rich men among them. For everyone else there would be justice. Fazlullah vowed to replace the slow and corrupt civil courts with sharia benches that guaranteed swift, moral decisions. On Fridays, up to 15,000 men would gather at Imam Dehri to hear him speak; their wives flung rings and gold bangles at his feet.

A helicopter buzzed outside; a young militant entered and whispered in Sirajuddin's ear. His gaunt face clouded over. An army offensive had started further up the valley, he said. He had to leave.

Musharraf's miscalculations played a critical role in the rise of the Taliban. His officials struck a series of disastrous 'peace deals' in 2004, 2005 and 2006 that only emboldened the militants. Then, in July 2007, an army-led siege of the extremist Red Mosque in Islamabad led to the deaths of over one hundred people and triggered a ferocious backlash. Taliban suicide bombers launched a firestorm of violence over the following months, killing hundreds of people, including – to widespread shock – ISI officials. The insurgency oozed across the frontier with a viral intensity. Inevitably, it reached Lakki Marwat.

In May 2008, three months after the election, Anwar Kamal came to visit in Islamabad. It was one of those rare balmy summer evenings in the capital, when the streets shine with a fresh slick of rain and the suffocating humidity has been mercifully punctured. But the atmosphere was tense. A day earlier, an al-Qaeda suicide bomber had rammed his vehicle into the Danish Embassy, about a mile from my house; plain-clothes security men loitered on street corners toting AK-47s.

To my surprise, Kamal had not retained his seat in the NWFP parliament. He had been nudged out by just forty-four votes, he said, grumbling something about two hundred dead voters who apparently rose from the grave to vote for the brother of his old nemesis, Kabir Khan. But that wasn't what was bothering him. Pulling out his phone, Kamal flipped past photos of his grandchildren and stopped at a video. It showed a young man lying motionless on the ground – eyes glazed and fixed on the heavens, blood trickling from his temple, one running shoe ripped off. The camera zoomed in. The dead man had Central Asian features, wore a small black turban and had a wispy moustache that suggested he was no older than eighteen. 'He's an Uzbek,' said Kamal. 'We killed him last week.'

The Taliban were banging on the gates of Lakki Marwat. A week earlier, a gang of armed militants swept out of Waziristan on a mission to kidnap the local *nazim* – mayor – for ransom. As they raced back towards the mountains with their catch, Kamal and his gunmen caught up with them. A shoot-out in a maze of irrigation canals near Tajori ensued, at the end of which six Taliban were killed. Kamal's young driver Akhtar, now sipping tea in my kitchen, had fired the decisive retort with a rocket-propelled grenade. 'He's a dead shot, you see,' said Kamal proudly.

The Taliban threat came from two sides. To the west lay Waziristan, the nerve centre of the Taliban insurgency. For centuries, Wazir raiders had harassed the Marwat, sweeping on to the plains from their mountain keep to plunder women, gold and livestock. Now the Taliban were seeking hostages to fund their insurgency. A dozen people, mostly officials, had been kidnapped; a mobile-phone company paid $50,000 to free two of its engineers. But the danger also came from within. The local Taliban had entirely overrun Shah Hassan Khel, the village in the bandit-infested hills which we had skirted during the election campaign. The militants had gathered behind Maulvi Ashraf Ali, a smooth-talking young cleric who had fought with the Taliban in Afghanistan, and had now returned to convert his home village into a Taliban statelet. Ali banned sports and television, closed the girls' school and teamed up with local bandits to rob trucks on the Indus Highway. He mounted roadblocks outside Shah Hassan Khel to search vehicles for government employees. Kamal considered them an isolated group, but was worried that they could link up with the Taliban in Waziristan. 'This is a war of nerves,' he told me.

To steel those nerves, Kamal convened a *qaumi jirga* – a grand meeting of the Marwat sub-tribes. On a sweltering summer morning, about three hundred tribesmen, agreeing to shelve their internecine feuds temporarily, gathered under a stand of trees. The police stood by an armoured vehicle parked a short distance away, watching impotently. Kamal held centre stage, fanned by a bodyguard as he addressed the men squatting around him. He turned on his heel and jabbed the air. 'If the government will do nothing, then we must take matters into our own hands,' he thundered. 'Now is the time for action!' The tribesmen roared their approval.

Afterwards, about twenty senior elders adjourned to a small police building. Suddenly, a young man with greasy black hair, a glittering prayer cap and a bandolier of bullets across his chest appeared at the door. Seeing me, he refused to shake my hand. He was a member of the local Taliban. He spoke briefly. The Taliban had no beef with the Marwats, he declared; their principal interest was to fight American soldiers in Afghanistan. Then the cocky young fighter tucked his pistol into its holster and walked out.

As Taliban violence engulfed the frontier, the conflict started to have an impact on Kamal's life. Fighting near Peshawar forced him to take a circuitous detour when travelling to Lakki. He left his aeroplane in its hangar, fearing it might be attacked if he flew home. Rockets fell on Bannu, a town to the north. After failing to show up for supper in Islamabad one evening, he sent me a text. 'Sorry. On my way to Peshawar. One of my friends died in a suicide attack today.'

Initially, Kamal favoured containment. He warned the Shah Hassan Khel militants to curb their ambitions; he organized patrols to fend off raiders from Waziristan. But then the army deployed five hundred soldiers, who camped on the lawns of Lakki Hospital, and Kamal was forced to tip his hand. He cooperated with the army and told the local clerics not to help the insurgents. 'I warned them that if I bleed, then so will you,' he told me on a visit to Islamabad. 'We do not fight holy wars in the settled areas.'

The Marwats' defiance brought them to the attention of Baitullah Mehsud, the Taliban leader holed up in the mountains of nearby south Waziristan, and Pakistan's most wanted man. A former bodybuilder, Mehsud had risen from humble origins to become a ruthlessly innovative guerrilla leader. He pioneered the use of suicide bombers; the ISI and CIA blamed him for the assassination of opposition icon Benazir Bhutto in December 2007. He had a gift for gun politics – dozens of smaller groups, such as Fazlullah's in Swat, had united under the umbrella of his Tehrik-i-Taliban Pakistan (TTP) group. But Lakki Marwat refused to bend before him. In January 2009, Mehsud demanded to meet the people who dared defy his advance. After some prevarication, they agreed.

The meeting was a highly secretive and carefully choreographed affair. Kamal denied to the local press that it had taken place, fearing retribution from the authorities. Piecing together accounts from several Marwat elders, I learned what had happened.

At midnight, a force of one hundred Marwat fighters rumbled into Jandola, on the border of Waziristan, to the agreed meeting place on a mountain slope; an equal-sized Taliban force was waiting for them. Guided by the light of their mobile phones, the Marwat elders stumbled through the dark, finding Mehsud perched against a rock, being tended to by a doctor. The Taliban emir was said to suffer from kidney disease, or diabetes, and required regular medical attention.

A Thermos flask with tea and a packet of biscuits were produced, and the two sides sat in a circle. They began to talk. Mehsud complained that the Marwats' obstinate resistance was preventing him from attacking the police and army in Lakki. 'You must permit me, I am at war with the government,' he said. Kamal parried that Mehsud's targets – the police, but also the health workers and teachers – were Marwats. Should they be killed or kidnapped, *Pashtunwali* would oblige Kamal to retaliate. 'You have your compulsions, I have mine,' one witness recalled him saying. 'As a Pashtun I cannot deviate from my tradition.'

It was effectively a debate between two visions of the frontier – Kamal representing the old traditions, Mehsud as the harbinger of a new order framed around a lumpen version of sharia law.

There could be no agreement. 'It's very simple,' Kamal reportedly told him. 'You kill two of my people; I will kill ten of yours.'

After a few hours the two sides rose, shook hands and departed. Kamal returned to the sandy plains of Lakki, where his tribesmen would redouble their fortifications; Mehsud slunk back into the inky mountains of Waziristan.

On 1 January 2010, I was on holiday in the west of Ireland when the radio brought news of a suicide bombing in Pakistan. Of itself, this was nothing new. Over 8,500 people had died violently in the northwest over the previous year, many in suicide attacks. But this one had an unusual twist: the bomber had targeted a volleyball game. Then the newsreader said something that riveted my attention: Lakki Marwat.

I phoned Kamal. He was fine, he said, but the situation in the dilapidated local hospital was dire: about two hundred people had been watching the volleyball in an enclosed courtyard when the bomber struck; at least half were dead and most of the others badly injured. I thought back to the game I had seen during the election campaign, and imagined the devastation of a blast in such a tiny space. The attack had taken place, Kamal added, in Shah Hassan Khel, the hillbilly village long controlled by the Taliban.

A month later, back in Pakistan, I went down to Lakki with Kamal. The journey was tense. Entering the district, we passed a culvert where a roadside bomb had killed the deputy police chief six months earlier. Further along was the rubble of a madrasa, destroyed by the army. As we neared Lakki town, a car with a single occupant crossed our convoy twice. Kamal's bodyguard, Mina, phoned from the lead vehicle. He worried it was a suicide bomber. If he saw the mystery car again, he said, he would open fire. Kamal grunted his assent. Mercifully, the vehicle didn't reappear.

Kamal's house was ringed with concrete barriers and protected by gunmen; regular traffic was not allowed to approach. That night we had supper with a senior security official. He arrived in secretive circumstances after dark, travelling in an unmarked car and wearing civilian clothes. He had reason to be cautious: the Lakki police chief had recently quit after the Taliban threatened to kill his children. 'The man got shit-scared,' said Kamal. 'Once that happens, you can't expect him to do any good.' The security official had just returned from United Nations duty in Liberia, where he taught best practice to local police. The reality at home was more messy. After supper two tribesmen joined us. The tall one was clean-shaven and wore a neat waistcoat and a crafty smile. Speaking English, Kamal explained they were Lakki's leading criminals wanted for a string of robberies and killings. But instead of arresting them, he proposed a deal: in return for a temporary amnesty from the law, the criminals would help patrol the hills against Taliban encroachment. 'You need criminals like this. They know where a Talib gets his food, where he sleeps, who are his friends,' he explained. The security official agreed. 'I'm turning a blind eye, for now,' he told me after they left. 'I told them, "You go and kill those terrorists, and we won't do anything against you."'

The elders of Shah Hassan Khel were also mobilizing. The following morning the so-called village 'peace committee' – a dozen grim men slinging Kalashnikovs – trooped into Kamal's courtyard. They were led by Mushtaq Ahmed, a bony-faced man with quivering hands. He explained the events leading up to the volleyball atrocity.

At first, he said, some villagers had supported the Taliban in Shah Hassan Khel. They were drawn to the charismatic young commander, Maulvi Ashraf Ali, and his flowery speeches about the beauty of sharia law and the decadence of Western culture. Youngsters were captivated by his dramatic yarns of fighting the infidel Americans in Afghanistan. But then the Taliban's popularity eroded. People didn't appreciate the ban on girls' schooling and volleyball. They realized the Taliban had another agenda. 'Ashraf Ali talked about sharia. What he really wanted was power,' one man said.

Then the Pakistan Army forced them to take sides. In mid-2009, troops surrounded Shah Hassan Khel and warned the villagers to flee. Then they began pounding the houses with artillery and sent helicopter gunships after the Taliban. A wounded Ashraf Ali was carted away in a wheelbarrow; his men slipped off to Waziristan. But they weren't safe: months later, seventeen Marwat Taliban died in a CIA drone strike near Mir Ali; the Taliban threatened to return. But the villagers were standing behind Kamal. 'Enmity went to the maximum level,' Kamal said.

The villagers celebrated New Year's Day with a game of volleyball, which the Taliban had previously banned. Ahmed's face darkened as he described what followed. The bomber, who was driving an explosives-laden jeep, was a local lad – a misguided nineteen-year-old who had fallen for the Taliban's tales. He careened into the volleyball crowd, crushing several people before detonating his payload. After the explosion, Ahmed found two relatives among the rubble and charred bodies. Everyone lost somebody, even the bomber: his own stepbrother was among the dead. Now, Ahmed said, the village had a gargantuan blood feud to settle – ninety-seven confirmed deaths. 'We are Pashtun and we want revenge,' he said in a quiet, cool voice. 'We will track them down. We will capture them. And we will kill them, one by one.'

But how? Kamal huddled with the 'peace committee', plotting to send fighters into Waziristan to hunt down Ashraf Ali. It seemed quixotic: the Marwats were a small tribe with limited means and Waziristan was crawling with ruthless Taliban. And the enemy had already scored a symbolic victory: the volleyball court in Shah Hassan Khel was empty, Ahmed said, since most of the players were dead.

On the way back to Peshawar, Kamal predicted that the Taliban wouldn't last. They were the 'rejected people', he said – the dregs of society, incapable of delivering on their promises. 'We have a saying,' he said in his gravelly voice, as Lakki disappeared behind us, 'If a man with a bald head grows nails, then tomorrow he will injure himself.' In other words: give power to foolish men and they will eventually destroy themselves.

He is right, to a degree. The Taliban revolution is faltering. In Swat, Taliban promises of redistributed wealth gave way to arbitrary violence that alienated ordinary people. Behind the showy Islamist rhetoric, the Taliban lack a viable political plan for delivering the promised revolution. Marxist revolutionaries they are not. The Taliban's military limits are also becoming clear. Overblown predictions of militants marching on Peshawar, made as recently as 2008, are rapidly receding. A sweeping army operation in summer 2009 drove the Taliban from Swat, although their leaders remain at large. Fazlullah slipped into Afghanistan; the last I heard, his spokesman Sirajuddin was on the run. Last October the military operations extended to south Waziristan; a few months earlier, in August, an American drone killed Baitullah Mehsud outside a relative's house. The last thing the CIA operative saw, before the missile obliterated Mehsud, was an image of a sick man, lying on a rope bed, hooked up to a drip.

Yet there is no denying it: the Taliban have shaken Pashtun society to its core. The revolt exposed the folly of the 1980s jihad, when north-west Pakistan became a laboratory for a dangerous experiment in religious and violent indoctrination. Seeds planted then, watered by America's post-9/11 policies, are sprouting into cancerous plants. Recently, two young Pashtun men, one from Afghanistan and the other from Peshawar, were implicated in plots to bomb the New York subway and Times Square. The Pakistani, Faisal Shahzad, is the son of a senior airforce officer. The revolt has laid bare other failings: the chronic neglect of the tribal belt; the foolish jihadist meddling of the Pakistani Army; the deep inequalities in Pashtun society; and perhaps, even, the limitations of centuries-old *Pashtunwali*.

Almost 125 years ago, Rudyard Kipling wrote 'Arithmetic on the Frontier'. Today that arithmetic is altered. Army offensives may kill the Taliban militants; Anwar Kamal vows never to give in to them. But the fault lines they have exposed are here to stay. ∎

Life and Time

We grow up
but do not comprehend life.
We think life is just the passing of time.
The fact is,
life is one thing,
and time something else.

Translated by Sher Zaman Taizi

A BEHEADING

Mohsin Hamid

KHADIM ALI
Untitled, 2005
Mixed media on wasli. 24.5 x 17.5cm
Photo by Vipul Sangoi
Courtesy of the Asal Collection, © Khadim Ali

I hear the window shatter. There's no air conditioner on to muffle the sound. I get out of bed. I wish I wasn't my age. I wish I was as old as my parents. Or as young as my son. I wish it didn't have to be me telling my wife to stay where she is, saying everything will be fine in a voice she doesn't believe and I don't believe either. We both hear the shouting downstairs. 'Put on some clothes,' I'm saying to her. 'It'll be better if you're wearing clothes.'

The electricity's gone so I use my phone to light the way. Already there's the sound of men running up the wooden stairs. I shut the bedroom door and lock it behind me. Shadows are jumping and stretching from multiple torches. I raise both my hands. 'I'm here,' I say to them. I want to say it loudly. I sound like a whispering child. 'Please. Everything is all right.'

I'm on the floor. Someone has hit me. I don't know if it was with a hand or a club. My mouth is full of liquid. I can't get any words out. I'm gagging and I have to let my jaw hang open so I can breathe. Behind my back my wrists are being taped together. It feels like electrical tape, the kind of tape you wrap around a tennis ball for street cricket when you're a kid. I'm lying on my face and there's a grinding pain from that so I make some noise before I black out.

I'm between two men. They're holding me under my armpits and dragging me out the front door. I don't know how much time has passed. It's still night. The electricity has come back so the gate lights are on. The gatekeeper is dead. He's an old man and he's lying folded in on himself. His face is so thin. He looks like we've been starving him. I'm wondering how they killed him. I'm looking at him, looking for blood. But I don't have enough time.

I think there are four of them. They have a copper-coloured '81 Corolla. We used to have a car like that when I was growing up. This one is in bad shape. They open the trunk and dump me inside. I can't see anything. My face is partly on a rough carpet. The other part is on the spare tyre. Its rubber sticks to me. Or maybe I'm sticking to it. The shocks are shot, and every bump slams through the car. I think of being at the dentist, when it's already hurting and you know it's going to hurt more and you just wait and try to think of mind tricks to make it hurt less.

I feel feverish, a high, malarial fever that makes me shiver and drift in and out of sleep. I hope they didn't kill my son and my wife and my parents. I hope they didn't rape my wife. I hope whatever they do to me they don't use acid on me. I don't want to die but I don't mind dying. I just don't want to be tortured. I don't want anyone to crush my balls with a pair of pliers and put his cigarette out in my eye. I don't want this car ride ever to end. I'm getting used to it now.

They take me out in the sunlight. They're big men. Bigger than me. They take me into a house with paint peeling off the walls and put me in a bathroom with no windows, just a skylight. I've already pissed myself and my legs itch from dried urine. I don't make a sound. I sit there and prepare to cooperate. I wish I could remember how to say my prayers. I'd ask them to let me pray. Show them we're the same. But I can't risk it. I'll make a mistake and if they see that, things will be even worse for me. Maybe I can just mumble to myself and they'll think I'm religious.

They come back when it's dark. They're speaking a language I don't understand. I don't think it's Arabic or Pashto. What is it? Is it fucking Chechen? What is that fucking language? Who the fuck are these people? Tears are coming out of my eyes. That's good. The more pathetic I look, the better. 'Sirs,' I say in the most grovelling Urdu I can manage. 'What have I done? I beg your forgiveness.' My mouth doesn't work properly so I have to speak slowly. Even then I sound like I'm drunk. Or like someone has cut off half my tongue.

They ignore me. One is setting up a video camera on a tripod. The other is plugging a light into a portable UPS unit the size of a car battery. I know this. I don't want this. I don't want to be that goat. The one we bought for Big Eid. I used to feed it after school. We kept it for a week. I would break shoots off the hedge, green shoots that stained my hands, and feed them to that goat. It was a nice goat, but with dead eyes. I didn't like its eyes. I liked the way it chewed sideways. It was like a pet. I never petted it, but it was like a pet. It had small feet. It could stand on a brick to reach the leaves. My parents let me watch a man come and wrestle it to the ground and say a prayer and sacrifice it to God.

'Look, don't do this.' I'm speaking English now, slurring, making no sense. The words are just dribbling out of my mouth. I can't stop them. They're like tears. 'I've always censored myself. I've never written about religion. I've always tried to be respectful. If I've made a mistake just tell me. Tell me what to write. I'll never write again. I'll never write again if you don't want me to. It doesn't matter to me. It's not important. We're the same. All of us. I swear it.'

They tape my mouth shut and pin me flat on my stomach. One of them gets behind me and pulls my head up by the hair. It feels sexual the way he does it. I wonder if my wife is still alive and if she's going to sleep with another man after I'm gone. How many men is she going to sleep with? I hope she doesn't. I hope she's still alive. I can see the long knife in his hand. He's speaking into the camera. I don't want to watch. I shut my eyes. I want to do something to make my heart explode so I can be gone now. I don't want to stay.

Then I hear it. I hear the sound of my blood rushing out and I open my eyes to see it on the floor like ink and I watch as I end before I am empty. ■

POP IDOLS

Kamila Shamsie

AYAZ JOKHIO
Detail, *Nusrat Fateh Ali Khan from Ten Musicians*, 2009
Acrylic and newspaper collage on board, gloss varnish. 30.5 x 23cm
Courtesy of the collection of Khurram Kasim. © Ayaz Jokhio

Before Youth Culture

In 1987 I had a lot in common with many other fourteen-year-olds. I watched the Brat Pack/John Hughes films, repeatedly; I knew the Top 10 of the UK chart by heart; I cut out pictures of Rob Lowe, Madonna, a-ha from teen magazines and stuck them on my bedroom walls; I regarded the perfect 'mixed tape' as a pinnacle of teenaged achievement and gave thanks for not living in the dark days of LPs. But in doing all these things I merely affirmed what every adolescent growing up, like me, in Karachi could tell you – youth culture was Foreign. The privileged among us could visit it, but none of us could live there.

Instead, we lived in the Kalashnikov culture. Through most of the eighties, Karachi's port served as a conduit for the arms sent by the US and its allies to the Afghan mujahideen, and a great many of those weapons were siphoned off before the trucks with their gun cargo even started the journey from the port to the mountainous north. By the mid-eighties, Karachi, my city, a once-peaceful seaside metropolis, had turned into a battleground for criminal gangs, drug dealers, ethnic groups, religious sects, political parties – all armed. Street kids sold paper masks of Sylvester Stallone as Rambo; East met West in its adulation of the gun and its hatred of the godless Soviets.

In those days, schools were often closed because of 'trouble in the city'; my school instituted drills to contend with bombs and riots, rather than fire. Even cricket grounds – those rare arenas where exuberance still survived – weren't unaffected; all through 1986 and for most of 1987, there was hardly any international cricket played at Karachi's National Stadium because of security concerns. The exception in 1986 was a Pakistan v. West Indies Test match. Still, my parents refused to allow me to attend. They were worried there might be 'trouble'. This was the refrain of my adolescence. My parents and their friends constantly had to make decisions about how to balance concern for their children's safety against the desire to allow life to appear as normal for us as possible. Like all teenagers, though, we wanted to go somewhere – and public spaces, other than the beach, held little appeal.

As a result, 'going for a drive' became an end unto itself. A group of us would pile into a car and we'd just drive, listening to mixed tapes with music from the UK and the US, singing along to every song. Sometimes these were tapes one of us had recorded straight off the radio while on a summer holiday in London, and we'd soon memorize all the truncated clips of jingles and radio patter as well as the songs. 'Capital Radio! Playing all over London!' we'd chant while navigating our way through Karachi's streets. 'There are tailbacks on the M25 . . .' We always travelled in groups. You heard stories about the police stopping cars that had only a boy and girl in them and demanding proof that the pair were married, turning threatening and offering an option of arrest or payment of a bribe when the necessary paperwork wasn't forthcoming. There weren't any laws against driving in a car with someone of the opposite gender, but there were laws against adultery – and the police treated 'sex' as synonymous with 'driving' for the purposes of lining their pockets.

That was life as we knew and accepted it. Then one day in 1987 I turned on the lone, state-run TV channel to find four attractive young Pakistani men, wearing jeans and black leather jackets, strumming guitars, driving through the hills on motorbikes and in an open-top jeep, singing a pop song. And just like that, Youth Culture landed in living rooms all over Pakistan.

Islamization

It didn't really happen 'just like that', of course. Nothing ever does. There are various contenders for Pakistan's first pop song, but everyone seems to agree what the first pop video was. It came to our screens in 1981. I was eight when a brother-and-sister duo, Nazia and Zoheb Hassan, released the single 'Disco Deewane' ('Disco Crazy'). I was too young then to know that something altogether new had arrived in the form of the 'Disco Deewane' video with its dream sequences, dancers in short, white space-age dresses and Nazia's sensual pout. I do remember being mildly embarrassed that a pair of Pakistanis were trying to 'do an Abba'. Somewhere I had acquired the notion that pop music belonged to another part of the world; if the term 'wannabe' had existed then I would have agreed that it applied to Nazia and Zoheb – and everyone who loved their music; never mind that the song played in my head as incessantly as anything Abba ever produced.

I'm fairly sure that I wouldn't have been so dismissive of the idea of Pakistani pop videos if I had been born just a few years earlier, and could recall the Karachi of the early seventies, which had no shortage of glamour and East–West trendiness: nightclubs; locally made films with beautiful stars and catchy songs; shalwar kameez fashions inspired by Pierre Cardin (who designed the flight attendants' uniform for Pakistan International Airlines); popular bands who played covers of UK and US hits at fashionable spots in town. It's true, a good part of this world was known only to a tiny section of Karachi society, but I grew up in that tiny section and yet, even so, by the start of the eighties, stories of that glamorous milieu seemed a million miles away from the reality around me.

The reason for this dissonance was the dramatic shift that took place in Pakistan's cultural life between the early seventies and early eighties. The shift had a name – 'Islamization' – and a face – heavy-lidded, oily-haired, pencil-moustached. That face belonged to Pakistan's military dictator, Zia ul-Haq, ally of the Saudis and the Americans. As the alliance with the Americans brought guns into Karachi, so the alliance with the Saudis brought a vast increase in the number of Wahhabi mosques and madrasas: these preached a puritanical version of religion at odds with the Sufism that had traditionally been the dominant expression of Islam in much of the subcontinent. Fear of the growing influence of political, Wahhabi-inspired Islam formed a steady thrum through my childhood, and early on I learned that one of the most derogatory and dismissive terms that could be used against another person was 'fundo' (as in 'fundamentalist').

By the time I was watching Nazia and Zoheb on TV, I already knew Zia ul-Haq stood for almost all that was awful in the world; he had placed my uncle, a pro-democracy politician, under house arrest. What I didn't know then was that the video of 'Disco Deewane', at which I was turning up my nose, was coming under attack by Zia's allies on the religious right; they had decided it was un-Islamic for a man and woman to dance together, as Nazia and Zoheb did in the video, even if they were siblings.

These were the early days of Islamization, when the censors were confused about what was permissible. A few years later, the process of Islamization was sufficiently advanced that a video such as 'Disco Deewane' would have no chance of airing. Although Nazia and Zoheb continued to release albums, the censorship laws and official attitudes towards pop meant they never gave concerts, received limited airtime on PTV, never released another video with the energy and sensuality of 'Disco Deewane', and were seen as a leftover from the days before Zia's soulless rule sucked the life out of Pakistan's youth culture. Or, from the point of view of my historically amnesiac adolescent world, by the mid-eighties, when pop music really started to matter to me, they were already dinosaurs from another era.

BB (Benazir Bhutto; Battle of the Bands)

But I was soon to learn that some dinosaurs can roar their way out of seeming extinction in a single moment. The person who taught me this was thirty-three-year-old Benazir Bhutto. As long as I could remember she had been the pro-democracy politician under arrest, house arrest or exile. Pakistan was Zia ul-Haq to me, after all; how could someone who spoke of replacing not just the man but the entire system ever be of relevance? Imagine then how my world must have turned on its head in April 1986 when Benazir returned to Pakistan a free woman, for the first time in eight years, and a million people took to the streets of Lahore to welcome her home.

Benazir's triumphant return was one of several watershed political moments that marked my young life. My earliest ever recollection is of my father showing me his thumb, with a black mark on it, and explaining that he'd just been to the polling booth, and that the black mark, indelible ink, was to guard against anyone attempting to cast more than one vote. I was three and a half then, and the start of Zia ul-Haq's dictatorship was just months away. I remember the day Benazir's father was hanged, the day women's rights activists marched on Islamabad to protest against misogynistic laws and were set upon by baton-wielding police, the day Zia held a referendum to extend his rule. So, the return of Benazir, after a decade of soul-wearying, dictatorial, oppressive political news was electrifying. For me, this is how it happened: at one moment she was far away, then she was in our midst and nothing was quite the same as before.

It seemed just that way with pop music, too. In the mid-eighties, in Lahore and Karachi (and in other pockets of urban Pakistan), groups of students came together in each other's homes for jam sessions; the names of some of those students are instantly recognizable to anyone following the rise of Pakistani pop in the eighties and nineties: Aamir Zaki in Karachi, Salman Ahmad in Lahore, Junaid Jamshed in Rawalpindi. In 1986, Lahore's Al-Hamra auditorium hosted its first 'Battle of the Bands', and the underground music scene cast off its subterranean nature. Some of the loudest cheers were reserved for a Rawalpindi-based group called the Vital Signs. But down south, in my home town, we paid little attention to 'the provinces' and so the Vital Signs remained completely unknown to me until that day in 1987 when I turned on the TV and saw the four young men singing in an open-top jeep.

The Vital Signs

Watching the video of 'Dil Dil Pakistan' ('Heart, Heart, Pakistan' or 'My Heart Beats for Pakistan') today, I'm struck by the void that must have existed to make pretty boys singing patriotic pop appear subversive. In a bid to circumvent growing restrictions, TV producer Shoaib Mansoor had the idea of getting a pop song past the censors by wrapping it up in nationalism. Vital Signs and 'Dil Dil Pakistan' was the result. The video, with its guitar-strumming, denim-clad twenty-something males, premiered on Independence Day – 14 August – 1987 and millions of Pakistanis, including my fourteen-year-old self, fell over in rapture.

Our reaction clearly wasn't to do with their dance moves. The Vital Signs boys of 1987 seem ill at ease, their gyrations arrhythmic, their posture self-conscious. This is particularly true of the lead singer, Junaid Jamshed, but still, I was in love. They were clean-cut, good-looking and, most shockingly, they were nearby. They were Pakistani after all; one day you might turn a corner and run into one of them. This scenario started to seem even more thrillingly possible the day gossip raced through the schoolyard, telling us that one of the boys at school – a boy I knew! – was Junaid Jamshed's cousin.

The first concert I ever attended was Vital Signs playing at a swanky Karachi hotel. It's a safe guess that some of the girls present hadn't told their parents where they were really going that evening. Mine was a co-ed school, and while all the boys and girls were entirely at ease in each other's company, many of the girls had restrictions placed on them by their parents about co-ed socializing outside school hours. Almost no one's parents were classified as fundo, but many were 'conservative' – the latter having more to do with ideas of social acceptability and 'reputation' than religious strictures.

The concert took place in a function room, one used for conferences, small receptions or evenings of classical music. I had doubtless been in that room many times for tedious weddings, but I don't suppose I'd ever entered it in jeans before – and that alone must have made the room feel different, unexpected. There was a makeshift stage placed at one end and neat rows of chairs set out for the audience by organizers who obviously had no idea what a pop concert was all about. But we did, we Karachi adolescents. We'd watched pirated recordings of Hollywood teen movies, and *Top of the Pops*, and we knew that when a pop group started singing no one sat down and politely swayed in time to the music. So, as soon as the band came on, all of us climbed atop our chairs and started dancing. 'You guys are great,' Jamshed said in surprised delight, before breaking into Def Leppard's 'Pour Some Sugar on Me'. I recall telling myself: *Remember this.* I had never before come so close to touching the Hollywood version of Teenaged Life.

By 1988, a slightly reconfigured Vital Signs, having replaced one of its original band members with the guitarist Salman Ahmad, was in the process of recording a debut album when a plane exploded in the sky, killing Zia ul-Haq and allowing Pakistanis to take to the ballot box to declare what we wanted for our nation after eleven years of military rule and so-called Islamization. The answer was clear: no to the religious parties; yes to the thirty-five-year-old woman.

Democracy and Status Quo

Given the state of Pakistan today, it is impossible to remember the heady days at the end of 1988 without tasting ashes. Elation was in the air, and it had a soundtrack. At parties my friends and I continued to dance to the UK's Top 40, but the songs that ensured everyone crowded on to the dance floor were 'Dil Dil Pakistan' and the election songs of both Benazir's Pakistan People's Party (PPP) and the Karachi-based Muhajir Qaumi Movement (MQM). There was little concern for political affiliation. At one such party I recall a young Englishman looking perplexed as Karachi's teens gyrated to a song with the chorus *Jeay jeay jeay Bhutto Benazir* ('Long live Benazir'). 'I can't imagine a group of schoolkids in London dancing to a "Long Live Maggie" number,' he said, and I pitied him and all the English teenagers for not knowing what it was like to see the dawn of democracy.

A few months into the tenure of the Bhutto government, with the new head of state's approval, Pakistan TV organized and recorded a concert called *Music '89*. Nazia and Zoheb Hassan hosted, fittingly; but the event also passed the baton to a new generation, including Vital Signs and the hot new talent, the Jupiters, fronted by Ali Azmat. Tens of millions of people tuned in and religio-fascists fulminated from every pulpit. Benazir, as she would go on to do time and again, gave in to the demands of the religious right and, despite its huge success, the tapes of *Music '89* were removed from the PTV library.

One of the most distinguishing features of the Bhutto government was the prevalence of the status quo precisely where there was the most urgent need for change. Islamization was no longer the government's spoken objective, but all the madrasas, jihadi groups and reactionary preachers continued as if nothing had changed, with the support of the army and intelligence services. Benazir's supporters argued that she had no room to manoeuvre given all the forces ranged against her; her detractors said her only real interest was in clinging on to power. Either way, the great social transformation we had expected to see, that Return to Before, never happened.

Even worse, many of the changes begun by Zia ul-Haq gained momentum. Almost all of rural Pakistan continued to hold fast to Sufi Islam, but the cities, where there was no deep affiliation to a particular religious tradition, became, perversely, more susceptible to the reactionaries. There were signs that a reactionary Islam, which entwined itself with world events, had made its mark on several of my schoolfellows – the male athlete who didn't want to run in shorts on the school's sports day because Islam demanded modesty in dress; the close friend of mine who held up a picture of Salman Rushdie in the months just after the fatwa and said, 'He even looks like the Devil!'; and, most notably, the other friend who told me, in 1991, that Saddam would win the war against the Americans. When I pressed him for his reasons, given the disparity in the two nations' armies, he shrugged and made some cryptic comment about Saddam having a 'greater' weapon. Chemical? I asked, and it was only when he continued to look straight at me, without expression, that I realized what he was thinking. 'Allah?' I said, and he raised both shoulders and dropped them – a gesture that told me I may not believe it, but it was so.

Everyone I knew at school had been closely following the Gulf War, though much of that had to do with the excitement of CNN broadcasting into our homes for the first time – after a lifetime of state-controlled TV, we were all hungry for images from around the world. At seventeen I knew certain basic political truths, even if they were never directly articulated on CNN: America had turned its back on Afghanistan after the Soviet withdrawal; the Gulf War was about oil; the same America that had embraced the religio-military dictatorship of General Zia was now turning frosty towards the new democratic government and imposing sanctions on the nation. None of this got in the way of the draw of America as a destination for my friends and myself – most of us, including the boy who predicted Saddam's righteous victory, were headed there for university. We knew that America was a wonderful place, if you were in it. There was no struggle to reconcile my conflicting views. I'd always known it was a country that produced both Rambo and Laura Ingalls Wilder.

By the summer of 1991, even though political disillusionment with Pakistan's democracy was rife, I viewed the world around me as a source of delight. University beckoned – almost all my friends would be on the East Coast by the autumn. We made plans for meeting in Boston on weekends and over Thanksgiving break. It didn't occur to me that I might be homesick, or that anything would seem remotely unfamiliar. It also didn't occur to me that henceforth Pakistan would be no more than a part-time home, and that I would eventually join the ranks of Those Who Left. I was going away for university, that was all; in four years, I'd return, and both Karachi and I would be much the same as before. And as for those pop stars of my youth – I assumed that some would fade away before others but that in the end they'd all be remembered as 'pioneers of pop'. I certainly never would have imagined that their lives over the next two decades would reflect Pakistan's shifting religio-political landscape.

The Sufi Rocker

Weeks before I left for university, I had one concert-going experience that was to prove more potent in retrospect than at the time. The group with whom I spent that summer included a boy called Sherry, whose brother Salman Ahmad had just left Vital Signs to start his own band, Junoon. Junoon's first album, released that year, was greeted with total indifference by critics and the public, but Sherry rounded up all the gang to go to a Junoon concert that summer. We went, but without much enthusiasm. Vital Signs was still the premier band in the country, and Ahmad, the guitarist, who was either jettisoned or parachuted out (accounts varied), had a whiff of second best about him. But onstage, Junoon was electrifying – thanks to both Ahmad and the singer, Ali Azmat, formerly of the Jupiters. Later, when Junoon became the biggest name in Pakistani pop, I would talk about that concert with an 'I heard them before they were famous' tone of superiority. But the truth was, soon after that I went to university and started to see the overwhelming maleness of Pakistani pop as alienating – my musical world now revolved around Natalie Merchant, Ani DiFranco and the Indigo Girls.

I started to pay attention to Junoon again in 1996, when they became megastars with 'Jazba-e-Junoon', the Coca-Cola-sponsored recording of the official Pakistan team song for the Cricket World Cup, and more or less simultaneously Ahmad started looking to Sufi Islam in an attempt to find a sound for Junoon that wasn't merely derivative of Western rock. My own interest in the mystical side of Islam had started at university when I took a course on Sufism and learned how absurd I had been to think subversion via music came in the form of boys in denim singing pop songs in which they pledged their heart to Pakistan.

In the Sufi paradigm, God is the beloved and the mortal is the supplicant/lover – the relationship between the individual and God is intensely personal and does not admit the intercession of 'religious scholars' or 'leaders of the congregation'. Small wonder that the Sufis have almost always stood in opposition to those who claim to be the guardians of religion. But the deep-rootedness of Sufi Islam in Pakistan has often meant that the orthodoxy don't dare take it on – through the Zia years, the great singers in the Sufi tradition, such as Nusrat Fateh Ali Khan and Abida Parveen, continued to perform, both in public gatherings where the crowds could exceed half a million and on state-run TV. Every note leaping from their throats was a rebuke to the orthodoxy. It wasn't until university that I saw the brilliance of those singers – particularly of Nusrat, who was a worldwide phenomenon by the nineties. You didn't need to understand a word he sang, or feel any religious stirrings, to be struck to the marrow by one of the greatest voices of the century.

Nusrat and other qawwals were such a potent force in Pakistan that it's not surprising that Junoon's attempt to encroach on Sufi musical ground deeply divided listeners at first. But within a few years, the term 'Sufi rock' was no longer something spoken with inverted commas hanging around it. Much as I loved the music, though, I was sceptical about the relentless Coke-sponsored marketing that went alongside it. It didn't sit too well with the Sufi idea of stripping away the ego.

Of course, there was no reason why musicians singing Sufi lyrics should live by Sufi rules. But Ahmad, who now affected the fashionable garb of a long-haired, bead-wearing, goateed mystic, spoke extensively about his immersion in Sufism. The critical acclaim for Ahmad's music began to fade at the start of the new millennium, and yet halfway through the decade he was more visible than ever before – performing at the UN, talking up Indo-Pak friendship, promoting HIV/Aids awareness, appearing on TV, playing at the Nobel Peace Prize ceremony. It is hard to separate sense of mission from marketing in all this. Whatever he has done in the last few years, and whatever he does in the future, Ahmad's legacy is Sufi rock, that electrifying blend of the deep-rooted mystical side of subcontinental Islam and contemporary, cutting-edge, rocking youth culture.

The Fundo

In Salman Ahmad's autobiography, *Rock & Roll Jihad*, it is unsettling how often he writes of receiving messages and signs from God, and of his certainty that he is doing God's work through his music. His old friend and former Vital Signs bandmate Junaid Jamshed would doubtless disagree. I still vividly recall the moment in the late nineties when I returned to Karachi after an absence of several months and one of my friends said, 'Have you heard about Junaid Jamshed?' I hadn't given him much thought for some years; other groups, not only Junoon, had come along since and eclipsed those pioneers of pop. 'He's become a fundo.'

Junaid Jamshed? The man who wanted Karachi's teens to pour some sugar on him? Surely not. But yes, my friend said when I questioned them – he had joined the Tablighi Jamaat, a proselytizing movement, which believed in following the example of the Prophet in the most literal ways – the length of your beard; the clothes in your wardrobe; the Arab inflection of your pronunciation; the exact words you used to say goodbye. The Tablighi Jamaat had been among the groups to benefit from the state sponsorship of Wahhabi Islam in the Zia years, though they always insisted they were completely apolitical.

Rumour had it that some personal crisis had propelled Jamshed into the arms of Tablighi Jamaat, who promised a clear path to salvation. There was no way of knowing if that was truth or conjecture. All I knew was that one day I turned on the TV and there was a man I didn't instantly recognize, with a long beard and white skullcap, quoting from the Quran. Nothing he said was objectionable; he spoke of peace, and the importance of education, and other perfectly right-minded things. But it filled me with despair.

Jamshed himself couldn't seem to decide how easily this mantle of righteousness sat on him. For six years, we all watched as he vacillated between pop star and proselytizing man of faith. He declared he was quitting the music business. Then he refashioned his beard into a neat goatee and appeared with Vital Signs at a tribute concert for Nazia Hassan, who had died tragically young from cancer almost twenty years after burning up screens in the 'Disco Deewane' video. When questioned, Jamshed claimed that there was nothing incompatible in Islam and pop music. Later still, he would insist that the U-turn at that concert was a sign that he had not yet been strong enough to do the right thing. At the time, he rationalized, he'd had four international concerts lined up, as well as a new album he'd already recorded, not to mention a one-year contract with Pepsi . . . it just hadn't been the right time to sever his ties with pop music, the pressures were too great. Once free of contractual obligations, Jamshed again declared pop music haram (forbidden) and soon after took to recording religious songs of praise.

Today, Jamshed's life is divided between proselytizing for Tablighi Jamaat, recording religious albums and running a very successful designer label – J. (Jay Dot) – with stores in the glitziest malls of Pakistan, and branches soon opening in the UK. According to his MySpace page, it is no problem to reconcile his religious devotion with his designer stores. As he reminds us, 'Our Prophet Muhammad, peace be with him, was also a merchant who sold cloth.'

There are other ways in which religion can pay. Last year, Jamshed appeared on TV speaking with a tone and urgency that suggested he was about to reveal some deeply important spiritual truth. His message: contrary to rumours, Lay's potato chips are made using only halal products. For this TV spot, which ends with Jamshed munching on a potato chip, he was reportedly paid 2 million rupees (£26,000 – though the comparatively low cost of living in Pakistan makes it a much larger amount in real terms).

That Jamshed was outspoken about his religious faith wasn't in itself worthy of comment. In the Pakistan I had grown up in almost everyone identified as Muslim; to do otherwise meant you were either of the 3 per cent of the population belonging to other religious groups, or had adopted a contrarian attitude. But one of my friends aptly put her finger on why the particular form of Islam espoused by the former pop star was so disquieting: 'In our grandmother's generation, when people became more religious, they turned devout. Now they turn fundamentalist.'

The Rock Star Fantasist

From his early days in the Jupiters, to his huge success as the voice of Junoon and, recently, his critically acclaimed solo career, Ali Azmat has always been the man who most lived up to the idea of the rock star. He remains the most charismatic performer on the pop scene, with a sartorial flair that sets trends, a turbulent relationship with a beautiful model, a reputation for brashness and a personality that is an appealing mix of contagious good humour and artistic suffering. When the journalist Fifi Haroon asked Azmat how many girlfriends he'd had, he replied, 'I'm a lover, not a mathematician.' While Junaid Jamshed was declaring pop music haram and Salman Ahmad delved into the Quran and Sufism, Azmat just focused on the music. He might have been singing Sufi rock, but he made it quite clear that it was the rock that mattered.

Then, in 2009, the rock star shifted his primary vocation from singer to that of cheerleader.

The man Azmat has been championing – introducing him at public events, singing his praises on TV, featuring him as the resident 'expert' on his talk show – is Zaid Hamid, a self-professed 'security consultant and strategic defence analyst'. An example of Hamid's strategic thinking was in evidence early in 2010 when he set out a vision for Pakistan's future. 'Pakistan will lead a bloc of Muslim nations known as the United States of Islam,' he declared to an approving, self-selected audience. 'Any nation that wants to lift a foot will first ask Pakistan's permission . . . We have good news for India: we will break you and make you the size of Sri Lanka.' And on and on it went, describing how Pakistani Muslims from 'the United States of Islam' would ensure the security of Muslims the world over.

A few weeks after this televised address, Azmat appeared on a talk show hosted by the model and actress Juggan Kazim; the other guest was the feisty actress Nadia Jamil, who savaged Azmat for his association with Hamid, whom she described as a hate-monger.

Azmat hotly denied this. 'We're not against any people,' he said. 'We're against a political ideology called Zionism . . . there are all sorts of Zionists. There are Hindu Zionists, Muslim Zionists, Christian and Jewish Zionists.'

'What is Zionism?' asked Kazim.

'We don't even know ourselves what it is,' Azmat replied, without a flicker of embarrassment. 'It's a political ideology where obviously these guys have taken over the world, through whatever means, through businesses . . .'

Hamid's star has imploded in the last few months, for various reasons, including a murder case against him and attacks from members of the orthodoxy who saw his popularity as a challenge. But the spectacular speed with which he rose to prominence, and the support he gathered, are very telling about the state of Pakistan. A country demoralized and humiliated by its myriad problems could either turn reflective, or it could simply blame everyone else. Large sections of Pakistan have chosen the latter option. Hamid's appeal to the young – who made up much of his following – was that while his talk of Pakistan's glorious future was entirely wrapped in religious-tinged rhetoric, he stayed away from social proscriptions. If the question is 'What kind of Muslim am I?' – and in Pakistan that is often the question – the Hamid answer is 'The kind who fights Zionism everywhere!' Whether you do so in jeans and T-shirt, and with or without a guitar, is largely beside the point. You can become a Better Muslim without disrupting your social life. What more could a Pakistani rock star ask for?

It's a strange business, growing up. Your teen idols grow up too, and you realize that the vast gulf of years which separated you from them is actually just a narrow ravine, and that you are all roughly part of the same generation. In the particular case of the Pakistani pop pioneers, you also realize that your nation is growing up with you too

– the Islamic Republic of Pakistan came into being in 1971, when the former East Pakistan became Bangladesh. Given the youthfulness of the nation, perhaps it isn't surprising that we of the 'Islamic Republic of Pakistan generation' look at each other and seek answers to the question: 'What do our lives say about the state of the nation?'

Largely, our lives say that polarity and discordance are rife. However, although they are few and sometimes difficult to identify, there are still spaces in Pakistan where difference presents opportunities to harmonize. Aptly enough, one of those spaces is the music studio. *Coke Studio*, to be specific. Corporate sponsorship has been an integral part of Pakistani pop music since Pepsi signed Vital Signs to sing their most famous tune with the slightly rejigged lyrics 'Pepsi Pepsi Pakistan'. Notably, despite the different paths Azmat, Jamshed and Ahmad followed, they all remained linked to corporate sponsors, a fact that didn't seem to get in the way of any of their religious or political beliefs.

Now in its third season, *Coke Studio* is a wildly popular TV show featuring live performances from Pakistan's biggest musical acts, as well as introducing some lesser-known singers. The most glorious thing about the show is the disparate traditions it brings together – pop, qawwali, rock, folk, classical. Qawwals and rock stars duet, the tabla and violin complement each other's sounds. And the man who makes it all happen? The somewhat reclusive and much sought-after producer Rohail Hyatt, who, twenty-three years ago was one of the four boys in jeans singing 'Dil Dil Pakistan' in my living room. More than any of his Vital Signs bandmates or Junoon rivals, he seems aware of one simple and persisting truth: in Pakistan, as all around the world, what we most crave from our musicians is music. ■

RESTLESS

Aamer Hussein

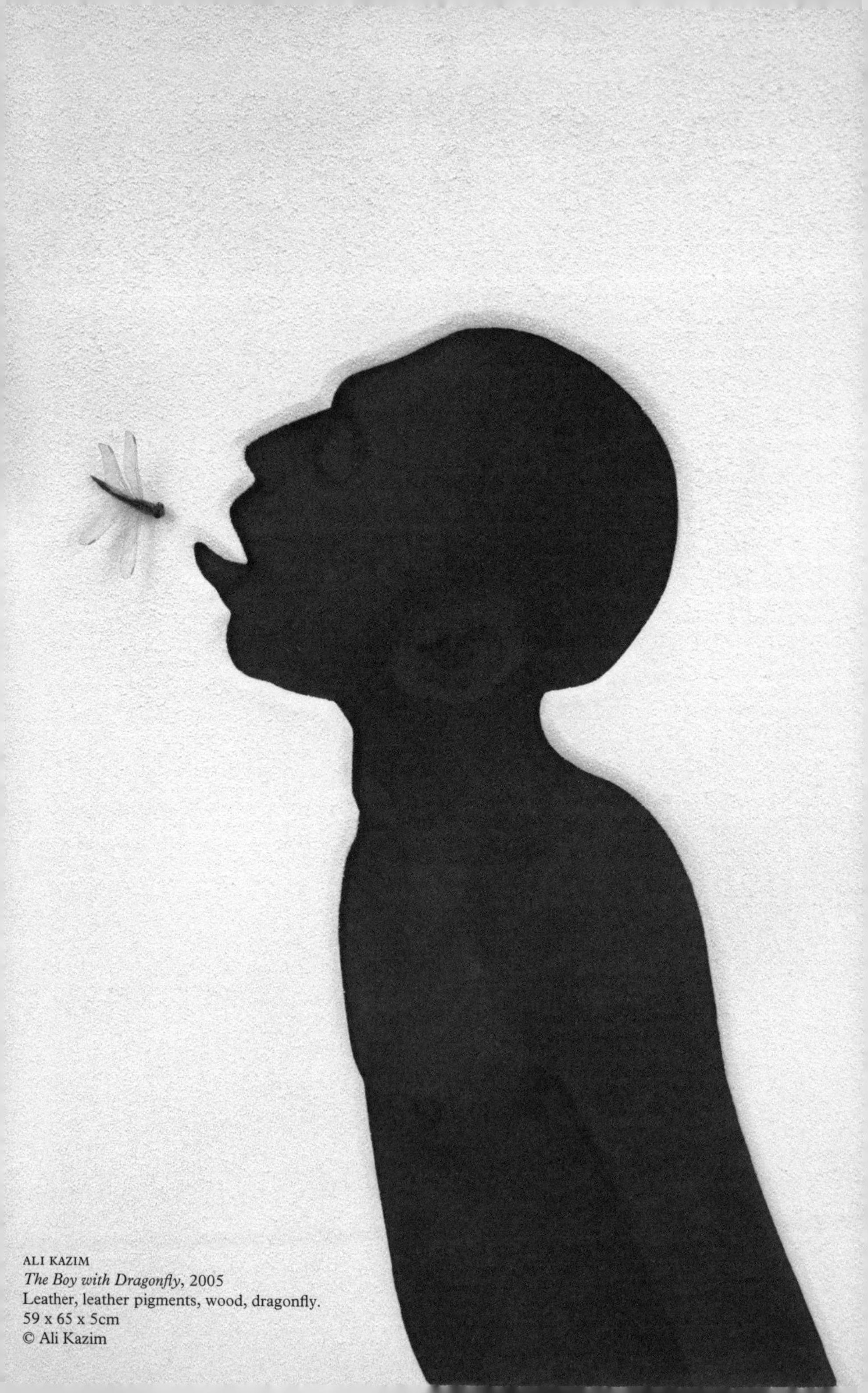

ALI KAZIM
The Boy with Dragonfly, 2005
Leather, leather pigments, wood, dragonfly.
59 x 65 x 5cm

No one to greet us at Heathrow. We'd arrived from Bombay, via Prague and Beirut, my two sisters and I. A relative who had come to pick up a cousin travelling with us gave us a lift. We drove past dark, cramped buildings to an address in Wimbledon where two-storeyed houses huddled. Lord, I said, have we crossed the Arabian Sea to live in a place like this? But it was only the relative's house. We saw Kensington Palace Gardens, the Albert Hall and the statue of Boudicca at Hyde Park Corner from the car window as we drove to Park Lane.

Our father and oldest sister hadn't received our cable. They weren't expecting us till June. They lived in a penthouse, with a sixth-floor view of parkland and hardly enough room for all. Our sister, who'd been in London for nearly two years and worked for the *Evening Standard*, knew the city centre well. She marched us around its bridges and alleys, stopping to buy us ices when we looked tired. We weren't used to long walks in the heat. I was overdressed for the warm London weather. (My mother had said it rained all the time, and made me pack tweed jackets and woollen trousers.) My hair flopped over my forehead and was cut short behind; my blue linen shirt flapped around me in the breeze: all wrong. My sister bought me a purple shirt that clung to my bony torso.

May 1970. I was fifteen years and six weeks old.

London was a little shabby. I had expected skyscrapers, glass and steel among the grey monuments.

We lived across from Hyde Park. Pop singers held free concerts there, near-naked office workers took sunbaths for lunch. Hippies smoked marijuana, preachers ranted at Speakers' Corner. Salvation Army Doris sang 'Puppet on a String' to the accompaniment of a tin can. If all that bored us, there was always the Serpentine to sail on.

Three or four cousins came over from Bombay and Karachi. We wandered around in packs, unaccompanied in the streets and public parks, for hours: impossible for them at home. Each day brought a discovery: fashion parades on Carnaby Street and the King's

Road, odorous cheeses and shelves of cheap bright paperbacks at Selfridges. London Bridge, the Tower. Bright skies till late – alarming for someone used to sunset before seven. No need to worry about being home before dark. We jumped on and off buses. We spoke fluent English but were unused to the ways of this city. We waved a twenty-pound note at a conductor who reprimanded us and told us to watch out for thieves. We discovered frozen fish and burgers. We broke bottles of ketchup and mayonnaise on Oxford Street. A passer-by told us in cockney: 'You'll have to clean all that up.' We thought he was serious, and knelt down to pick up bits of broken bottle with scraps of soggy brown paper until a street cleaner shooed us away. My very tall cousin and I fell off a moving bus on the Strand.

On rainy afternoons we went to see *Anne of the Thousand Days*, *The Taming of the Shrew*, *Mary, Queen of Scots*. There was a Garbo season at the Classic, King's Road. Films were expensive, but we sat in the cheap seats near the screen, which we never would have done at home. I always chose historical films. (I unconsciously identified Englishness with costume dramas.) The first play I saved to see at a matinee was *Hedda Gabler*, with Maggie Smith intense as Ibsen's anti-heroine. Mahalia Jackson and Mungo Jerry performed in Hyde Park. At home, in the evenings, serialized on TV: Sartre's *Roads to Freedom*, Flaubert's *Sentimental Education*.

Summer. Grandes dames, gospel, pop groups, divas.

'M ight I remind you, you're not on holiday,' my father said. He took me to Westminster, the public school he'd selected for me. (I was meant to follow him to Magdalen in Oxford, and study law there.) I'd spent a year and a half at an all-male school in India, suffering through science classes; when, at Westminster, they told me I'd have to repeat a year and study Latin and maths, I protested. I was sent instead to a tutorial college on the other side of the park, between unfashionable Gloucester Road and Earls Court. The principal, a grey-haired lady with fancy spectacles, suggested I attend a summer class in English before term began. I took the 74 bus from Park Lane to the West London Air Terminal every morning to attend lessons in a language that, although not my mother tongue, was the one I knew best.

My classmates were Japanese, Greek, Venezuelan, Nigerian, Persian. A curly-haired, bespectacled boy called Giovanni sat next to me. He'd ask me to walk with him to Earls Court station. Though I preferred to take the bus, I'd go along, to be companionable. On Fridays he'd borrow two shillings from me. 'I go to the seazside to zleep with de girls. You come with me? Do you zleep with de girls?' I didn't sleep with girls, not yet. I did fancy one, Kumiko, a very pretty Japanese girl who sometimes rode on the bus with me to Hyde Park Corner. But I soon found out she had an Iranian boyfriend – older than me, and, I thought, better looking.

I didn't make other friends in the summer class. My cousins went home, one by one. I depended on books for company. I read about the opera and the theatre in the public library, borrowed, one after the other, Yukio Mishima's cruel tales, Cyprian Ekwensi's lowlife chronicles of Lagos, Baldwin's sexual jigsaw: *Another Country*.

Summer ended. The family moved to a first-floor apartment in Hyde Park Place, with picture windows looking right into the park and enough rooms to house all the relatives who wanted to visit. My mother had joined us and for a while all six of us lived there. Then my mother and one of my sisters went off to Karachi for several months. I had my own room, space to read quietly. I learned to fry frozen fish and burgers, eat stuffed vine leaves from cans, make hummus and pitta sandwiches and cups of good instant coffee.

Late at night, I watched films on TV, *Yang Guifei* and *Onibaba*. Polanski, Antonioni, Wajda. Sometimes, on Sundays, my sisters and I watched Indian films at Her Majesty's, Haymarket. I didn't enjoy them as much as I once had. I wasn't homesick. I'd left Karachi and the sea before I was thirteen, to spend two years in small-town India and holiday in Bombay: I couldn't say where home was any longer. Perhaps the films reminded me of what I didn't want to lose: I enjoyed speaking and listening to my mother tongue, but I had no need to be English or anything else. London was just another place I'd landed in.

Classes began in September. I still took the 74 every day, but from another stop. Along with English grammar and composition, I studied biology, history, scriptures and literature. Our teacher of English literature was an elderly dyed blonde who said she was descended from an Indian princess. I found her inspiring; the others laughed at her. I made friends: Lamie, the Palestinian boy; Japanese Naoko; and Yunie, the Korean girl. Naoko, like me, lived with her family; they had a ground-floor flat on Exhibition Road where she sometimes served us Japanese tea and bean cakes. Lamie and Yunie lived in bedsit land around Kensington where foreign students rented narrow single rooms, cooked on single gas rings, shared bathrooms and were allowed two baths a week (no showers). Lamie wanted to be a doctor. He often took me to his room behind our school to share his supper of fried cheese and bread with oil and thyme, while we listened to the plaintive songs of Lebanon's Fairuz. Yunie's Earls Court flat was full of friends who brought bottles of cheap wine to supplement the tea, biscuits, crisps and cigarettes she served in abundance.

Through the autumn, I wrote poems about Naoko, because I needed someone to write poems for. I showed them to Yunie. But that was only after Naoko left for Tokyo in December. Yunie told me that Naoko wouldn't have responded to my interest: she was dating Lamie and didn't find me very interesting. Yunie was two years older than I was, and had two boyfriends she couldn't decide between: one her age, the other ten years older.

I'd never known leaf-piled pavements and slate-black afternoons. Sometimes I spotted a pale moon rising at three.

News that winter: JAPANESE NOVELIST MISHIMA COMMITS SEPPUKU, RITUAL SUICIDE.

Because I'd read so many of his books I felt, somehow, tainted.

At Christmas, snow: as if London had staged a white pageant, become an ice rink for newcomers. I wore a sheepskin coat and didn't mind the cold that first year.

Naoko, before she left, had introduced me to her best friend. Norma was a Colombian with a warm Hispanic manner, near-perfect English and two other languages. She wanted to be an interpreter. Her mother made Japanese prints and sketches.

I picked up Norma from their maisonette in Olympia, took her for walks in the leafless park. We kissed by the frozen pond in Kensington. Neither of us had money. Easiest to talk in my room, but my sister didn't like that. 'Norma has a lazy left eye,' she said. 'She wears ugly fur-lined boots and I bet she washes her frizzy hair with Fairy Liquid.'

We dated through January. Then Norma said she didn't think we could last as a pair. 'You're a good-looking guy but you're a virgin. You need to learn how to kiss. Let's just be friends.' I didn't really want that, though in some odd way I was relieved.

Yunie, who didn't like Norma, found the story of our relationship funny. Yunie was with me in A level English lit now. She had a mysterious way of disappearing for weeks, but when she was around we were best friends. We'd spent hours listening to her favourite singers. Janis Joplin. James Taylor, Carole King, Melanie, Cat Stevens, Leonard Cohen.

I went out with other friends when she wasn't around. Lamie surfaced at Easter and competed with me for girlfriends. We saw *Ryan's Daughter* and *The Music Lovers* in 70mm. We both dated a Thai girl for a while, who dumped us in turn for an older Iraqi boy. Then Lamie heard that his sixteen-year-old brother had been imprisoned and tortured in Israel. He left our company and moved to Manchester.

Another summer. Yunie went away again, leaving her stereo and albums in my room. I read less now, and spent more time listening to her records. I saw *Hair* and *Oh! Calcutta!* at the theatre with visiting friends. I was sixteen and my hair was shoulder-length. I smoked cheap Player's cigarettes, offered them around. I walked barefoot by the Serpentine, with friends or alone.

The library had a collection of Urdu poems by Faiz, who'd lived up the road from us in Karachi. They'd called him a dissident, an internal exile and a communist. He wrote better about restlessness and loss than anyone I'd ever read. One of his prison poems had been set to music; my sister used to sing it when we were children, and we'd imitate her.

Though I spoke Urdu well, I'd been forced in India to do exams in Hindi, which now I read and wrote much faster. The Faiz book had poems in English and Urdu on facing pages. It helped me to relearn my native script.

Pakistan divided. East Wing, West Wing, we'd called its distant limbs, but the body that lay between them belonged to another vehicle, almost all of India: and how long could we fly together with unmatched wings?

My mother left Karachi before war broke out. My sister returned to London while it was raging. Friends turned their backs on one another, and a few swore enmity.

At the end of '71, when Bangladesh declared its independence, I joined a rally at Trafalgar Square, but that was my protest against the role General Yahya, who'd only replaced Ayub as President a couple of years before the troubles began, had played in the conflict.

Soon after Trafalgar Square, a pneumatic pothead from Boston took me to her bed after a matinee performance of *The Devils*. (An arranged seduction, I later discovered: a Bangladeshi boy had bet her she couldn't have me.) I'd thought, as I told Yunie later, that I should rid myself of my irksome virginity with someone willing to teach what I needed to learn before I turned seventeen in April. Not that I'd needed to learn much. Yunie laughed, but I think she found it less amusing than she pretended to.

A few days later, Yunie and I spent a whole night in bed together after a party, kissing and touching. It was only the second time I'd tried alcohol. I was high on champagne, she on hash cookies. Santana music played in the background. I assumed she wasn't ready to go 'all the way'.

She came to stay in my flat for two or three days at a time. We'd end up in bed, in each other's arms. At some climactic point, she'd push me away.

'I love you, Yunie.'

'I don't love you. Oh, not in that way, you're like a brother. We're just randy.'

She left for Boston in March.

I sat my English A level in summer; I'd been in hospital with mumps when Yunie left, and only got a B. I failed history. We gave up the Hyde Park Place flat. (My father was travelling, two of my sisters studying near Nantwich, the third with my grandparents in India. My mother and I were lost in its corridors all winter: there were never more than three of us living together at any given time.) We moved a mile down the road to Sussex Gardens. My English teacher suggested I read literature at Sussex, but my father insisted I prepare for law at Oxford.

I shifted to a college in Bloomsbury, danced away Saturday nights at parties with my journalist sister's friends, and drifted away from Kensington.

I wrote poems for Yunie, but I had a new girlfriend: Pakistani, she lived across a bridge over the Thames. She played piano and guitar. We sang duets, tried to set Faiz to guitar music, performed at a club together. We stayed together for a year. I didn't learn to love her.

After classes, I wandered from store to store in Soho, searching for the music that echoed in my head, spending my pocket money on songs in distant languages: Turkish, Malay, Xhosa, Catalan. At home I'd listen to the singers' soulful voices and sing along with them, though I didn't know the lyrics or understand the words.

I was eighteen, bad at history and British Constitution, turned down by Oxbridge, restless in an open city, bored of being young. ■

LITQUAKE
SAN FRANCISCO'S LITERARY FESTIVAL

SEE   HEAR   SPEAK

San Francisco
OCTOBER 1-9

litquake.org

New York
SEPTEMBER 11

litcrawl.org

"Hipsters, word nerds and wordsmiths crawl out from behind their books and computers to mingle" -- San Francisco Chronicle

Litquake
San Francisco's Literary Festival

MORE INFO
www.litquake.org

SUBSCRIBE NOW
RECEIVE FOUR ISSUES A YEAR
SAVE $22

USA
$45.99

Canada
$57.99

Latin America
$65.99

GRANTA

MANGHO PIR

Fatima Bhutto

I was seven years old the first time I visited a Sheedi neighbourhood in Karachi. I had accompanied my grandmother on a campaign tour, visiting homes and receiving applications from men who needed legal aid to fight cases in the perpetually clogged city courts, from others who had lost their jobs and had no way of feeding their families, and from widows seeking stipends from the state. I felt nervous at the sight of crowds, preferred my car rides free of screaming men chanting slogans and wanted desperately to sit at home and talk without the noise of loudspeakers, megaphones and microphones. My grandmother, Joonam – 'my life', as I called her in her native Farsi – had been thrust into party politics after the assassination of her husband, my grandfather, Zulfikar Ali Bhutto, and had been jailed, beaten and elected to congress before I lost my first tooth. I adored Joonam and relished time spent with her, even if it meant engaging in campaigning.

Karachi was, in my imagination at least, a bustling metropolis. Palm trees lined the city's wide avenues, children thronged Clifton Beach, buying roasted corn smeared with lime and chilli from street vendors and sidling up to the men who sold camel rides for a couple of rupees. But there were millions who would never benefit from its occasional munificence, even though there should have been plenty to spare. There were no Sheedi on Clifton Beach, smack in the middle of the affluent old Clifton neighbourhood where my family lived. There were no Sheedi in the new electronics stores, buying CD players or shiny fabric from the city's up-and-coming designers. And yet, although they lived in the shadows, they refused to go unnoticed. The poverty and political dispossession could not hem them in. That first visit with Joonam was a jolt to my mental shaping of a city that I had, until then, only seen on its best and most welcoming behaviour.

Karachi, like all port cities, is a hub for travellers, traders and settlers. It is a sweltering mix of those who have been brave enough to settle on its shores – Parsis, Jews, Baha'is, Pushtun,

Afghans and so many more. The city has no majority; but even in this outrageous muddle of people and shades and colours, the Sheedi are unusual – an ethnic minority displaced among the swell of Karachi's various populations. While the most successful of the Sheedi – and there are not many who escape the deprivations of their community – enjoy a reputation that spans the world of arts, politics and athletics, they are best known for the northern Karachi shrine they protect and serve. A shrine built upon centuries of myth and modern-day fables that proclaim living breathing avatars of their lost saint and inspire spiritual searching. But no visit to this holy site of pilgrimage can ignore the impoverished environment of the surroundings. The glorious, the divine, and then the rot.

Mangho Pir, home of the Sheedi shrine, and its environs are covered in white mist. Men walk across haphazardly constructed pedestrian paths in rubber slippers and frayed shalwar kameez, coated in the white talc, dark hair lightened and skin powdered. This is a quarry town – dust escaping from the mines announces that you have arrived at the largest marble market in the region.

The gritty stone comes from across Sindh Province: from Thar, Sehwan, Jamshoro and Dadu, from Balochistan and, for some reason, perhaps owing to the desolate nature of this conveniently forgotten town, ends up in Mangho Pir. The marble slabs are lined neatly in towers with jagged shards that look sharp enough to cut through skin. Onyx is sold here too but marble is what makes a man's business in Mangho Pir.

The keepers of the shrine are ethnically African Pakistanis whose ancestors settled on the Balochistan coast and the Sindhi shores around 628 CE. One narrative identifies them as the descendants of opulent traders. They arrived, the story goes, through Bharuch, a seaport in Indian Gujarat fabled for its spice and silk trade, a crossroads through which traders from the Levant, Ethiopians seeking westward winds, Greeks, Persians, Carthaginians and Romans all passed. Alternative histories identify them as the progeny of brave warriors, descendants of soldiers who came a hundred years later (in approximately 712 CE), combatants loyal to Muhammad bin Qasim's conquering army that landed on the banks of the Indus, at Bhambore in Sindh, when bin Qasim was only seventeen years old, bringing Islam to the Hindu and Buddhist subcontinent. Bin Qasim's soldiers were known as *Habshi* (Abyssinian) or *Zinji*, 'Negro' in the warrior's native tongue. Still another story points to a forced migration of Bantu-speaking peoples (largely Swahili, a language still heard in Sheedi poetry and folk songs) of East Africa. They were transported to the still flourishing seaport of Bharuch in the seventeenth century by Portuguese slave traders who thought their human booty suitable gifts, to be offered in exchange for protection, as baksheesh if you will, for the Nawab of Junagadh. Those who were not presented to the local ruler were said to have been sold at the port. There are grounds, perhaps, for all three legends to be true. Linguistic, mercantile and political trajectories can be traced in support of all three narratives – soldier, trader or slave.

Maulabux is a Sheedi political activist whose maternal grandfather came to Karachi when the British were transforming the city into a mega seaport at the time of the Bombay Presidency. Although my parents, and indeed my grandmother, knew him from his work as a dedicated political activist, I remember meeting Maulabux at a funeral; I was eleven years old, maybe twelve. A Sheedi man, another grass-roots worker, had been killed by the Karachi police. He had been tortured and held without charge in police custody. He left behind two small children and a shy, young wife. The mourners screamed angry curses at the government that had killed one of their best organizers, the women wept and hurled their tattered plastic slippers at the police vans perennially parked in the area, the men sat huddled together over a table and worked on a statement condemning the murder and drew up plans for a shutdown of local businesses in protest. Maulabux was one of those men. I remember him, calm but shattered, working quietly that day to ease the grief of the man's family and planning the community's response.

Maulabux is from Lyari, one of Karachi's oldest Sheedi settlements. He is a tall man, his hair clipped close to his scalp and his face clean-shaven. Although I have never seen him chew paan, his stained teeth betray its use – his smile a reminder that for all his serious political background (and his background is serious) he is a raconteur. Maulabux isn't sure which line about his people's antecedents he buys, but he tells me stories passed down to him by his father and grandfather. 'They brought us over as slaves,' he says over tea one afternoon in a Karachi garden. 'They put us in ships and forced us to row to our new prisons – like in the movie *Amistad*. Have you seen *Amistad*?' I nod, more perplexed by the fact that Maulabux watches Spielberg films than anything else.

I ask him about bin Qasim's army, and he wagers that there were indeed African troops but that they can't possibly account for the large population of Sheedi in Pakistan today. He doesn't call himself Sheedi, he doesn't use the term the way I do – to refer to an ethnic group. He says *blackion* instead, adding the Urdu suffix *-ion* denoting the plural to black, a Minglish – Urdu/mixed English – construction. 'There are *blackion* in the Rann of Kutch in India, in Iran, Bahrain, Oman and in the Gulf.' Maulabux acknowledges that the *blackion* didn't face the same sort of discrimination in places like Oman, where they 'practise the European style of accepting different races', so tolerant and accepting are the Omanis of anyone who is willing to come and build their sultanate by the sea. The Sheedi Maulabux knew who had settled there were all 'highly educated, visible in government posts like immigration offices and customs'; they were not shamed into hiding like the *blackion* in our country.

I say, 'There are Sheedis in the Punjab too, aren't there?' We are playing hide-and-seek with geography and migration, and I feel I must have trumped him now. Maulabux smiles, points to his curly hair and thrusts his fingers at me. 'They are not the original *blackion*.' Case closed, he leans back and gingerly sips his tea.

Sakhi Sultan Mangho Pir Rehmat Ullah Alaih, whose birth name was either Hasan or Kamaluddin, was an Arab descendant of Hazrat Ali, the Prophet Muhammad's son-in-law and progenitor of the Shiite line of Islam. It was during his long pilgrimage at the site of Mangho Pir that Hasan or Kamaluddin became elevated to sainthood, proclaimed enlightened by the respected teachers who oversaw his spiritual journey and the devoted followers who believed in the power of the would-be saint's prayers spoken straight to God. The stories of Hasan or Kamaluddin's sainthood are filled with the fantastic. After his death, according to the best legend, the lice living in his long dreadlocks fell to the ground and were reborn as crocodiles.

For as long as the shrine of Mangho Pir has been part of Karachi's Sufi culture, it has been tended to by Sheedis. Today the shrine is teeming with devotees and guardians alike. The majority of the faithful are Sheedi – in fact, I am the only non-Sheedi on the day I visit – men, women, teenagers, children. While pockets of Pakistan fall to Islamists, filling the vacuum created by decades' worth of corrupt government, and the country becomes a state synonymous with fundamentalism, there are millions who would shake their heads and say that there is another Pakistan, that the one spoken of in BBC headlines isn't the Pakistan they know at all, that the one they know is tolerant and diverse and always has been. The shrine of Mangho Pir is proof of that alternate, retiring society.

I am met at the shrine by Haji Ghulam Akbar, who lives in the adjoining Sheedi Goth ('town'). A former campaigner and political activist who successfully stood for local office in the late 1970s, Akbar has a thin moustache dyed mandarin orange with henna and eyes lined with *kajal*. Everyone we encounter seems to defer to him, though he takes little notice as he hurries along. The site is packed with people; women gather in front of an old man selling salt in a steel bowl outside the shrine's doors, a *shifa*, or treatment, that they hope will cure them of all sorts of diseases – depression, rheumatism, kidney stones, skin ailments, all are dashed by either ingesting a good amount of the water from the hot springs here or bathing in it. The faithful also come to the shrine to seek blessings from the crocodiles, avatars of the saint that have made their home here for centuries. Many families will spend three days, sleeping on the cool marble floors, purchasing salts, incense, gifts for the saint to enhance the effectiveness of their treatments.

The short distance from Mangho Pir to Sheedi Goth is unpaved; the ground beneath not made to withstand traffic. If the shrine is blessed with spirits imbued with the powers of healing and access to the divine, it is an oasis enclosed within a much more earthbound reality. Half the town's inhabitants' homes are illegal. There are plain, unpainted brick houses, shaped like concrete boxes with no windows; there are homes made out of tents that gypsy Sheedi sleep in when the annual *urs* (festival) rolls around; filthy swathes of cloth haphazardly sewn together to provide the bare minimum of what would loosely be considered shelter for the local homeless. Everything standing seems to be made of mud, of dust and dirt and stones. There are no pavements, no *chaikhanas* (tea houses), no playgrounds. The children are barefoot. There are a hundred to a hundred and fifty homes here, and a population of five hundred souls.

'You know, in these non-registered homes are some of our best footballers, cyclists and boxers. Though our name hasn't come forward in cricket yet . . .' Akbar says, his head bent and eyes fixed on the ground – the usual pride that accompanies the fact that the Sheedi are among the nation's most gifted athletes seems curiously missing, reserved for giants such as Syed Hussain Shah, who won a bronze in boxing at the 1986 Olympics, Mehar Ali Shah, a boxer who represented Pakistan at the Asian Games, Aziz Baloch, who plays football on the national team. 'But we live in an invisible community. There are no options open to us – only sports, and that only because we break through; they cannot stop us. And this *urs*.'

The residents of the goth are the curators of the festival that marks the death of the saint through a celebration of his life – very unlike the usual manner of marking deaths in Pakistan, where songs and drumming are not encouraged. The *urs* will happen any time between May, June and July, lasting for four or ten days – however many the residents can afford. The crocodiles will be showered with rose petals and offerings, Sheedi Goth's residents will beat the drums strung up on maypoles across their run-down town and sing and dance in troupes traditionally led by women. The *urs* is held at a different time each year and newspapers, both local and foreign, only publish news of it, along with photographs of the revellers and crocodiles, once it is over and done with. This year, the UK *Daily Mail* ran a photograph of a man and his infant son, brought to be blessed at the shrine and standing precipitously close to the famous reptiles, with the caption 'Make It Snappy, Dad!'

The government gives the custodians of the shrine 3,000 rupees (£40) a year for the *urs*, a pittance considering how much is extracted in monthly hot-spring rent. It is an amount designed to placate the powerful bloc of Baloch and Sindhi voters across the city. 'We can't even buy one goat for that amount,' Akbar tells me. 'There are many other groups, religious or community or *jo bhi* [whatever], who get lakhs' and lakhs' worth of financial support. We only get pity.'

This is a community set in a wasteland. The nearest school is a town away and does not teach in the languages – Sindhi and Balochi – spoken by the majority of Sheedi. There is no transport to ferry the children to the school, no buses or cars to return them home. Without an education, this generation of Sheedi is stuck. There is a hospital but it has no ambulances. As I walk with Akbar, the locals gather to talk to me and soon it seems we are moving in a procession. Women grab at my sleeve; they speak over each other and interrupt my questions with answers they know by heart. They see me as a messenger who will tell their troubles to someone I happen to be related to; they don't particularly care so long as the word gets out. They are thinking, I know, of my grandfather Zulfikar. He was killed in 1979, but ghosts live long in Pakistan.

As we walk through the narrow alleyways, we are hurried towards an empty plot. Farida's house has just burned to the ground; she stands in front of debris that looks like much of the disorder one sees everywhere in Sheedi Goth. 'I was at work,' she says, clutching her dupatta in a closed fist. She is a young woman, but looks worn. Along with much of Sheedi Goth's working population, she works miles away from home, travelling two hours each way, when the traffic cooperates, longer when there are transport strikes or VIPs clogging up the roads. 'My children were alone – there is no one to look after them – and they are very young so they cannot tell us how the fire started.' I ask if it could have been a gas leak. 'I had no gas connection,' Farida replies, stone-faced. She has the clothes on her back, her dupatta, creased from her clenched hands and dirty from days of wear. Farida is living with neighbours who have taken her family in. Mercifully, her small children were unhurt by the blaze. 'Who was there to call? There is no fire department here. No one from the city government to come and help me build a new house. No one.' Farida continues to stand in front of the charred remains of her home; several minutes pass like this in silence.

I had come to talk about the long-ago journey that brought the ancestors of the Sheedi from their home to this place. I wanted to ask about the famous *urs*, where women sing in a language that is part Swahili and part Balochi, and about the *dhammal* and its relation to traditional East African *ngoma* drum music, which is awfully similar, but I can't. My quest for Sheedi lore and legend remains unspoken as the residents gather to tell me a different sort of story, the kind that won't eventually end up on the front of a foreign newspaper with a heart-warming photo and amusing caption to go along with it.

At the shrine, our prayers offered and received, Akbar and I walk down the small hill towards the crocodiles. Along the short distance to the pool there are small, simple, whitewashed graves marking the terrain – the final resting places of Muhammad bin Qasim's followers. We walk silently between the graves and Akbar breaks our awkward solemnity by telling me that there are 'two hundred crocodiles here, *takreeban*'. Approximately.

The crocodiles are mostly middle-aged, the elders somewhere between forty to sixty years old. 'They live here like a family,' says Akbar. The head of the family – they are Pakistani crocodiles after all – is named 'Mor' and he is the reason people come to offer bags of bloody meat to the creatures. He is the head avatar, the alpha incarnate. 'What happens when Mor dies?' I ask, not sure how far the lifespan of a Sufi crocodile goes. Haji Akbar shrugs. 'When one Mor dies, another takes his place and becomes the new Mor.' I don't dare ask how the process of dynastic crocodile succession is carried out.

The less brave (or less faithful?) can climb some well-placed rocks and peek from a safe distance, but those who mean business walk through a small corrugated-iron gate and into the crocodiles' lair. I count fourteen of them. Mor, his thick scaly neck garlanded with roses, sits in the shade of a gazebo built for his comfort. He barely moves to acknowledge our arrival and Akbar tells me he's a very calm beast, *takreeban* in his fifties although he looks younger.

'There are no facilities for our devotees,' Akbar complains, pointing around him. 'The Sheedi come from across Sindh and Balochistan in the thousands during our *urs*, but there is no help given to us by the government. We arrange everything ourselves, even though during the *urs* we have a *dhammal* and traditions so unique that the world media comes to film and photograph us, we have no assistance. We provide the water, the food, the lodging, everything.' It is hard not to remark on the fact that I am the only non-Sheedi at the shrine that afternoon, difficult not to leap to conclusions as to why the state has no interest in funding and supporting Mangho Pir's shrine.

For eight hundred years, *chashmas* (hot sulphur springs) have run underground filling the pools at Mangho Pir's shrine. This is the one part of the holy site that is frequented by Sheedi and non-Sheedi alike. Men and women line up with old gasoline canisters that will carry the magical waters of the spring back home with them.

But first they fill up with the water and retreat into small stalls to shower privately and pray for whatever cure they seek. The water, Akbar whispers, cures *kharish* – skin diseases ranging from scabies to eczema – purifies your kidneys if you drink it, softens your skin and inspires full body rehabilitation if you are regular in your visits.

The most famous spring, the Mamma Baths, is bedecked in light blue porcelain tiles and, save for the large pool of scalding water in the middle of the room, resembles a Middle Eastern hammam. The area is administered by an aged Sheedi woman named Fatima who stands outside the doors of the Baths collecting the fees – eight rupees, or ten pence, for fifteen minutes. Ladies have their time, then filter out so that the men may come in and have theirs, and on it goes. Fatima is a round old lady, pear-shaped, and she moves cumbersomely, shifting her weight on to each foot as if she must tread carefully to avoid veering off in the wrong direction. I ask where her family came from, if they travelled in the footsteps of the saint. 'From here,' she answers, stomping the ground. 'Before?' I ask, trying to place Fatima within a migration of warriors or slaves. '*Before?*' She looks at me as if I make no sense whatsoever. 'Sindh. Always Sindh,' she says, stomping her foot again emphatically.

The water in the Mamma Baths, swirling around in a porcelain mini-pool, is *takreeban* 100°F. Abdul Malik Rind, whose local expertise and range of influence covers the Mamma Baths, has appeared between the two Fatimas, the Baths' bouncer and me, and beckons me towards the large bath in the middle of the room; I slip out of my sandals and walk towards the water. He takes a plastic flask and fills it with water and asks me to hold out my hands. I do so, and hot water is poured over me. I stifle a yelp but notice that in fact my hands do feel instantly softer and smoother. Feeling braver, I step closer to inspect the pool and slip, almost plunging head first into the frightening hot waters. Fatima catches me by the elbow, pats me on the back and snickers. She's been on duty here for the last forty years and – desperate to move on from my near gaffe – I ask her what those years have been like. She tells me that they've never run out of *chashma* water here, nor out of visitors.

Here, Rind jumps in to the conversation and adds that people from all over the world have come to the shrine to be healed and blessed by its spiritual powers. 'What kind of people?' I ask. 'Oh, American women come with boils on their chests,' he answers, puffing out his own chest with pride. 'They come here to be cured and after a few days of visiting the Mamma Baths then they are fully fine. No boils, no marks, nothing.' Rind wipes his hands together, illustrating the impressive healing potential of the springs. 'They are Republicans,' he adds, throwing in a worldly smile.

It is five thirty in the evening and the doors of the Sindh Government Hospital in Sheedi Goth are padlocked. A young man who asks not to be named, wearing a black-and-white keffiyeh around his neck, has accompanied me here. He runs his finger along the lock and it is soon caked in dust. The lock hasn't been opened in a while. There are other gates and windows, all sealed.

Behind the hospital are bungalows built for absent doctors. Khadim, a gatekeeper who has worked here for the last twenty years, tells me as we walk to his quarters behind the neat bungalows that the local doctors and persistently abbreviated bureaucratic medical support staff – EDOs, MLOs, MOs (executive district officers, medical legal officers, medical officers) – all eat the hospital's budget. There's nothing left for the actual facility or its patients. The bungalows were built from funds meant for the upkeep of the hospital, the refurbishment merely an ornamental indication that the facility was an up-and-running operation, and that's it, nothing has been spent on medical equipment, lodging for the ill or medicines. My guide tells me that the police officers next door have a small-time drug-running business here, hence the padlocked doors. They sell *chars* – heroin-laced marijuana – to supplement their meagre salaries.

Khadim, who has eight children, takes me to his home. He has a nine-year-old daughter with one blind eye, her socket pinched shut. His eldest daughter, Naheed, who is my age, has polio and lies on a mattress on the floor. She tells me she's just recently had an operation. So the hospital does work? No, Naheed corrects me, she went to Jinnah Hospital in central Karachi.

This is the rot. The oppressive poverty that is the story of the Sheedis in Pakistan, more a part of their lore than the exploits of bin Qasim's warriors, clearer than their confused Ethiopian-Tanzanian-Kenyan-Zanzibarian heritage, and just as easily ignored as they are.

I have made arrangements to visit another Sheedi neighbourhood where in a week's time there will be a *mela*, a festival celebrating their distinct culture. This will be strictly a community affair, not open to outsiders. The men, from Akbar to all the young boys I meet at Sheedi Goth, insist I also visit their boxing grounds, where the greatest train for matches held at midnight in hidden porticos around Karachi. I make arrangements to visit them later in the week. As I drive out of Mangho Pir, my car is stopped by a spontaneous riot. Sheedi and the Pathans living in townships near the shrine, in a rare show of solidarity, have set fire to tyres and closed the roads out of the area in protest over the lack of water in the neighbourhood. Traffic is at a standstill. Men on motorcycles, some sitting three to a vehicle, pull their shirts up to cover their noses and mouths. I notice them first, before I see the smoke. I see them bracing themselves for the obligatory burning that comes with any protest riot. There are no TV cameras here, no press vans or state officials in their standard heavy motorcades, there is no one to witness the riot who can do anything about it. This is a demonstration of anger, grief and frustration, pure and simple.

Three days after my trip to Mangho Pir, I meet Maulabux in a garden and he brings three friends. One of them, Habib, is in his early to mid-twenties; he is soft-spoken and polite. A police officer serving in Lyari, where he and his family have always lived, he is at pains to explain the recent violence and police incursions in his neighbourhood – an area known for its radical politics, secular history and multi-ethnic population. Life is always interrupted –

festival dates, school exams, Mondays, Tuesdays, Wednesdays – by this sort of warfare. State v. community, Sindhi v. Baloch, Sheedi v. everyone else.

'There are very few Sheedi in the police force,' Habib says when I ask if he feels safe in his posting. 'People don't like to be confronted by us in positions of authority. Where did they come from? Who are they? They don't see us as being part of their communities.' In 2009, Habib was part of a police team that arrested a member of the powerful Muttahida Quami Movement (MQM), a quasi-ethno-fascist political party known for its militant tactics, catering to the *muhajir*, Urdu speakers who migrated from India during partition. 'They gave a press conference against me afterwards,' Habib says. Only he was mentioned in the MQM's media attack – not other members of the squad who carried out the arrest. 'I'm a local, I'm not corrupt, I know the people I serve,' he says. 'Maybe that's what made me threatening.'

Maulabux's two other friends are Ghulam Hussain, a heavy-set professor, and Sabir, a banker turned sociologist. Professor Hussain is the eldest of the four men; he wears a crisply starched shalwar kameez and carries a set of pens in his breast pocket. 'One fellow in our community, his son – born in 1986 – had an FIR [police First Information Report] cut against him for dacoit activities when he was three years old. In 1989.'

'Let me tell you a story,' Maulabux begins. 'A friend studying at Karachi University was asked by some classmates how on earth he had made it into the university, coming as he did from Lyari and being a *blackie*. And he replied, "First I got off my slave ship, then I got on a camel, then I came to the big city . . ." and they believed him! It's like people who stop us on the roads in Lyari and ask how to get to Lyari. "You're here," I tell them and they don't believe me because we're standing on wide roads, people are out shopping, there are grocers selling fruit on the streets. They expect only horror from us.'

Maulabux is a born storyteller; he laughs and jokes his way through the most disturbing tales, even when he speaks of racism and a policy of exclusion that confines us to a private garden on a day when we ought to be on the streets enjoying a festival.

'People see us, black with *ghungaroo baal*, curly corkscrew hair, and they hear we are from places like Lyari or Mangho Pir – out of eighteen districts in this city we are only in four! It's not like we've overrun the place – and they feel like a *zulm*, an injury, has been done to them, like they're insulted by us.'

One of the Prophet Muhammad's earliest companions was a freed slave named Bilal, afforded the respectful honorific *Hazrat* on his death. Professor Hussain sees this religious heritage as a duty upon Muslims to ignore caste, creed and race. 'In front of Allah,' he intones, 'we all say the same *kalma*, the same prayers – there's no difference between dark or light, rich or poor.'

'There is no room for us to progress,' Maulabux continues, changing tack. 'Maybe we get postings here and there, but that's just for show. Where is the way up? People say, "Oh, these *kalas*, they're everywhere in sports – in boxing, in football." Yes, we are! *Lekin, jidd-o-jehad hai*. But it's a struggle. Pakistan has only ever won one gold medal in anything' – at this everyone laughs; knowing nothing of our sporting history, I'm impressed we have any medals at all – 'in boxing. And it was a Sheedi who won it. But people still pretend we don't exist. Watch people's eyes when they think you're an African foreigner in their country. Their eyes widen. You can see the yellows, the pinks and the white corners of their eyes.'

Habib interjects, 'You know, in Sheedi communities you see the young idolizing Muhammad Ali, the Brazilian football team, the West Indies cricket team. These are our role models.' 'Bob Marley too,' adds Maulabux nodding seriously. 'Oh, and we were very, very upset when Michael Jackson died.' Professor Hussain solemnly bows his head as he remembers the king of pop, a reference that is pointedly ignored by the others.

They tell me that the only time there was hope among the Sheedi was in the 1970s. Lyari, the largest of the four Sheedi districts, was spruced up. Hospitals, schools, sports stadiums were built and scholarships encouraged. 'All our local heroes made their names then,' Maulabux says. 'Abbass, a famous traditional dancer, Asghar Baloch, a sports champ, the poet Noon Meem Danish [whose first name translates simply into the letters N and M], Malang Charlie and Zahoor Azad, two other great dancers. Azad didn't think he'd ever get out of Karachi and see Mirpur Khas, let alone the rest of the world. He was sent to the United States on cultural tours.'

But all that changed. In 1977, General Zia ul-Haq overthrew the democratically elected government and ruled for the next ten years with an authoritarian Islamist creed, one that didn't look kindly upon male dancers, or dancers of any sort. Karachi's Sheedi community was at the forefront of resistance to the dictator and paid for their protests and campaigns with jail sentences and public torture. Hundreds were arrested, Maulabux and his comrades included, for defying martial law regulations and censorship, and speaking and acting against the government, whether by supporting lawyers' movements, political rallies or student uprisings. Maulabux tells me how he and several other men put up posters of Nelson Mandela, at the height of South Africa's apartheid, in Karachi's central Regal *chowk*, or roundabout. 'People here were shocked that this man of colour was fighting the whites in South Africa, they had no idea it was possible. Imagine, forgetting so quickly the lessons of partition . . .'

What about Obama? I ask Maulabux. Will his posters be put up on roundabouts? He looks sideways at me, a tug forming at the corner of his lips. 'That's politics. He's American, they're killing our people. White, black, it makes no difference in the White House.'

Habib, the police officer, isn't bothered about Obama or Mandela or about the state that consigns the Sheedi to the periphery, simultaneously fighting them through police violence and ignoring them by depriving them of a stake in their country. 'At the end of the day,' he says, 'we Sheedi are a community. If one person is in trouble, he has twenty people around him. That's what we are, what we do. We take care of each other.' ■

WHITE GIRLS

Sarfraz Manzoor

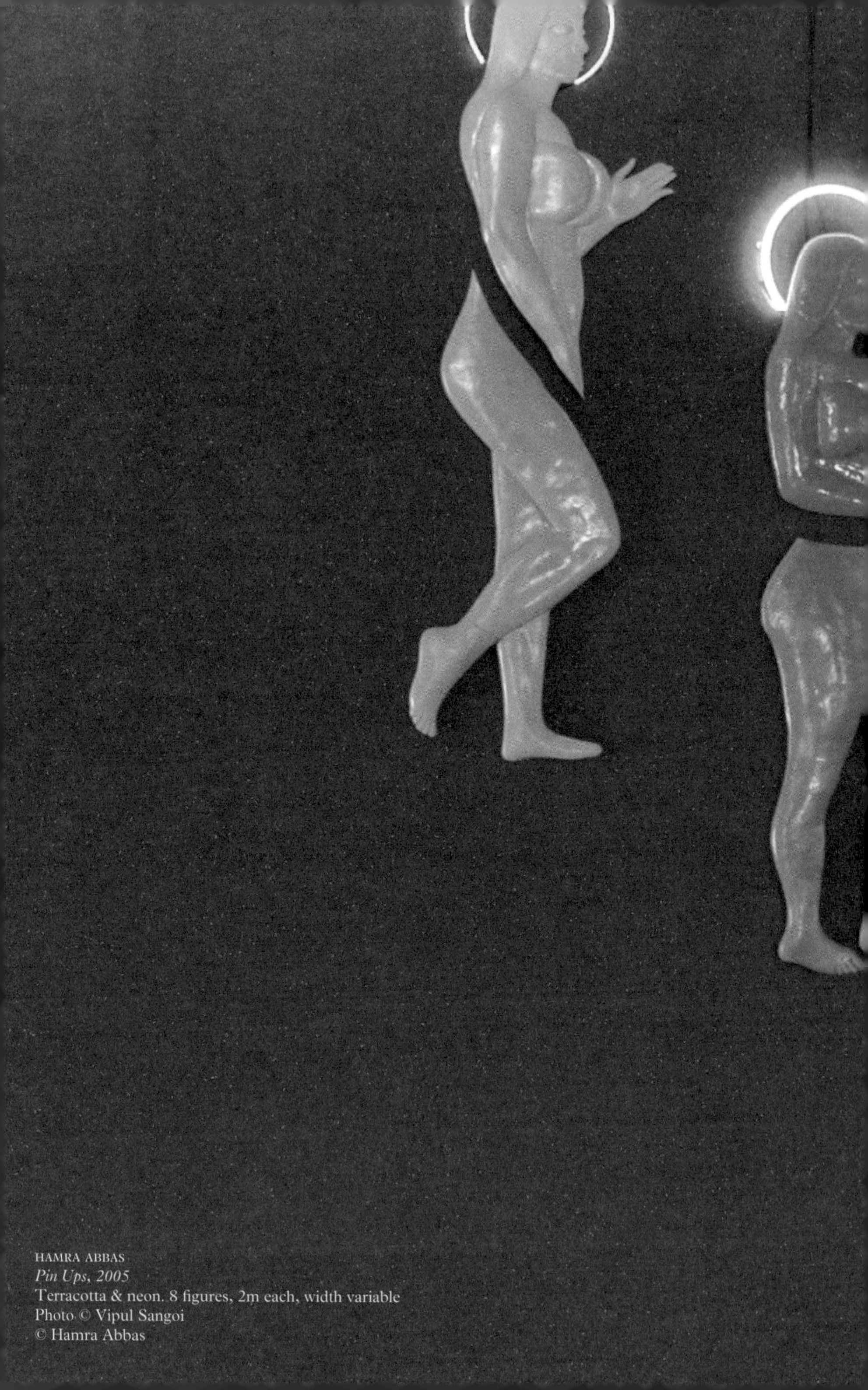

HAMRA ABBAS
Pin Ups, 2005
Terracotta & neon. 8 figures, 2m each, width variable
Photo © Vipul Sangoi

Her name was Bo and she was the first girl I ever loved. I was ten years old, a shy skinny brown boy with a mop of black curls, and Bo wasn't just out of my league – she had descended from another universe. Bo was tall and beautiful, with sparkling white teeth and golden hair that swung in braids when she ran. I loved her but knew she would never be mine. She did not live in Luton, for a start, she was somewhat older than me, she was married and – the highest hurdle – she was white. Even at the age of ten I knew that while I could possibly have persuaded her to leave her husband, swap Los Angeles for Luton and consider being with a younger man, I could not make Bo brown. The futility of my adoration did nothing to dampen my feelings. 'I love you, Bo,' I would whisper as I gently caressed her photograph. The boys at school all loved Bo too, but I was the only one who took the trouble to write to her. One afternoon I strode into my local library and pulled out an edition of *Who's Who* from which I located a Los Angeles address. That evening, while my family was downstairs watching television, I composed my first-ever love letter. 'Dear Bo,' I wrote, 'I am writing to you because we both have something in common: I am ten years old, and you were in a film called *10*.' There was no response. I was hurt at first, but I persuaded myself that it was for the best. We had always been doomed, Bo and I.

I was the son of working-class Pakistani parents, and they assumed I would have an arranged marriage with a fellow Pakistani Muslim. To them, white people were to be tolerated – but socializing was discouraged and forming relationships with white girls was unthinkable. I suspect my parents knew the scale of the challenge. Their favoured tactic to encourage me to stay away from the Caucasian menace was to relate stories, supposedly drawn from real life, which featured Pakistanis they had known who had drifted into relationships with white girls. The location of the stories could vary but the narrative was suspiciously similar in every tale. The story would begin with a gullible Pakistani boy who thought he knew better than his parents. This brazen lad would somehow be introduced to a white girl. In my parents' retelling of these stories, the girls never had names and they seemed more like villains in a Grimm fairy tale than recognizable human beings. This nameless white girl would lure the poor Pakistani boy with her base charms until the fellow was helplessly under her spell. She would then proceed to fall pregnant, or bleed him dry of his money, or introduce him to hard drugs. 'And do you know what happened after that?' my mother would ask, her voice trembling and her eyes widening at the horror she was set to reveal. I would shake my head nervously, suspecting that whatever she was about to relate was unlikely to involve a happy and successful marriage. Sure enough, my mother would explain how the foolish Pakistani son had ended up becoming a heroin addict, or had been forced to sell several of his internal organs to repay his girlfriend's debts, or had moved to Hitchin and become a taxi driver. These stories all finished with the same tragic coda. 'And, you know, his parents . . .' my mother would whisper darkly, her eyes reddening, '. . . they never speak about him – he is dead to them.' I was raised on these miserable parables and so learned early on the barely veiled moral: if you find a white girl, you will lose your parents.

The consequence of my parents' warnings was that I radiated extreme unease whenever I was around the white girls at my school, even as I was helplessly drawn towards them. The first was Julie. She wasn't in my class and I was too shy to talk to her, so I simply tried to be around her as much as possible. A bit player in someone else's romantic comedy. At home I would idle away hours in happy daydreams about Julie, but even then she was not my girlfriend; she would be my neighbour or my adopted sister. I imagined that Julie's parents would end up buying the house next door to us or that they would be tragically killed and that my father would somehow adopt Julie so that she would be my sort of sister.

I was already a teenager around this time and lurking in the distance, like a shark's fin slicing through the ocean's surface, was the threat of an arranged marriage. Both my older brother and sister had married in Pakistan and it was thought inevitable that I would be married off to a Pakistani girl, someone with whom I shared a common religion, ethnic origin and possibly some of the same family members. Before this day came my parents believed it was their responsibility to ensure I was safely protected from temptation. My father discharged this responsibility admirably by driving his family around in a sunflower-yellow Vauxhall Viva while encouraging me to retain the soft fuzz above my upper lip at a time when everyone else had started shaving. I remained single throughout my time at home.

I finally left home at the age of eighteen to study at Manchester University. In my first week I attended the Freshers' Fair, where I was given a welcome pack. I opened it later that afternoon when I was back in my room and inspected its contents. There was a guide to the various societies that were available to join, a handy map with all the university buildings and some other sheets of paper. I reached deeper into the pack to make sure I had not missed anything and found myself holding what looked like a soft lozenge. I looked closer and realized that it was not a sweet – it was a condom. I had heard of such things but never held one. It seemed an act of malicious cruelty to include the condoms – it turned out there were three – in the welcome pack. 'Dear God, please let me get a chance to use them,' I muttered as I unpeeled it and noted that it looked like a deflated balloon.

Sophie was one of the girls who lived in my residence hall. She had a face full of freckles and a mop of chestnut hair that fell in ringlets around her face. She also had a fearsome dope habit. Sophie was pale-skinned and she hid from direct sunlight by wearing long shapeless jumpers, obscuring her face behind fat clouds of cannabis smoke. She was only nineteen, but she seemed so much more experienced than I was; her bloodshot eyes and Charles Bukowski novels hinted at a world-weariness I found incredibly alluring. The most appealing thing about Sophie was that she didn't drink. I discovered this early in the first term when I was sitting in a pub with some other students, all of whom were guzzling lager. Sophie was drinking orange juice. 'How come you're not drinking?' I asked. 'It just doesn't agree with me,' she said. It was then that I knew she was the girl for me. 'It doesn't agree with me either,' I said with delight. Our shared disagreement with alcohol was, I hoped, a sign for Sophie that we had so much else in common.

During those first few months I spent many hours in Sophie's bedroom. She would be huddled under the blanket, an ethnic tapestry on the wall and the Velvet Underground on her cassette player. I would sit on the edge of the bed, staring at her through plumes of smoke, secretly wondering what sort of boy was allowed to get into bed with her. The answer to that question, I later found out, was a boy called Robert, who had multiple piercings, a bristle of a haircut and Sophie's dope habit. In evenings at the pub I would sit with Sophie and Robert, chatting away amiably, and then at the end of the evening I would return to my room and listen to my Tracy Chapman CD while Sophie and Robert retired to her room to have noisy sex. Robert wasn't the only boy I heard Sophie having sex with; as the weeks of that first term dragged on, other boys – some with smaller tattoos, some with more piercings – would wind their way back to Sophie's room and I would have to increase the volume on my CD player and hope that Tracy's plaintive voice would drown out the ecstatic cries from down the corridor. In the end, it wasn't Sophie's prodigious promiscuity that convinced me we did not have a future; it was the time I saw her splayed on the floor of the communal kitchen, passed out in a puddle of lager. My love for Sophie was, it turned out, as short-lived as her tryst with teetotalism.

Not drinking was disastrous for my love life because most sexual encounters seemed to demand that both parties were sufficiently inebriated to fall into bed with each other. While I was languishing in a two-decade-long dry spell, my friend Tariq was having much better luck. Tariq was tall, with long flowing hair and soulful brown eyes. He was a British Pakistani like me but he came from money – his father owned restaurants in Birmingham – and he treated Islam more as a buffet than a set menu. The only time he stopped drinking was for Ramadan. Tariq was an astonishingly successful ladies' man and his technique for sleeping with girls was ruthlessly simple: he pretended to care. It did not matter if it was apartheid, animal rights, student loans or Palestine; there wasn't a fashionable cause that Tariq did not lustily support. 'These white girls will fuck a Paki and tell themselves they're doing it for political reasons,' he would laugh. 'And if you throw in a mention of the Raj they'll do it on the first night.' Tariq recruited his girls carefully – he'd spend lunchtimes at tedious student union meetings, casting his languid gaze in search of the prettiest girl in the room, and he would then make it his business to win her attention by delivering an impassioned speech which invariably included a quote from Khalil Gibran or Gandhi. I would look at the rapt expressions on the faces of the white girls and I could practically hear their knickers sliding to their ankles. It was more than a decade after we had both left university when I ran into him again, in Birmingham outside a cricket ground amid a sea of Pakistan supporters. His hair was shorn and his face appeared heavier; his eyes had lost their old humour. He told me that despite all his university frolics there was no Verity or Lily in his life; my old friend had returned to Birmingham and married a Pakistani solicitor with whom he had three children. 'I had my fun, mate,' he told me. 'It was time to grow up.' He explained that he had been seeing a white girl for whom he had begun to develop something that threatened to turn into love, but he had been unwilling to go any further. 'Take my advice – have your fun with the white girls and then marry someone from back home,' he said to me. 'You know what you're getting from them.'

In the years since graduating I'd had a modest succession of relationships and at least some of the modesty was through choice. I avoided any white girl who had 'a thing for Asian men' as I might someone with a violently communicable disease. When friends tried to set me up with single Asian girls I would berate them. 'Stop trying to put me in a box,' I would say. 'Is my colour all you see about me?' They soon stopped suggesting any friends at all. With every girl I dated, I did so believing we shared something in common: there was the girl who liked the same music as I did, the girl who worked for the same employer, the girl who lived in the same part of London. In the end, every relationship died, in part because of how I was raised. Since leaving home at eighteen I had become, outwardly at least, a thoroughly integrated British Pakistani whose friends and work colleagues were overwhelmingly white. And yet when it came to love and marriage I could not discard the advice of parents who had raised me to believe that the only thing a man and woman need to have in common for marriage is a shared race and religion. I could dismiss it intellectually, but intuitively it made sense. How could I really be true to myself with someone who did not understand the maddening peculiarities that came with being a British Pakistani Muslim? I also did not want to end up with a white girl because I worried about the look of sadness on my mother's face when she realized that her new daughter-in-law would not be able to speak to her in Urdu. I fretted about the identity confusion inherent in having mixed-race children. There was another, even less well-thought-out, reason for why I ultimately knew I would not marry a white girl: I did not want to be a cliché. I loved nothing more than to luxuriate in moral superiority. I was not going to sell out my tribe. I was not some self-hating Asian who believed that validation had to have fair skin and blonde hair. There was something disgustingly needy, I felt, about all those bourgeois Asians who ended up marrying white women. That would not be happening to me – I was old school. I was also single.

Trying to find a British Pakistani woman with whom I had something in common was never going to be easy. My father had died from a heart attack three days before my twenty-fourth birthday and my mother was ill-qualified to find Miss Right. I would not have trusted her to pick out a sweater, much less a wife. Call it a sixth sense, but something told me that my mother was keen to see me married.

There were the tiny clues: the floods of tears and hysterical wailing that greeted me whenever I returned home; the refusal to leave the house because 'How can I explain why I have failed as a mother?'; the strange phone calls that came at all hours which my mother would answer by giving cryptic responses such as 'Thirty-five', 'He has a flat in London' and 'Yes, he still has his own hair'. These phone conversations led nowhere and, in the face of my mother's subtle suggestions, I began to delve into matrimonial websites.

The Internet was where many other single Asians were retreating in their search for someone with whom they had something in common. I clicked on one of the more popular sites, registered and uploaded a photograph. Once logged in, I began to trawl for a potential bride. In my everyday life I knew hardly any other Pakistanis, but online I was deluged with choices. Each entry was accompanied by a postage-stamp-sized photograph and a brief paragraph in which the woman invariably mentioned how hard it was to reduce her personality to a few sentences before revealing that, in fact, a few sentences were more than ample to describe her job in local government and her fondness for R&B. There were suggested ways to filter possible candidates on the basis of star sign, monthly salary, profession and even skin tone, but not being a superficial vulgarian with a fondness for astrology meant this was no help at all. The website, I concluded, was offering a twenty-first-century method of finding partners that my parents would approve. I began to fantasize about a website where, alongside members' photographs, one could upload photographs of book, music and film collections, where one could search for someone based on a shared love of eighties power ballads and late-period Philip Roth.

But, sadly, the websites did not offer such search functions. Instead they threw up interminable pages of women who all wanted to tell prospective partners that they enjoyed the same dreary list of interests – travelling, keep-fit and socializing – while reassuring them that they were as happy curled up with a good book. Everyone seemed to want someone who was ambitious, did not take himself too seriously and did not play games. I signed off from the website and began actively to try to meet other British Pakistanis. I accepted invitations to book events and parties in search of an eligible woman. By now most of my friends were married or in serious relationships; it felt like time was running out.

I went on a succession of dates.
One woman was an observant Muslim who was disgusted by my lax attitude towards fasting and prayer. Another was appalled by how traditional I was in not drinking. 'So let me get this right,' she said, circling the rim of her wine glass with her index finger. 'You've never tasted alcohol in your life?'

'That's right,' I told her. She looked at me like I was a living example of a species long believed extinct. 'So do you like old Indian films?' I asked, trying to change the subject.

'I did when I was young, but who watches that shit any more?' she said, lighting a cigarette, 'I mean, all the best cinema is coming out of Korea right now.'

She was a beautiful girl with a heart-shaped face and indecently full lips, but every time she opened her mouth she became less attractive. 'I don't have anything in common with you,' I remember thinking. 'All we share is a skin colour.' The things that connected me to my heritage – my mother tongue, eighties Indian films, Asian food, a working-class preoccupation with money – failed to find resonance in this girl or in any of the other Pakistani girls I met. I wanted to believe I had more in common with them than I did, perhaps because I wanted to believe I was more Pakistani than I was.

By this stage, my family was engulfed in a fog of gloom. 'Some people never get married,' my mother said, staring out of the window with a look of disappointment.

'I *want* to get married,' I told her. 'But it's not easy meeting the right girl, someone I have something in common with.' My failure to find anyone who was British Pakistani was leading me finally to countenance what had always been impossible. 'Maybe she doesn't need to be Pakistani,' I said to my mum, releasing the kite to see if it would catch the wind or be ripped to shreds.

'You're getting old,' she said. 'You don't have time to waste. You need to get on the last train before it leaves without you.'

It was a warm Sunday afternoon in the first weekend of June and the train was about to leave. I leapt out of the taxi and ran, the wheels of my rollercase rattling along the platform. The whistle screamed and I boarded the train as it slowly pulled out of Hereford station. I turned to find the nearest spare seat in the carriage and that was when I first noticed her. She had wild green eyes and golden-blonde hair and she was reading a copy of *Mary Barton*. I was returning to London from the Hay-on-Wye book festival and, from the fabric bag at her side, I knew she too had been at the festival. 'She is beautiful and she likes books,' I remember thinking. I stared intently at the front page of my newspaper and pretended to read it while all the time stealing glances at the girl and thinking, 'Who gets to be with someone as beautiful as you?' She was not just out of my league – she looked like she had descended from another universe.

In any other situation I never would have had the confidence to talk to her, but somehow that day I stumbled upon a hidden stash of courage. I still don't know where I found my voice that afternoon and, given the way it all turned out, I cannot help but speculate how tragically different my life would have been had I failed to strike up a conversation. That day the wind was behind me; something was saying to me that this was one of those times when the universe hands you a gift and all you need is the confidence to take it.

I looked at her again. I took a deep breath, forced my mouth into a smile and said, 'Hello.' She looked up from her book, smiled and said, 'Hello.' We started talking and I learned the following about her: that she lived in London; that she had a buttery smile that spread easily across her face; that she was learning Hindi, having spent time in India; that she was funny and smart and entertaining;

that she was single.

The train rumbled towards London and I knew that if I let this opportunity pass I would spend years wallowing in regrets. 'I'd like to see you again,' I said, with a boldness that surprised me. 'Here's my number, I won't take yours – that way it's up to you if we meet again.'

I told myself that I was not really dating her. Yes, we had met the following Saturday and, true, we had gone to see films and concerts and had meals in those first few weeks, but she could not be my girlfriend – because she was white and any relationship with a white girl was always going to be doomed. Except that when I was with her the fear of being a cliché evaporated in the heat of lived intimacy. 'Why do you preclude the possibility that I could make you happy?' she asked me one afternoon after I had spent some time bemoaning how much I hated being single. We were sitting in a park in east London, watching a band we both loved. 'We don't really do happy in my culture,' I told her. 'We try to find reasons to be miserable.' It was true, but it was not an answer. I had grown up being told that white girls only brought misery and so being with a white girl was unimaginable. Yet now I was with someone who was making me happier than I had ever been and the only thing unimaginable was not being with her.

And so we kept seeing each other and I became accustomed to the idea of her as my girlfriend. I was deliriously happy but that happiness came at a price: in traditional Pakistani families like mine, the power of love was eclipsed by the expectation of duty. I had always assumed that my wedding day would be the saddest day of my life because I could not envisage being able to marry someone I truly and completely loved. Now I had met the girl I wanted to spend the rest of my life with – the girl I would end up marrying – and after thirty years of living in fear I have finally decided to place my faith in love. ∎

THE TRIALS OF FAISAL SHAHZAD

Lorraine Adams
with Ayesha Nasir

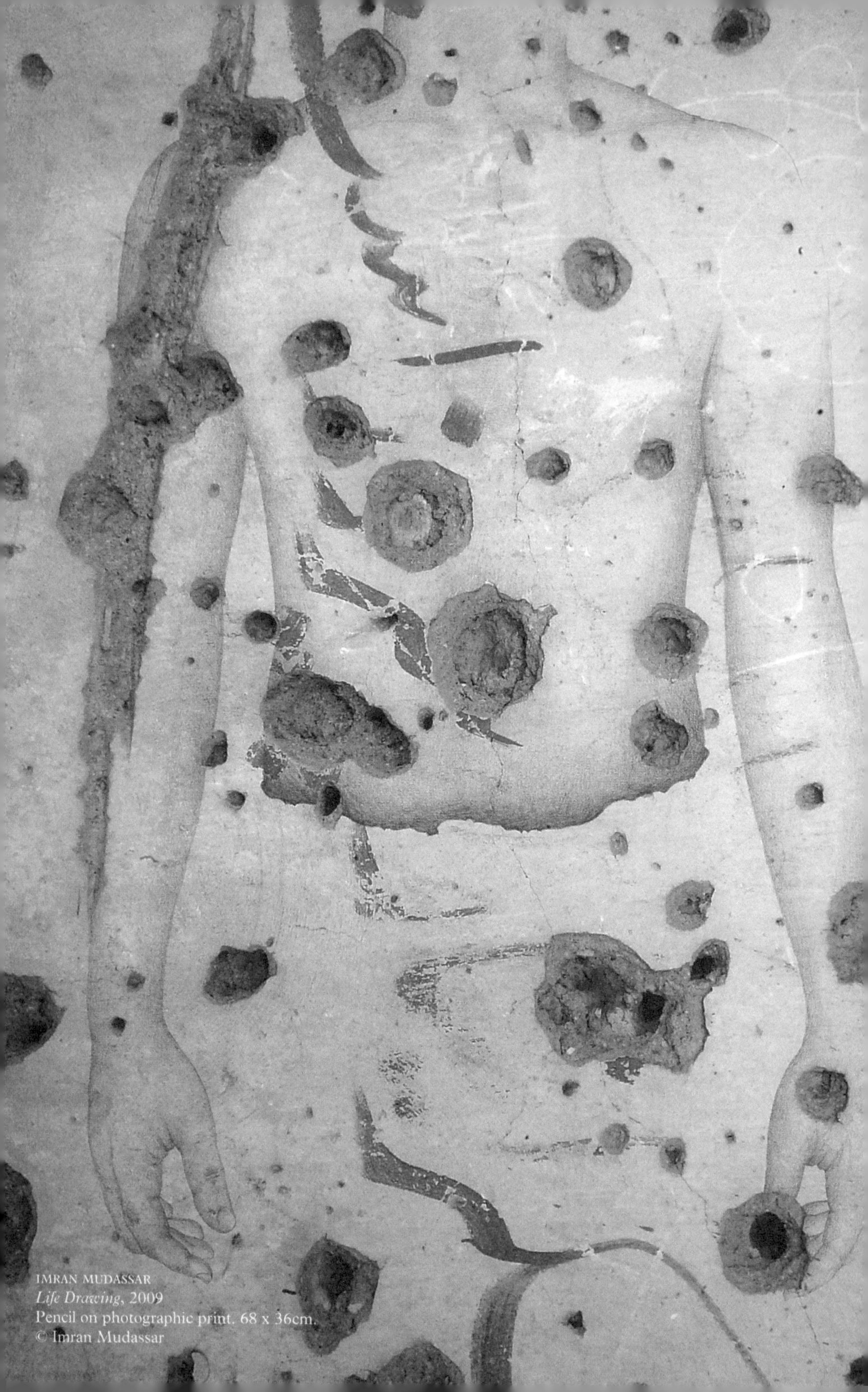

IMRAN MUDASSAR
Life Drawing, 2009
Pencil on photographic print. 68 x 36cm.

On 1 May 2010, Faisal Shahzad, a Pakistan-born naturalized American citizen residing in Bridgeport, Connecticut, drove an SUV loaded with explosive devices to the corner of 45th Street and Seventh Avenue in Times Square, New York. He began the detonation process, walked away, and took a train back to his apartment. The bomb failed to ignite. Police found him easily through the car's Vehicle Identification Number. He was arrested on 3 May 2010 on board an Emirates flight to Dubai that had pulled away from the gate but had not yet been cleared for take-off.

Bridgeport is a beaten-down city of 140,000, only a half-hour away from yacht-friendly Westport on the Manhattan-bound commuting coastline. An abandoned port hobbled by lower-than-average incomes and education, it seems an unlikely place to call home for Faisal Shahzad, the thirty-one-year-old, MBA-graduate son of an eminent Pakistani father. Shahzad rented a second-floor apartment (for $1,150 a month) in a three-storey tenement similar to others on the block. Recently renovated, his was the cleanest. Even so, its pale biscuit siding was gimcrack vinyl, its chalk-white trim a flimsy metal. The garage in the back, where he assembled the bomb inside his Nissan Pathfinder, was missing its door and guarded by a barking dog on a heavy chain.

This apartment was a month-long way station for Shahzad. He spent most of his ten years in America in Shelton, Connecticut, a slice of exurbia fifteen minutes north of Bridgeport. His house there is empty and strewn with discarded toys and two lawnmowers. A front window is smashed, another above the front door gone. He abandoned it exactly one summer ago. His income as an account analyst – a position which pays on average $50,000 a year and sometimes as much as $70,000 – wasn't enough to sustain making payments on the $218,400 mortgage. Shahzad's American career began in disappointment and mired in that house. With two degrees from the University of Bridgeport, a school so poorly rated by its peers that it doesn't even have a ranking in the *US News and World Report* college list, the best work he could find was a series of jobs as an account analyst, the last of which he quit last summer. By his own account, Shahzad was ditching Shelton to return to Pakistan with his family.

Shahzad's father, Baharul Haq, began life as the son of a servant in Mohib Banda, a poor village near Peshawar in Khyber Pakhtunkhwa, formerly called North West Frontier Province. He trained as an airman and rose to one of the highest posts in Pakistan's air force. In a country where who you know is far more important than what you know, Haq defeated phenomenal odds. Shahzad, one of four children, grew up on military bases in Peshawar, Sargodha and Karachi, studying at air force schools. His grades were average; he developed a weakness for fast cars and a taste for the Eurotrash look. 'He was a loafer, always wasting his father's money,' said Faiz Ahmed, a villager who knew the family. 'There were problems between him and his father – *Bahar sahab* was tight-fisted while Faisal was a spendthrift.'

Baharul Haq's economizing paid off. When he retired he moved into Hayatabad, a Peshawar neighbourhood of palatial villas staffed by guards, servants and chauffeurs, favoured by foreigners, military grandees and business notables. Shahzad's Shelton neighbours, by contrast – among them a dental technician, a computer consultant, a schoolteacher and a nurse – drive their own mid-range cars and mow their own lawns. 'He was here by himself at first,' his next-door neighbour, a Shelton native, told me. 'Then, he got married. It was an arranged marriage. She was very quiet. I talked to him more than her. We used to talk when he was mowing the lawn. She'd had a really good job. He told me they were getting the children phase over and then she was going back to work.

'He worked in Norwalk. It's about thirty-five minutes away, but it's a terrible commute, and he used to talk about that. Much worse than he expected. I could tell he wasn't happy . . .'

I asked about visitors.

'It was always her family. There was a sister who came from Massachusetts, and she was always in traditional dress. I don't know what you call it, but the kind of clothing you see in India.'

It was the house, the neighbour said, that increasingly preoccupied him. Records show that Shahzad had bought it in 2004 for $273,000. He tried to sell in 2006 for $329,000, in 2008 for $299,000, then dropped the price again. Trapped in the collapsing American housing market, he took out a second mortgage for $65,000 in January 2009.

I asked why they wanted to sell.

'He told me his parents were in Pakistan; he was the youngest child and it was the custom in their culture that it was up to him to go back and take care of the parents.'

What, I asked, is the most lasting image she has of him? The videotape capturing him buying fireworks? The mugshot after his arrest?

'I see him in the yard with her.'

His wife?

'The little girl. He was so good with her.'

Ajani Marwat is an officer in the New York Police Department's Intelligence Division, formerly Special Services, or the 'red squad'. After 9/11, Adam Cohen, a streetwise Boston native formerly of the CIA, came out of retirement to revamp the Division. Marwat is an unlikely Cohen acolyte. He has a sinking feeling that Jewish financiers control the world. He thinks the United States is being used by Israel to do its dirty work. But Marwat is also a man in possession of the highest level security clearance. He is fluent in seven languages and three of them – Urdu, Pashto and English – he shares with Faisal Shahzad. The other four – Hindi, Farsi, Dari and Tajiki – enable him to work with informants or witnesses from India, Iran and Afghanistan.

Today Marwat is sitting in my kitchen drinking tea and eating cherries. He does not want his birthplace or real name mentioned in this story; Intelligence Division officers are not allowed to talk to the media. What he will do is offer a window into what he thinks motivated Shahzad, and what his New York-born colleagues do not, and perhaps cannot, understand about the Shahzads they encounter. Marwat lost eight brothers and sisters to starvation, rocket strikes and bombings in his native country. One day when he was eleven, he had to go to the market to buy bread. At that time, any such excursion was a risk. His best friend went with him.

'There's a big noise. All I see is smoke. Then I can't hear anything. I look at my friend. He's running. But he has no head.'

The damage that United States aerial bombing causes in Pakistan is most heavily concentrated where ethnic Pashtun live. Shahzad's family was Pashtun, and he married one. The village of Shahzad's father is only a twenty-minute drive from one of the largest madrasas in Pakistan, the Dar-ul-uloom Haqqania, widely considered the incubator for the Taliban movement. But the village itself is in Nowshera, one of the most secular districts in Khyber Pakhtunkhwa, where the liberal Pakistan People's Party regularly wins elections. It is also not an area saturated in drone attacks. That distinction belongs to a belt of villages further south-west along the Afghanistan border.

In 2009, the year Shahzad abandoned his Shelton home and was living with his parents in their posh neighbourhood in Peshawar, approximately forty-seven drone attacks killed 411 people in Waziristan. Peshawar, however, suffered no drone attacks. The violence there is different. In the last year, Taliban suicide bombers have struck an average of three times a week, killing civilians in markets, mosques and police stations. As a military man, Shahzad's father's allegiance would be to the government, his sympathies with the victims of the suicide attacks in the city where he and his wife now live.

These intricacies are beyond esoteric for most NYPD police officers. Disrupting plots is more about interpretation than enforcement. But what if, as is so often the case, a man's history is not enough to fathom his future intentions? Marwat is a striking example. Like Shahzad, he too left for the West as a teenager. But Marwat didn't arrive the way Shahzad did – a proficient English speaker in designer sunglasses with a university scholarship. Marwat was a seventeen-year-old who slept in train stations. His life story, not Shahzad's, should have produced a militant.

Instead, Marwat's exposure to atrocity and poverty galvanized him. He laughs at what some might consider Shahzad's minor deprivations – a suburban house that wouldn't sell, a lousy commute. And he doesn't think they had much to do with Shahzad's radicalization.

'If I put myself in his shoes, it's simple. It's American policies in his country. That's it. Americans are so closed-minded. They have no idea what's going on in the rest of the world. And he did know. Every time you turn on Al Jazeera, they show our people being killed. A kid getting murdered. A woman being beaten. 24/7.'

'We don't have to do anything to attract them,' one terrorist organizer in Lahore explained to me. 'The Americans and the Pakistani government do our work for us. With the drone attacks targeting the innocents who live in Waziristan and the media broadcasting this news all the time, the sympathies of most of the nation are always with us,' he said. 'Then it's simply a case of converting these sentiments into action.'

Marwat's fellow counterterrorism colleagues on the force mean well but they don't always know what to look for. 'They're constantly looking to see if a guy goes to a mosque,' he says. 'I tell them, people who go to mosque, don't worry about them. People who go to mosque, they learn good things. People who don't go to mosque – you have to worry about them.

'A lot of times when cops are interviewing people, they think everyone's a terrorist. I have to tell them, actually, the way this guy's talking, it's nothing. Every Muslim in the world thinks what this guy thinks. This is the problem. If you train American-born guys, spend a lot of money teaching Arabic, the culture, the most they get, even after all that, is 30 per cent.'

Martin Stolar was one of four lead attorneys in *Handschu* v. *Special Services Division*, a landmark federal civil rights case filed on behalf of Barbara Handschu, a political activist and lawyer who represented the Black Panthers and other groups under surveillance in the 1960s. The 1985 decree that resulted prohibited unfettered police monitoring of religious or political groups. In 2002, when Adam Cohen was revamping the Intelligence Division, the police department sought a weakening of the Handschu decree from the original judge, paving the way for the surveillance of Muslims. They won it in 2003.

Today, I'm sitting across from Stolar in his grotty fourth-floor law office above lower Broadway between a carry-out called New Fancy Food and a store that sells 'Hats & Sun Glass'. He is smoking Merit cigarettes, still hippie skinny with a beard now silvery grey. He has agreed to talk to me about the only other convicted Pakistani bomb-plotter in New York City.

His client, Shahawar Matin Siraj, was found guilty by a federal jury of participating in a conspiracy to attack the Herald Square subway station in 2004, three days before the Republican National Convention was to begin at Madison Square Garden. Twenty-three at the time, Siraj was sentenced to thirty years in prison. Today he's in a federal prison in Terre Haute, Indiana.

Siraj's mother, Shaina Berbeen, who was a physician with her own clinic in Karachi, told me her family had left Pakistan for the US in 1999, the same year as Shahzad. They had fled persecution for being Ismailis, a branch of Shias sometimes referred to as Agakhanis. Berbeen and her daughter Saniya Siraj, now twenty-four, told me about severe physical punishment of Ismaili students, including Siraj, at the hands of Sunni teachers. Berbeen also shared with me a forensic psychological evaluation of her son, which placed his IQ at seventy-eight, 'the borderline of intellectual functioning . . . [a level]

surpassed by 93 per cent of the population'.

In 2002, Berbeen's husband became severely ill and Siraj was the family's sole support. He worked first at fast-food chain Blimpie, and then as a clerk in his uncle's store, Islamic Books and Tapes, next door to the Brooklyn mosque known as Masjid Musab Bin Omayer.

'Cohen,' Stolar tells me, 'instituted a programme directed at the Muslim community to develop confidential informants and undercover agents. By the time we get to Siraj in 2004, I don't think there's a mosque in New York City that doesn't have a CI or an undercover.'

Police sources tell me that foreign-born nationals are easy to turn into CIs – confidential informants. If a taxi driver gets into a tussle over a fare, gets reported and turns out to have immigration issues, the police can threaten him with deportation. 'You become a CI and you won't be deported.' It's a method the police have used for decades. Siraj had a CI assigned to him, an Egyptian nuclear engineer named Osama Eldawoody who had been drawn in because he had run a number of failed businesses out of his Queens apartment, prompting neighbours to call the police. The government paid Eldawoody's expenses, as well as $94,000 for his work as an informant on the case.

The undercover officer in Siraj's case was a native of Bangladesh who used the pseudonym Kamil Pasha. 'He's recruited in the classic NYPD way,' Stolar says. 'They troll the police academy to find someone who fits the targeted group. They started doing this with the Black Panther Party back in the sixties. So they get someone who's, number one, young, and number two, not known on the street. And they say, we promise you a gold shield, a detective's shield, if you do this.'

The cop and the CI had no knowledge of each other. July 2003 they began visiting the bookstore where Siraj was working. Eldawoody, fifty at the time, was old enough to be Siraj's father; Pasha, at twenty-three, was more of a buddy. In seventy-two visits with Siraj, he was able to cull what the jury considered 'radical statements', such as Siraj praising Osama bin Laden as 'a talented brother and a great planner'.

None of Pasha and Siraj's conversations were tape-recorded, and Eldawoody only began recording their encounters after he'd been meeting with Siraj for nine months. It's hard, therefore, to gauge what role the two men played in the conversation about the planned bomb attack.

In April 2004, the images of torture and abuse from Abu Ghraib prison in Baghdad surfaced in the media. When Siraj saw the image of the hooded Iraqi prisoner, attached to wires, standing on a box, he became hysterical. 'Turn it off, Mommy! Turn it off!' Siraj shrieked. Trial testimony showed that Eldawoody gave him photographs of a Muslim girl being raped by a dog. He is soon discussing the placement of the bomb with Siraj and his co-defendant, a twenty-one-year-old schizophrenic Egyptian who turned state's evidence in the case. Siraj, in this recording, says, 'No killing. Only economic problems.' He explains, 'If somebody dies, then the blame will come on me. Allah doesn't see those situations as accidents.' In earlier audio recordings, however, he has said, 'I want at least a thousand to two thousand to die in one day.'

At one point, under pressure from Eldawoody, the mildly retarded Siraj puts him off by saying, 'I'll have to check with my mother.' He never did. Berbeen said she never met either of the men who spent so much time with her son. But her daughter did. 'He was suspicious,' Siraj's sister said. 'First of all, nobody helps anyone in America. He's giving my brother rides all the time. It costs a lot of money to drive from Bay Ridge to Queens.

'One time Eldawoody told my dad, "Your son is a diamond. A hero." I think no one ever saw Matin that way. You know, it's like Batman. He wanted to be a superhero. Honestly, all my brother did in his spare time was video games. I think, on some level, he wanted to be in one of them.'

'This guy was a nebbish,' Stolar tells me. 'Look, I'm a defence attorney. I know how to make shit up and bend the facts, but this wasn't bending the facts. This was classic entrapment.'

On Monday, 21 June 2010, I was among the reporters filing into the courtroom of federal judge Miriam Goldman Cedarbaum in lower Manhattan. We'd come for Faisal Shahzad's arraignment after a federal grand jury had returned a ten-count terrorism indictment. We expected a five-minute perfunctory exchange; Shahzad would probably enter the typical 'not-guilty' plea.

Shahzad was cuffed and shackled, and Cedarbaum removed her reading glasses each time he answered a question so she could study his face. After the preliminaries, Cedarbaum began, 'I have to discuss some other things with you . . .'

'Sure.'

'. . . because I want to be sure that this plea is entirely voluntary and that you are entering it with full understanding of the consequences of entering a plea of guilty.'

He was going to plead guilty. The reporter next to me turned, his eyes opened wide. Meanwhile, Shahzad was interrupting.

'Before you do that . . .'

'Yes.'

'. . . can I say to you my plea of guilty? I just want to say a small statement.'

'I think you should wait.'

'OK.'

After several questions, Cedarbaum asked, 'Why do you want to plead guilty?'

'I want to plead guilty and I'm going to plead guilty a hundred times forward because until the hour the US pulls its forces from Iraq and Afghanistan and stops the drone strikes in Somalia and Yemen and in Pakistan and stops the occupation of Muslim lands, and stops killing the Muslims and stops reporting the Muslims to its government, we will be attacking the US, and I plead guilty to that.

'OK,' he went on, fumbling with some paper. 'With the assistance . . .'

'Oh, please,' the judge said. 'Don't read it. I want to know what happened. Tell me what you did.'

Shahzad tried again to read something because, he said, 'It covers all the elements.' But then he gave up and just started talking.

'Tehrik-e-Taliban Pakistan,' he said uncertainly. 'I . . . with them, I did the training to wage an attack inside United States of America.'

'I see. How to make a bomb or how to detonate a bomb? What were you taught?'

'The whole thing; how to make a bomb, how to detonate a bomb, how to put a fuse, how many different types of bombs you can make.'

Shahzad went through the previous year's timeline with her. He became a US citizen in May 2009, and then left on 2 June for Pakistan ('for good') with the intention of 'trying to figure out a way to get to the Taliban'. He stayed with his parents in their Peshawar house. Finally, on 9 December, he and two friends made contact with the Taliban in Waziristan where he stayed until 25 January 2010. His actual bomb-making training lasted only five days.

At times their conversation lapsed into a seminar, with Shahzad the tutor on Taliban politics.

'Is there a particular Taliban?' Cedarbaum asked at one point.

'Well, there are two Talibans; one is Taliban Afghanistan, the other is Taliban Pakistan. And I went to join the Taliban Pakistan.'

'I see. Has that always been there?'

'It recently . . . they . . . the organization was made . . . was made like six years ago when the first time Pakistan took a U-turn on the Taliban Afghanistan, and obviously the tribal area in Pakistan is the . . . was the harbouring for the mujahideen fighting in Afghanistan. So the Pakistan took a U-turn and they became allied with the US and they went against the Taliban and start fighting and killing them. So during that time, the Afghan Taliban made a group to counter the Pakistan government forces, and that's when Taliban Pakistan came into being. Six years ago, maybe.'

'Do the people you dealt with in the Taliban all speak English?' she asked him.

'No, they speak Pashto. Pashto is my mother language. I am Pashtun ethnically.'

'I see. And all the Taliban are Pashtun, all the Afghans are Pashtun?'

'Or most of them; not all of them. Majority. So I did speak with them in Pashto when I was communicating with them.'

'I see. Pashto is spoken in Pakistan?'

'Yes. Peshawar, the whole North West Frontier Province is all Pashto speaking, which was part of Afghanistan before the British broke it.'

The operation's financing was under $10,000. Shahzad supplied $4,500 of his own money, the Taliban added $4,900. 'When I came back on February 2nd, I started . . . started planning on the plan,' he explained. 'So I started looking for a place first to rent and slowly got together what I think could make a bomb . . . It took me from February up to end of April to do all that.

'The bomb was – it was in three sections that I made the bomb. The major was the fertilizer bomb. That was in the trunk. It was in a cabinet, a gun cabinet. The second was . . . if that plan of the actual, that didn't work, then the second would be the cylinder, the gas cylinders I had. And the third I had was a petrol, a gas to make fire in the car. But seems like none of those went off, and I don't know the reason why they didn't go off. And then . . .'

'When did you expect them to go off? How long did you think it would take?'

'Two and a half to five minutes. I was waiting to hear a sound but I couldn't hear any sound, so I thought it probably didn't go off, so I just . . . walked to the Grand Central and I went home.'

'You took the train to Bridgeport.'

'Yes.'

Cedarbaum, perhaps confused by the prosaic act of catching a suburban train after planting a lethal bomb, asked whether he did intend for the bombs to go off. Oh yes, Shahzad told her. And he chose Times Square on a Saturday night so he could maximize the mayhem? 'Yes. Damage to the building and to injure or kill people. But again, I would point out one thing in connection to the attack, that one has to understand where I'm coming from, because this is . . . I consider myself a mujahid, a Muslim soldier. The US and the Nato forces, along with forty, fifty countries has attacked the Muslim lands. We –'

Cedarbaum interrupted. 'But not the people who were walking in Times Square that night,' she said slowly. 'Did you look around to see who *they* were?'

'Well, the people select the government. We consider them all the same. The drones, when they hit –'

'Including the children?' the judge interrupted him once again.

There was a long pause.

'Well, the drone hits in Afghanistan and Iraq,' he finally said, 'they don't see children, they don't see anybody. They kill women, children, they kill everybody. It's a war, and in war, they kill people. They're killing all Muslims.'

'Now we're not talking about them; we're talking about you.'

'Well, I am part of that. I am part of the answer to the US terrorizing the Muslim nations and the Muslim people, and on behalf of that, I'm avenging the attacks because only . . . like and the Muslim people, and on behalf of that, I'm avenging the attacks because only . . . like living in US, the Americans only care about their people, but they don't care about the people elsewhere in the world when they die. Similarly, in Gaza Strip, somebody has to go and live with the family whose house is bulldozed by the Israeli bulldozer. There's a lot of aggression . . .'

'In Afghanistan?'

'In Gaza Strip.'

'I see.'

'We Muslims are one community. We're not divided.'

'Well, I don't want to get drawn into a discussion of the Quran.'

Shahzad's reasoning – shared by suicide bombers in Gaza, Sri Lanka and elsewhere – was that his act was a war tactic. Aerial bombing by states cannot avoid killing children. Hence, terror bombings by militants that kill children are a logical response.

The anti-terror police have a programme – so far successful – to prevent another 9/11, but it cannot address root causes – American foreign policy – and the chances that the mediocre son of a self-made military man will try to show his father what's what. Some attacks don't need the authorities to prevent them, however. Shahzad was as sub par a soldier as he was a financial analyst. In court, he told Judge Cedarbaum that he still didn't know why his triple redundant bomb failed to ignite sometime after six thirty on a Saturday night. 'The timer on the detonator, it was on military time,' a police source later told me. 'He set it for seven. That was 7 a.m. on this thing. For 7 p.m., what he wanted, it should have been 19.00.'

The New York Police Department declined to comment on the case of Shahawar Matin Siraj or the Times Square bomber and its counter-terrorism programme. ■

Naiza H. Khan

Rossi & Rossi Gallery – London
www.rossirossi.com

Naiza Khan, one of Pakistan's foremost artists, has exhibited internationally. Her work, examining society's views of women, has won various prizes. Recently she documented the changes to Manora, an island close to Karachi, exploring its poetry, history and spirit, as well as its decline.

'The Manora Project' represented by Rossi & Rossi.

Miniature Worlds Collide, 2010
Watercolour and graphite on paper 100 x 70 cm

Move: Choreographing You

Hayward Gallery – London
13 October 2010 – 9 January 2011
www.southbankcentre.co.uk/move

Use your mind and body to gain a new understanding of perception and movement. Become a participant – and in some cases a dancer – in installations and sculptures by internationally renowned visual artists and choreographers from the last fifty years. Featured artists include Mike Kelley, Isaac Julien, Robert Morris, Trisha Brown, Bruce Nauman and William Forsythe.

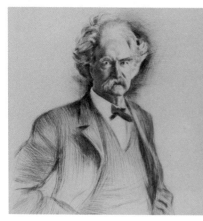

Mark Twain: A Skeptic's Progress

The Morgan Library & Museum – New York
17 September 2010, through 2 January 2011
www.themorgan.org

Samuel Langhorne Clemens – better known by his pen name, Mark Twain – was the quintessential American author, humourist, lecturer, essayist and master of satire. The Morgan and the New York Public Library are presenting this joint exhibition that includes more than 120 manuscripts and rare books, letters, notebooks, diaries, photographs and drawings.

THE SINS
OF THE MOTHER

Jamil Ahmad

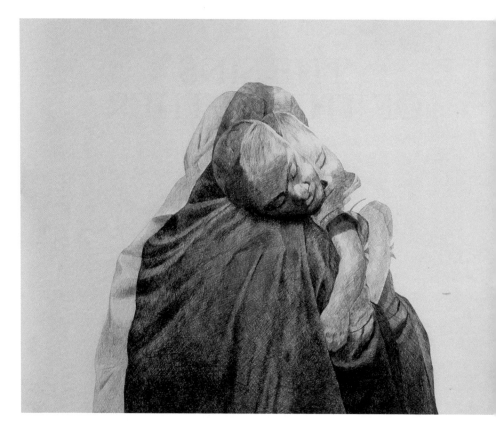

In the tangle of crumbling, weather-beaten and broken hills, where the borders of Iran, Pakistan and Afghanistan meet, is a military outpost manned by about two score soldiers.

Lonely, as all such posts are, this one is particularly frightening. No habitation for miles around and no vegetation except for a few wasted and barren date trees leaning crazily against each other and no water other than a trickle among some salt-encrusted boulders which also dries out occasionally, manifesting a degree of hostility.

Nature has not remained content merely at this. In this land, she has also created the dreaded *bad-e-sad-o-bist-roz*, the wind of a hundred and twenty days. This wind rages almost continuously during the four winter months, blowing clouds of alkali-laden dust and clinker so thick that men can barely breathe or open their eyes when they happen to get caught in it.

It was but natural that some men would lose their minds after too long an exposure to such desolation and loneliness. In the course of time, therefore, a practice developed of not letting any soldier stay at this post for two years running so that none had to face the ravages of the storm for more than four months.

It was during one of these quiet spells that the man and woman came across this post hidden in the folds of the hills. The wind had been blowing with savage fury for three days and if its force had not suddenly abated, they would have missed the post altogether and with it the only source of water for miles around. Indeed, they had steeled themselves to travel on during the approaching night when the impenetrable curtain of dust and sand seemed to lift and reveal the fort with its unhappy-looking date trees.

The soldiers, who had remained huddled behind closed shutters while the wind blew, had come out into the open as soon as the sky cleared. Sick and dispirited after three days and nights in darkened airless and fetid-smelling rooms, they were walking about, busy cleaning themselves and drawing in gulps of fresh air. They had to make the most of this brief respite before the wind started again.

Some of the men noticed the two figures and their camel as they topped the rise and moved slowly and hesitantly towards the fort. Both were staggering as they approached. The woman's clothes, originally black, as those of the man, were grey with dust and sand, lines of caked mud standing out sharply where sweat had soaked into the folds. Even the small mirrors lovingly stitched as decorations into the woman's dress and the man's cap seemed faded and lacklustre.

The woman was covered from head to foot in garments but, on drawing closer, her head covering slipped and exposed her face to the watching soldiers. She made an ineffectual gesture to push it up again, but appeared too weary to care and spent all her remaining energy walking step after step towards the group of men.

When the veil slipped from the woman's face, most of the soldiers turned their heads away, but those who did not saw that she was hardly more than a child. If her companion's looks did not, the sight of her red-rimmed swollen eyes, her matted hair and the unearthly expression on her face told the story clearly.

The man motioned the woman to stop and walked up, by himself, to the subedar commanding the fort. He kept a frenzied grip on the barrel of an old and rusty gun that he carried across his shoulders.

He had no time to waste over any triviality.

'Water,' his hoarse voice said from between cracked and bleeding lips. 'Our water is finished, spare us some water.' The subedar pointed wordlessly towards a half-empty bucket from which the soldiers had been drinking. The man lifted the bucket and drew back towards the woman who was now huddled on the ground.

He cradled her head in the crook of his arm, wet the end of her shawl in the bucket and squeezed some drops on to her face. Tenderly, and feeling no shame at so many eyes watching him, he wiped her face with the wet cloth as she lay in his arms.

A young soldier snickered but immediately fell silent as the baleful eyes of his commander and his companions turned on him.

After he had cleansed her face, the Baluch cupped his right hand and splashed driblets on to her lips. As she sensed water, she started sucking his hand and fingers like a small animal. All of a sudden, she lunged towards the bucket, plunged her head into it and drank with long gasping sounds until she choked. The man patiently pushed her away, drank some of the water himself and then carried the bucket up to the camel, which finished what was left in a single gulp.

He brought the empty bucket back to the group of soldiers, set it down and stood there, silent and unmoving.

At last the subedar spoke. 'Do you wish for anything else?'

A struggle seemed to be going on within the man and after a while, very reluctantly, he looked back at the subedar. 'Yes, I wish for refuge for the two of us. We are Siahpads from Killa Kurd on the run from her people. We have travelled for three days in the storm . . .'

'Refuge,' interrupted the subedar brusquely, 'I cannot offer. I know your laws well and neither I nor any man of mine shall come between a man and the law of his tribe.'

He repeated, 'Refuge we cannot give you.'

The man bit his lips. He turned as if to move but then, once again, faced the subedar. 'I accept your reply,' he said. 'I shall not seek refuge of you. Can I have food and shelter for a few days?'

'That we shall give you.' The subedar hastened to atone for his earlier severity. 'Shelter is yours for the asking. For as long as you wish it, for as long as you want to stay.'

There was a long line of rooms some distance away from the fort. These had been hastily constructed during the First World War when the strength of this fort had, for a short period of time, increased almost a hundredfold. Sand had started collecting against the walls as soon as the construction was raised. Slowly and steadily, it had risen. Most of the walls and roofs caved in under its crumbling pressure. Mounds of sand now occupied these rooms. However, there still remained a few rooms which had not yet caved in.

It was in one of these rooms that Gul Bibi and her lover were provided their shelter. For a few days, the couple hardly stirred outside their one small room. The only signs of life were the opening and closing of shutters as the wind died or strengthened or when food was taken to the hut by the soldiers. Some time after the food had been left at the doorstep, the door would open furtively and the platter would be dragged in, to be pushed outside a while later.

As days passed, the couple appeared to gather more courage. They would occasionally leave the door open while the man stepped outside to look after his camel. Then one day the girl too came out to make a broom out of some thorn shrubs for sweeping the room. After a few days of inactivity, the man, of his own volition, started fetching water for the troops on his camel. He would load up the animal with water skins and visit the springs twice a day. Once he brought to the fort, as a gift, a few baskets, which the girl had woven out of date palm leaves. 'They are to keep your bread in,' he explained to the soldiers. And this is the pattern life followed as time rolled by. Days turned to weeks and weeks to months. Winter gave way to summer. Some soldiers left as their period of duty ended. Others arrived to serve their turn at this outpost.

With each change – even the most minor – the couple appeared to withdraw into themselves for a while. They hardly ventured outside, and none of the shutters would open. Then, after some time, they would cautiously emerge and slowly adjust to the change. In this state, they reminded the soldiers of small frightened desert lizards which rush frantically into their burrow at the slightest sign of danger.

As each party of soldiers left, some would leave behind for the couple anything they could spare out of their meagre possessions. A pair of partly worn-out shoes, a mended bed sheet, some aluminium utensils. These they would tie into a parcel and place at the doorstep of the hut before the army truck drove them back to the headquarters. Then the soldiers also started taking up a collection on every payday and insisted on handing it over to the man for fetching their water. He refused the money the first time, but as the soldiers appeared to get upset at this rebuff, he forced himself to accept without expressing his gratitude in words. With no discernible expression on his face, he would take the proffered money, stuff it into a pocket of his tattered waistcoat and walk away. Indeed, there were times when his look of infinite patience, his aloofness and lack of expression made some new arrivals among the soldiers feel uneasy. But as time passed, each new group would accept him, though they failed to breach the barrier he had drawn around himself.

The real change came with the birth of their child.

They had become accustomed to the same collection of drab buildings with their sullen and frustrated dwellers, each begrudging the days wasted at this bleak outpost and desperately longing for a return to more habitable places, to the sights and sounds of crowded bazaars, the smell of water and vegetation, the feel of clean, freshly laundered clothes. But with news of the birth, the air of resentfulness and bitterness, which seemed permanently to envelop this post, appeared to lighten.

To most of the soldiers, there was sheer wonder in the wizened looks of the infant with his black locks of hair, as he was carried around by the mother. The baby's thin, plaintive cries brought back memories of their own families whom they had not seen for years.

With the birth of their son, the couple too seemed to shed their fears. Indeed, they appeared to be relieved finally of their worries and tensions.

As soon as the season of sandstorms was over, the woman wove an awning out of desert scrub and rigged it over the door to provide protection from the strong sun during the coming summer months. She mixed some clay and water and coated the room, the floor and the door front with it. She did more than that. She made a low wall about six inches high and enclosed an area, the size of two beds, in front of their room. She also made a gate into this small courtyard of hers – a gate with two small towers each topped with a small round knob. After completing it, she stood proudly waiting for her man to return in the evening to see her handiwork.

She had to wait for a long time because his camel had wandered away while grazing. When he finally returned, he looked at her work for a long time before speaking. 'My love, take away the towers, there is something about them I do not like.'

She stood still for a while and then, as the meaning sank in, she rushed frantically towards them and crumbled them back into clay.

Subedar followed subedar as each year ended and a new one began. Indeed, the couple measured the passage of time by the change of subedars. When the sixth one arrived, they realized that the boy was five years old.

A sprightly and active child he was too. Fed on army rations, he looked older than his years. He spent his days inventing games and playing them by himself or skipping from boulder to boulder, following the soldiers on their patrols. By evening, he was tired and would creep into his mother's lap and sleep for a while before they started the meal.

One evening, when the man returned with water from the springs, the boy was still asleep in his mother's lap.

She turned as if to get up but the man stopped her with a gesture. 'Stay for a while, I like looking at you. There is an air of peace around you.'

'I wonder what his life shall be when he grows up. What would you like him to be?' He looked at the woman.

She thought for a while. 'Let him be a camel herder, handsome and gentle as his father,' the woman murmured.

'And fall in love with the Sardar's daughter, his master's wife,' the man countered.

'And carry her away,' continued the woman.

'Into misery and sorrow and terror,' flung back the man.

'Don't ever repeat this. You must never talk thus,' she whispered.

The sleeping boy suddenly opened his dark eyes and said laughingly, 'I have been listening to you and I shall tell you what I shall be. I shall be a chief, I shall have horses and camels. I shall feast your friends and defy your enemies wherever they be.'

Gently the woman pushed the boy away from her lap and started getting the evening meal ready.

One winter morning, while the couple were sitting in front of their hut, a camel rider suddenly appeared and rode his camel straight up to the fort. His arrival was so unexpected that it left them no time to hide. So they remained sitting impassively while the man finished his business and rode away without casting a glance in their direction. Nevertheless, as soon as the stranger rode over the crest, the couple gathered the child, who had been playing in the dust of the courtyard, and moved inside the hut as though its chilly interior suddenly offered more warmth than the sun outside.

A little later, the subedar walked up to the hut and called the man outside. He wasted no time on preliminaries.

'That rider who has just left the fort was a Siahpad,' the subedar said. 'He asked questions about you. You know what that means?'

The man nodded dumbly.

'If you wish to leave,' continued the subedar, 'collect some food from the canteen. The men have packed a bag for you. If God wills, we shall meet again one day.'

The couple departed on their camel at early dusk, the man sitting in the middle with the boy perched in front and the woman behind him. Once again the old familiar smell of fear was in his nostrils. The woman had asked no questions. She packed and dressed quickly, first putting warm clothes on both herself and the boy, and then making a light load of the few things which they needed to carry for their journey. The rest of her possessions, those collected over the past years, she neatly arranged in a pile in one corner of the room.

Her man had brought the camel around to the doorstep and made it kneel. He had cleaned his gun and it was back on his shoulders. As she stepped out to mount the camel, she cast a quick backward glance inside the room, her glance briefly touching the firmly packed clay floor, the date palm mats she had woven over the years and the dying embers in the fireplace. Her expression remained as calm and serene as if she had been prepared for this journey for a long time.

The lone camel followed the telegraph line for about twenty miles before the man decided to strike eastwards into the broken country.

They tried to use their knowledge and wits to the full. They varied their pace, changed direction frequently and also the time of travel. They never spent more than the very minimum time at any waterhole. When they rested, they chose the most secluded spot and would pile up scrub and thorn brush to hide them and their camel.

They saw no signs of their pursuers and after five days the woman became a little sanguine. 'Perhaps the stranger was not a Siahpad. Perhaps we were not recognized,' she remarked hopefully. 'Perhaps he kept the news to himself. Perhaps they did not chase us. Perhaps they have lost us,' she chanted.

'No,' the man said, 'they are after us. I feel it in the air.'

The man was right. On the morning of the sixth day, as the couple were filling the water skin at a waterhole, they saw their pursuers top the horizon.

It was still early morning, when the desert air was unsullied by the eddies of sand and the whirling of dust devils. The party was a considerable distance away but there could be no mistaking who they were. The woman's husband and her father were riding their camels a short distance in front of the main body of men.

The man called Gul Bibi close to him. He placed his hand on her shoulder and looked into her eyes.

'There is no escape for any of us. There was never any escape. You know what I have to do now?'

'Yes,' she replied. 'I know. We have talked about this day many times. But I am afraid, my love.'

'Do not be frightened,' spoke the man. 'I shall follow you. I shall follow you soon.'

The woman walked away a few paces and stood there with her back towards the man. Suddenly she again spoke out. 'Do not kill the boy. They might spare him. I am ready.'

The man shot her in the back while she was still speaking. He then reloaded his gun and looked reflectively at the boy who stared back at him with unblinking eyes. With a shrug the man turned away, walked up to the kneeling camel and shot it dead. He then stood together with the boy waiting for the pursuers to reach him.

The party rode up to the waterhole and dismounted. The old man was in the lead. He glanced at the sprawled body of his daughter and looked at her lover.

'Who is the boy?' he asked. His voice was cold and without emotion. The voice of a stranger. The inky black folds of the headgear hid half the face, but the eyes were the old familiar eyes, which each man of the tribe knew. Eyes that could show anger, hatred, love, laughter, fondness and humour more vividly than anyone else. Now they showed nothing.

'Who is the boy?' the Sardar asked again, his voice remaining flat, not even showing impatience.

'Your daughter's son,' replied the man.

The boy stood shivering as the two men talked about him. He was nervously fingering a small silver amulet which hung around his neck on a grey-coloured string.

The husband of the dead woman approached.

'Whose son is he?' he growled. 'Yours or mine?'

The lover did not reply but his eyes again met those of the old man. 'He is her son,' he repeated. 'That silver amulet is hers. She must have placed it around his neck before her death. Do you not recognize the amulet? You gave it to her to ward off evil spirits.'

The old man said nothing, but picked up a stone. His companions did likewise. The lover stood still as the first shower of stones hit him. He started bleeding from the wounds on his face and temples. There was another shower of stones and yet another, before he fell.

At first, he lay half sitting and half sprawling. Then he lay with only his elbow supporting him. Finally, that small gesture of pride too failed him and he lay stretched on the ground, his clothes darkened with blood and small rivulets of it running across his back and staining the ground. The hail of stones continued with the circle of men moving closer and closer. The agony ended only with death, the bones broken and the head crushed beyond recognition.

After they had killed the lover, the offended husband turned to his companions.

'Now we start with the boy.' The boy, who had been standing next to the dead camel, heard this and started whimpering.

'No,' admonished the old man, 'the boy's death is not necessary. We shall leave him as we found him.'

Some of the other men murmured their agreement. 'Yes, let him stay as he is,' they agreed. 'The Sardar is right.'

They dragged the two bodies a short distance away and entombed them separately in towers made out of sun-blackened stones which lay scattered in profusion all around the waterhole. They used mud and water to plaster the towers so that their work might endure and provide testimony, to all who cared, about the way in which the Siahpad avenged insults. The old man took no part in the burial but walked about by himself. He did, however, interrupt his walking for a while and stood at the spot where the bodies had lain.

As soon as the men had finished, they mounted their camels and rode away. After travelling but a short distance, the father of the girl suddenly reined in his camel.

'I should have brought the boy,' the older man said, shading his eyes with his hand and staring in the direction of the waterhole.

'Death would be best for the likes of him,' burst out the son-in-law. 'The whelp has bad blood in him.'

'Half of his blood is my blood. The blood of the chiefs of this tribe. What mean you by bad blood?'

'I still say what I said before,' answered back the husband. 'He has bad blood. Nothing good shall come out of him.'

The older man moved his camel up to the other man's as the rest watched him. He looked around. 'Let me tell you all now,' he shouted. 'My daughter sinned. She sinned against the laws of God and those of our tribe. But hear this also. There was no sin in her when she was born, nor when she grew up, nor when she was married. She was driven to sin only because I did not marry her to a man.'

He pointed a shaking finger at his son-in-law. 'You know well enough what I say,' he thundered, his emotions suddenly bursting out. 'Marry another woman, marry as often as you like. Every one of them shall be driven to sin, for reasons you are aware of.'

At this insult, shouted in his face before the men of his tribe, the face of the other man darkened with rage.

'You should not have said such things, old man, even if you be our chief,' he shouted as he drew his sword and slashed at Gul Bibi's father. Once, twice, thrice he swiped and the old man was already dead as he slid down in small jerks like a broken doll from the saddle to the ground.

With his death, the party scattered. The men did not wait to bury their Chief's body in a proper grave but left it covered under a thin layer of sand, hoping the approaching sandstorm would bury it deeper. Whether fearful of the evil they had seen or afraid of being involved in another feud, or maybe weary of each other's company, they just rode away hurriedly.

At the waterhole, the boy had stopped shivering after the party departed. He had overcome his fear and was sitting between the two towers playing with some stones and quartz crystals. At first he had tried to prise some stones away from the towers, but they were too tightly wedged together and his fingers made no impression.

As the sun rose higher, he sat quietly watching the clouds of sand-grouse which appeared in the sky. Flight after flight alighted at the edge of the waterhole, dipping their beaks in the water and flying away back into the sun. Their peculiar chuckling calls and the whirring of countless wings provided him some diversion from the horror he had just witnessed.

Then he was completely alone. The thousands of birds, which had kept him company for a while, had disappeared. With nothing to keep him occupied, he became aware of his thirst and hunger. He tried to resist it for a while, but as the pangs of hunger grew sharper, he finally walked over to the dead camel and opened the bag containing food. He ate a little, drank some water and then lay down squeezed against the dead camel as the sandstorm approached. ∎

Manchester Literature Festival 2010

14 – 25 October

www.manchesterliteraturefestival.co.uk

Catch some of the most acclaimed and inspirational writers from across the globe, including **Martin Amis, Bernard Cornwell, Carol Ann Duffy, Lyndall Gordon, Seamus Heaney, Caryl Phillips, Lionel Shriver, Barbara Trapido, Saul Williams** and **Jeanette Winterson**, at the fifth Manchester Literature Festival.

Visit the festival website for full programme details or call 0161 236 5555 to order a brochure.

Supported by
ARTS COUNCIL ENGLAND

MANCHESTER CITY COUNCIL

About the Cover

From the ornate horse-drawn carriages of the Raj to the pioneering craftsmanship featured on the Kohistan Bus Company's fleet in the 1920s, Pakistan has a long-established tradition of decorating vehicles. The idiosyncratic designs serve as both moving advertisements and indicators of cultural affiliation. Truck artists transform village rickshaws, city buses and commercial trucks into a procession of moving colour.

The cover for *Granta* 112 was created by Islam Gull, a truck and bus artist of Bhutta village in Karachi, as part of a greater collaboration with Pakistani artists for the issue. Gull, born in Peshawar, has been painting since the age of thirteen. Twenty-two years ago he settled in Karachi, where he now teaches his craft to two young apprentices. In addition to trucks and buses, Gull decorates buildings and housewares and has worked for several consulates in Karachi, as well as travelling to Kandahar, Afghanistan to paint trucks there. Commissioned with the assistance of the British Council in Karachi, Gull produced two chipboard panels to be photographed for the magazine's cover, using the same industrial paints with which he embellishes Pakistani trucks.

CONTRIBUTORS

Lorraine Adams is the author of two novels, *Harbor,* winner of the *Los Angeles Times* Book Prize and *The Room and the Chair* (Portobello/Knopf). She lives in New York City.

Jamil Ahmad was born in Jalandhar, Punjab in 1933. A civil servant in the frontier areas and a minister in the Pakistani embassy in Kabul, his first book, *The Wandering Falcon,* will be published in 2011 (Penguin India/UK).

Nadeem Aslam was born in Gujranwala, Pakistan, and now lives in England. He is the author of the novels *Season of the Rainbirds, Maps for Lost Lovers* and *The Wasted Vigil* (Faber/Vintage).

Fatima Bhutto was born in Kabul, Afghanistan, in 1982. She is the author of three books including *Songs of Blood and Sword* (Jonathan Cape/Nation). She lives in Karachi.

Hasina Gul is a broadcaster at Pakistan Broadcasting Corporation's Peshawar station. She is the author of two collections of poetry – *Shpoon Shpole Shpelai, Khutah Khabray Kava* and *Da Hum Hagasey Mausam Dey.*

Yasmeen Hameed, Urdu poet and translator, has produced four verse collections and won the Allama Iqbal Award.

Mohsin Hamid lives in Lahore and is the author of *Moth Smoke* (Granta/ Farrar, Straus and Giroux) and *The Reluctant Fundamentalist* (Penguin/ Harcourt), shortlisted for the Man Booker Prize in 2007.

Mohammed Hanif was born in Okara. A former head of the BBC Urdu Service, he is the author of *A Case of Exploding Mangoes* (Jonathan Cape/Vintage). He lives in Karachi.

Intizar Hussain was born in 1923 in the north Indian state of Uttar Pradesh and migrated to Pakistan in 1947. He has published six collections of short stories and four novels in Urdu. He is the recipient of the Sitara-i-Imtiaz, Pakistan's third highest governmental honour.

Aamer Hussein was born in Karachi in 1955 and moved to London in 1970. He is the author of five collections of short stories and a novella, *Another Gulmohar Tree.*

Uzma Aslam Khan was born in Lahore. She is the author of *The Story of Noble Rot* (Penguin India/Rupa & Co); *Trespassing* (Flamingo/Picador) and *The Geometry of God* (Haus Publishing, 2010).

Waqas Khwaja, professor of English at Agnes Scott College in Atlanta, has published three collections of poetry and edited three anthologies of Pakistani literature, most recently *Pakistani Short Stories*.

Hari Kunzru is the author of three novels, *The Impressionist, Transmission* and *My Revolutions* (Penguin).

Sarfraz Manzoor is a journalist and broadcaster. He was born in Pakistan and migrated to Britain in 1974, at two. His memoir, *Greetings From Bury Park* (Bloomsbury/Vintage), was published in 2007.

Daniyal Mueenuddin grew up in Pakistan and Wisconsin. His first short-story collection, *In Other Rooms, Other Wonders* (Bloomsbury/ W. W. Norton), won the Story Prize and was a finalist for the Pulitzer Prize and National Book Award. He lives on a farm in southern Pakistan.

Ayesha Nasir is a journalist based in Lahore, Pakistan.

Basharat Peer is the author of *Curfewed Night* (Harper/Scribner), a memoir of the Kashmir conflict. He is a fellow at Open Society Institute, New York.

Jane Perlez is a Pulitzer Prize-winning correspondent for the *New York Times* who has covered Pakistan for the last three years.

Kamila Shamsie is the author of five novels, including *Burnt Shadows* (Bloomsbury/Picador), published last year. Born in Karachi, she lives in London.

Declan Walsh is the *Guardian*'s correspondent for Pakistan and Afghanistan. His book *Insh'Allah Nation: A Journey Through Modern Pakistan* will be published in 2011 (Random House).

Sher Zaman Taizi, born in Pabbi, is the author of fifteen books in Pashto and twenty-four in English. He was awarded the Nobel Peace Prize Certificate in 1981 and the Tamgha-e-Imtiaz in Literature in 2009.

Green Cardamom, founded in 2004, is a London-based not-for-profit organization and gallery specializing in international contemporary art viewed from an Indian Ocean perspective. The images in this issue are a collaboration between *Granta* and Green Cardamom curators Hammad Nasar, Anita Dawood and Nada Raza.